messiness with a holistic and transformational message characterized by its pursuit of righteousness and justice. Here is no unrealistic fantasy, but rather a truly hopeful appeal in a world mired in hopelessness and despair.

William W. Klein, PhD
Professor Emeritus of New Testament Interpretation,
Denver Seminary, Colorado, USA

Social ills are, arguably, the chief ethical and apologetics issues of our time. But American evangelicalism, on the whole, has aligned with political tribes to determine our approach to these problems. Instead of setting culture, we have chosen sides in societal schisms. In *Authentic Engagement*, Dr. Dieumeme Noëlliste challenges the church to address social matters on the king's terms. We do not have the privilege of indifference or idleness, but kingdom ethics should determine our participation. God has equipped us with an eternal message that is temporally relevant. It allows us to have hope in tumultuous times. I commend this book to anyone who desires to embody Christ's kingdom-minded message and mission.

Brandon Washington
Pastor of Preaching,
Embassy Christian Bible Church, Colorado, USA

Authentic Engagement

Authentic Engagement is clear and straightforward, but it is not an easy read. It is truthfully and painfully prophetic, but it is hopeful. It is not an easy read because Noëlliste unflinchingly identifies, describes, and grapples with ways in which the church too often fails to be the church and fails to be the church in the world. Yet it is hopeful because Noëlliste's vision of and prescriptions for the church are grounded in the reality of the Triune God and are unswervingly shaped by the redemption available to the world in Jesus Christ. When his clear-eyed analysis stings, it is "the wound of a friend," and when he issues constructive calls to action, they are informed by his own authentic engagement in the life of the global church. Throughout, this is a book of biblically grounded theology – theology about the church, for the church, and for the world.

W. David Buschart, PhD
Professor of Theology and Historical Studies,
Denver Seminary, Colorado, USA

This volume is a clarion call for the church to be all that it was meant to be *in* and *for* the world. Biblically thoughtful and theologically thorough, with interaction from an array of global voices, *Authentic Engagement* argues that the Christian faith has social import: being a constructive agent of social change is necessary for the church's witness and indispensable to its mission. It has been so from the beginning. This book returns us to this fundamental truth.

M. Daniel Carroll R. (Rodas), PhD
Scripture Press Ministries Professor of Biblical Studies and Pedagogy,
Wheaton College and Graduate School, Illinois, USA

Professor Dieumeme Noëlliste's fiercely intelligent, deeply committed, dynamic personality guided the Caribbean Graduate School of Theology from its inception, and his ever-expanding influence on global theological education spread from there. Now, four decades into a notable ministry of preaching, teaching, and cross-cultural leadership, he offers us a bountiful harvest – his biblical and theological reflections on the church's call to social transformation. While his own life story might be held up as an inspiring example of radical transformation, Dr. Noëlliste deliberately grounds his arguments in Scripture, reason, and the historic teachings of the church. What we see in this book is not Dr. Noëlliste, the Haitian prodigy, but the rich fruits of a carefully disciplined mind that is subservient both to the word of God and to the will of his heavenly Father. Thus, a humble submission to God's word and will undergirds this prophetic call to Christian social transformation. His partnership in this project with his gifted niece, Dr. Mirlenda Noëlliste, signals the way their message spans genders and generations. Read this and renew your prayers for God's will to be done here on earth, as it is in heaven – faithfully, lovingly, justly, and joyfully!

Timothy Paul Erdel, PhD
Associate Professor of Religion and Philosophy,
Bethel University, Indiana, USA

Dieumeme Noëlliste and Mirlenda Noëlliste have done it again, this time in English! This is a well-researched and carefully argued volume that demonstrates in a theologically rich fashion how the Christian church can authentically engage with the wider world to bring positive transformation to all. I particularly value how the two authors bring the voices of a wide range of important theologians around the world into the conversation about the church's role in the world. This is an important and valuable resource for scholars in ecclesiology and theological ethics. It will also work well as a textbook in theological ethics at graduate and undergraduate levels.

Rev. Knut M Heim, PhD
Professor of Old Testament,
Denver Seminary, Colorado, USA

The church endures scathing criticism from both insiders and outsiders. As the church's ranks decline, many view it as irrelevant. But rather than merely lament the past, and especially the current state of the church's ineffectiveness in the world, Dr. Noëlliste and his niece show how the church can recapture its Christ-ordained mission. In this robustly resourced, historically nuanced, and theologically informed treatise, they put forward this challenging proposal – the church can advance the cause of social transformation by being *authentically engaged* with the present social order. Both italicized words are crucial for their project: the church must truly be the church as God's alternative society (no compromise of its nature and character); and the church must fully engage the world in all its

Authentic Engagement

The Role of the Church in Social Transformation

Dieumeme Noëlliste

with

Mirlenda Noëlliste

GLOBAL LIBRARY

© 2023 Dieumeme Noëlliste and Mirlenda Noëlliste

Published 2023 by Langham Global Library
An imprint of Langham Publishing
www.langhampublishing.org

Langham Publishing and its imprints are a ministry of Langham Partnership

Langham Partnership
PO Box 296, Carlisle, Cumbria, CA3 9WZ, UK
www.langham.org

ISBNs:
978-1-83973-800-5 Print
978-1-83973-801-2 ePub
978-1-83973-802-9 Mobi
978-1-83973-803-6 PDF

Dieumeme Noëlliste and Mirlenda Noëlliste have asserted their right under the Copyright, Designs and Patents Act, 1988 to be identified as the Author of this work.

All rights reserved. No part of this publication may be reproduced, stored in a retrieval system or transmitted, in any form or by any means, electronic, mechanical, photocopying, recording or otherwise, without the prior written permission of the publisher or the Copyright Licensing Agency.

Requests to reuse content from Langham Publishing are processed through PLSclear. Please visit www.plsclear.com to complete your request.

Scriptures unless marked otherwise are taken from the Holy Bible, New International Version®, NIV®. Copyright © 1973, 1978, 1984, 2011 by Biblica, Inc.™ Used by permission of Zondervan.

Scripture quotations marked (ESV) are from The Holy Bible, English Standard Version® (ESV®), copyright © 2001 by Crossway, a publishing ministry of Good News Publishers. Used by permission. All rights reserved.

Scripture quotations marked (NET), are from the New English Translation (NET). NET Bible® copyright ©1996–2006 by Biblical Studies Press, L.L.C. www.bible.org. Used by permission. All rights reserved worldwide.

Scripture quotations marked (NKJV), are from the New King James Version (NKJV). Copyright © 1982 by Thomas Nelson, Inc. Used by permission. All rights reserved.

British Library Cataloguing-in-Publication Data
A catalogue record for this book is available from the British Library

ISBN: 978-1-83973-800-5

Cover & Book Design: projectluz.com

Langham Partnership actively supports theological dialogue and an author's right to publish but does not necessarily endorse the views and opinions set forth here or in works referenced within this publication, nor can we guarantee technical and grammatical correctness. Langham Partnership does not accept any responsibility or liability to persons or property as a consequence of the reading, use or interpretation of its published content.

Contents

Foreword xi

Preface xv

Acknowledgments xvii

1   Introduction: The Transforming Vocation of the People of God. 1

Part One: Models of Transforming Engagement

2   Major Views on the Church's Role in the World 15

3   Authentic Engagement 35

Part Two: Ecclesial Consciousness for Transforming Engagement

4   Society of the Triune God 51

5   Ambassador of Heaven 67

Part Three: Acts of Transforming Engagement

6   Exemplar of a New Order 81

7   Herald of Transforming News 101

8   Catalyst of Human Well-Being. 115

Part Four: The Stance of Transforming Engagement

9   Hope-Filled Realism 145

10   Expectancy 159

11   Prayer. 167

Bibliography. 171

Subject Index 179

Author Index 181

Scripture Index 183

Foreword

More than seventy years ago, H. Richard Niebuhr articulated an enduring taxonomy of ways of relating Christ to culture. He identified five main approaches, which included "Christ against culture," "The Christ of culture," "Christ above culture," "Christ and culture in paradox," and "Christ as the transformer of culture."[1] More recently, Don Carson has evaluated these options in light of biblical theology, observing how Niebuhr's options and preferences might have looked different had he himself come out of a very different culture, particularly in the Majority World.[2] What, then, of precisely such a Majority World voice? What would someone who grew up in and ministered for about half of his adult life in the Caribbean, but who also studied in and taught during the other half of that life in the United States, have to say on these topics? What would anyone, updating the cultural mandate *of the church*, and not just Christ or the individual Christian, have to say? What would such a writer in the third decade of the twenty-first century need to modify, if anything, from either Niebuhr or Carson? What if their perspectives began with neither of these books nor other secondary literature, but with a combination of the study of Scripture, rigorous theology and lived experience? Theologian Dieumeme Noëlliste provides answers to all these and related questions in this succinct yet profound work on the church's authentic engagement with the culture and society around it. From different but complementary angles, he agrees with Niebuhr and others who argue that transformation is the ultimate goal.

Noëlliste was born and grew up in Haiti, the most impoverished of all the nations in the Western hemisphere. He later served as the president of Jamaica Theological Seminary, and as dean and then president of the Caribbean Graduate School of Theology, both located in Kingston, Jamaica, for many years. For some time now, he has been a professor of systematic theology and ethics at Denver Seminary in Littleton, Colorado, holding the Vernon C. Grounds Chair of Pastoral Ministry and Social Ethics. He also directed the Vernon C. Grounds Center for Public Ethics during a significant majority of that time. Noëlliste received his bachelor's degree in theology from William Tyndale

---

1. H. Richard Niebuhr, *Christ and Culture* (New York: Harper Torchbooks, 1951).
2. D. A. Carson, *Christ and Culture Revisited* (Grand Rapids: Eerdmans Publishing Company, 2012).

College in Farmington Hills, Michigan, his Master of Divinity from Trinity Evangelical Divinity School in Deerfield, Illinois, and his PhD in theological studies from Northwestern University in Evanston, Illinois, specializing in modern and contemporary Christian thought. In fact, I first heard about Dr. Noëlliste from our former professor there, Dr. Don Carson, who was lauding his ministry. Just a few years ago Noëlliste received the alumnus of the year award, bestowed on him by TEDS.

Dr. Noëlliste has written numerous scholarly and practical articles, along with editing, co-authoring or authoring several other books, in both English and French, and he is fluent in those languages, as also in Creole and Spanish. He has traveled throughout the world, regularly organizing and/or speaking at theological conferences as well as helping with the accreditation and reaccreditation of Bible colleges and seminaries, especially in the Majority World, and helping them to build up their facilities and resources. For a period of time, he served as director and chairman of the International Council for Evangelical Theological Education, the major accrediting body for evangelical theological schools in the Majority World. He belongs to the Latin American Theological Fraternity, the International Council for the Promotion of Christian Higher Education and the Oxford Round Table, an organization that sponsors interdisciplinary conferences with diverse attendees, usually on matters of public policy.

In a world of unprecedented political polarization within individual countries with the resurgence of far-right and far-left organizations in both political and socio-economic contexts, and in a world of greater international warfare and threats of war than we have seen in three-quarters of a century, the Christian church needs to present a credible and compelling witness to the truth as well as the practical livability of its faith. With virtual anarchy in Haiti, the one nation in Latin America that has received the greatest amount of Christian missionary efforts since the arrival of the Europeans(!), we have to do better. We need to avoid the extremes and work at moving toward a center that is deeply rooted in Scripture and its mandates, which recognizes politics as the art of compromise, which can support the lesser of two or more evils when choices in political and ethical decisions do not present clear-cut cases between right and wrong, good and bad. We need to recapture Jesus's vision for the arrival of the kingdom of God, with the church as a countercultural witness to the possibilities for the flourishing of human life both in this world and in the next. We need to recognize the already-but-not-yet arrival of that kingdom with Jesus's first coming, which will one day make way for its full arrival at his second coming. We dare not underestimate the depths of evil and opposition to

God's kingdom that currently remain and will always remain prior to the end of the age, but we also dare not underestimate the possibilities of transforming our planet, with the help of God's Spirit, into new, more moral environments, complete with all that is required for human persons to flourish. We have to allow God to determine the limits of what he will allow on the one hand, and inspire on the other, rather than over-optimistically or over-pessimistically act as if we could make those decisions for him.

Alternating between the theoretical and practical levels, and drawing widely on key biblical passages and theological texts, Dr. Noëlliste challenges our minds and touches our hearts. Just when we think he has given us about all we can manage *notionally* in one sitting, we discover he is also giving us about all we can handle *emotionally*. Yet this is not because this book is either unrelentingly optimistic or pessimistic. Noëlliste is profoundly realistic. Even when he challenges our thinking as to the good that could happen, he then gives us glimpses from his lived experience when it has actually happened for a time in Christian circles. What we have here is actually a manifesto for ecclesiastical possibilities in our time as the church seeks authentic engagement with the world in hopes of its transformation for the better, in whatever ways God chooses to bring it about. Read it for encouragement, motivation and inspiration. It deserve nothing less.

Craig L. Blomberg
Distinguished Professor Emeritus of New Testament,
Denver Seminary, Colorado, USA
October 2022

Preface

Ancient philosophers spent a great deal of time talking about the nature of reality. Is realty made of water, air, or fire or something else? Their discussion often turned around the notion of movement. Is reality static or is it dynamic? In other words, do things remain the same, or do they keep changing?

For a philosopher like Parmenides, the static view *seemed* the correct description of the world, while his fellow philosopher, Heraclitus defended adamantly the contrary position. Reality, he believed, is always in flux. It never remains the same.

Very good arguments can be offered on behalf of both men. But humanly speaking, Heraclitus appears to have the edge. We seem to live in a sea of change. Some even say that, if there is one constant, it is change itself. This is an overstatement, of course, since the only One who can claim absolute immutability is God (Mal 3:10; Jas 1:17). But you get the point. Every now and then, I look at my pictures of thirty, twenty, and even ten years ago, and can barely recognize my own self.

Yet in giving the nod to Heraclitus, we must caution against a concept of change that seems to construe it as aimless and purposeless. To what end is the river changing so constantly to the point that we can never set foot in the same mass of water? Is the motion an end in itself? Are the wheels just turning, but never moving?

Such a view of change doesn't seem attractive to us. The change that gets us excited is the one that eggs us along toward a destination – a better place than the one we now occupy. It is teleological in nature. We believe that it is this sort of change that Christian faith endorses and champions. It is a dynamic movement that pushes the created order, including ourselves, towards what it and us need to be. It is a change that presses forward towards a goal that is better. It is a change that's not content with a reality that insists on being confirmed as the ideal, although it is in fact the very opposite of it!

Scripture tells us that God, the immutable One, is the power that propels reality towards that much desired destination. He is the One who will ultimately make all things new (Rev 21:1ff). Yet, although he is the Ultimate Mover, in his sovereignty, he uses lesser agents in the process of prodding reality in the direction of his ideal for human life, and among such instruments are his people – the church.

If this is true, this recognition raises (or should raise) several questions in our minds. What position must his people adopt in order to play a meaningful part in that divine project? How must we view ourselves in order to muster the confidence to contribute effectively to the execution of the grandiose plan? What concrete actions can we pose to foster the forward movement of that project without causing harm to our identity as his people, and to the cause itself? What posture should we adopt when our effort doesn't seem to yield the outcomes we desire? These are the issues that we will endeavor to explore in the pages of this book. If our meagre attempt prompts you, our readers, to join us in the examination of these questions, we will consider our effort worthwhile.

Dieumeme Noëlliste
Littleton, Colorado, USA
Advent 2021

Acknowledgments

This book has been in the making for some time. The first musings occurred in an address I delivered at the 2005 Congress on the Evangelization of the Caribbean (CONECAR), in the Bahamas. The talk was entitled "The Caribbean Church: A Successful Agent of Change" and it stirred up a great deal of interest among the participants. Then, as is well known, in 2010, a massive earthquake devasted the country of Haiti. That catastrophic event pushed a segment of the Haitian church to launch a movement called La Mobilisation de l'Eglise autour de son Rôle Prophétique (The Mobilization of the Church for Its Prophetic Witness). As part of the movement, I had the opportunity to deliver talks and present seminars on the church and its role in the social domain. Some five years later, I revisited the topic for a series of lectures I delivered to the students and faculty of the Séminaire de Théologie Evangélique de Port-au-Prince. In addition to all this, for several years my responsibilities as a member of the Faculty of Denver Seminary included providing leadership to the Vernon Grounds Institute of Public Ethics. The Institute was a think tank that reflected on the church's role in addressing some of the thorniest issues confronting American society. During its ten years of operation, it tackled health care, immigration, creation care, child poverty, racism, capital punishment, and economic justice.

In all these settings, I received much that helped inform my thinking on the issues addressed in this book. The contributions came in the form of feedback, pushback, insights, and sharing of differing perspectives, from a wide cross section of persons: students, church leaders, Christian activists, and fellow academics. To all of them, I owe a debt of gratitude. The names are way too numerous to mention, but I must give a shout-out to a select few. Among them are M. Danny Caroll Rodas, Erin Heim, Michelle Warren, Brandon Washington, the late Felix Gilbert, and Dr. Gary Vander Ark who served with me on the steering committee of the Vernon Grounds Institute. Besides these, I must mention my friends Edouard Lassegue and Rony Joseph, fellow Haitians with whom I frequently lament the situation of our country.

All this means that the ideas that have made their way into the pages of this book have been running, in one way or another, in my mind for years. Putting them down on paper required concentrated time. I am deeply grateful to the board of trustees of Denver Seminary who afforded me the time to do that by granting a sabbatical during the spring of 2021, during which the lion's share of the manuscript was produced, amid the disruption of the COVID-19 pandemic.

In 2019, I teamed up with my niece Mirlenda to produce a volume in French on Afro-Caribbean religions, entitled *Les Religions afro-caribéennes à la lumière de la foi chrétienne*. The experience was a delight. I am grateful that Mirlenda accepted the invitation to be a contributor to this book.

This is our second book with Langham. Once again, the people at this innovative publishing ministry have shown grace and patience toward us. When COVID-19 interfered with our writing plan and prevented us from meeting the original deadline, our editor Mark Arnold was kind enough to grant us an extension. For this we are grateful.

In the process of writing, I find nothing more invigorating than the encouragement of family. I am grateful to my wife Gloria and daughters Leila and Nicole for their moral support while working on this project.

In 1 Corinthians 15:10, Paul says: "By the grace of God I am what I am, and his grace to me was not without effect." I share these sentiments. I am deeply grateful to God for manifesting his grace once again in my life by enabling me to bring this project to completion. To him be the glory!

1

Introduction: The Transforming Vocation of the People of God

It is common to hear criticism leveled at Christianity for its alleged complicity in some of the ills that beset the world. To the proponents of the New Atheism, for example, the gods, and particularly the Christian God, are the cause of all the intractable problems that confront humanity.[1] Some in the environmentalist movement also join the fray and lay the ecological crisis squarely on the shoulders of Christian faith.[2] Often, the reason Christianity's feet are held to the fire is because of the conservative stance it adopts on some issues considered prejudicial to the enhancement and flourishing of life.

Now, if by conservatism one means conformity with, and allegiance to, the spirit, attitude, values, ideology, policies, and actions of a given prevailing social order, at first blush the charges are not without merit. Sadly, history is replete with examples of Christianity's acquiescence with the reigning ideologies and the prevailing mindsets which have been the causes of suffering for untold millions of the earth's inhabitants. To make the point one need only think of the support that such abhorrent systems as the slave trade and slavery in the

---

1. This indictment has been made by several contemporary atheist thinkers, among them Christopher Hitchens in his *God Is Not Great: How Religion Imprisons Everything* (New York: Twelve, 2007), 56; Richard Dawkins, *The God Delusion* (New York: Houghton Mifflin, 2008), 36; and Sam Harris, *Letter to a Christian Nation* (New York: Knoft, 2007), 87.

2. Lynn White's charge that Christianity is responsible for the abuse of the creation has become well known since the publication of his article "The Historical Roots of Our Ecological Crisis," reprinted in *Ecology and Life: Accepting Our Environmental Responsibility*, ed. Wesley Granberg-Michaelson (Waco: Word, 1988), 125–37. For some environmentalists, White's position seems to have become an article of faith. Recently, for example, Susan Power Bratton wrote, "If we assume Judaism, Christianity, and Islam are inherently anti-environmental, we will not expect them to make positive contributions to solving the environmental problems." See her chapter entitled "The Undoing of the Environment" in *Earth at Risk*, eds. Donald B. Conroy and Rodney Lawrence Petersen (Amherst: Humanity Books, 2000), 231.

Americas, colonialism in various parts of the world, the Nazi regime of Hitler's Germany, the apartheid system of South Africa, and segregation in the United States received from Christians and official Christendom.

Inconvenient though it may be, the plain truth is that the history of Christianity includes a bleak and horrific strand that should not be whitewashed or explained away. Integrity demands nothing less than the humble naming and acknowledgment of the misdeeds of the past in sincere repentance and with the firm resolve to avoid making similar missteps in our own time and contexts. And, for such an attitude, we have the examples of some choice servants of God to emulate. The posture of humble acknowledgment of a Nehemiah and a Daniel, for example, clearly revealed in the fervent prayers they addressed to God at critical moments of their country's history, is instructive (Neh 1:4–11; Dan 9:4–19).

Yet, such humble recognition is not tantamount to the blanket and wholesale indictment of the Christian faith proffered by Christianity's merciless critics. The same integrity that compels us to acknowledge Christianity's past misdeeds demands that the honest thinker recognizes that the Christianity that is complicit in these abhorrent ills falls far short of the real and ideal Christian faith. Sadly, it is a Christianity that often shows signs of being captive to the ruling cultural mindset, and which is practiced in places that often fail to live up to Christian ideals and values.[3] Theologian Alister McGrath has pointed out that it is the plight of an ideal to be perverted and abused. When this happens, he argues, the right thing to do is to confront and correct the deformation with a view to making the corrupted reality conform to the ideal. What should not be done, he contends, is to interpret the perversion as the negation of the reality and validity of the ideal itself.[4]

Transformation: A Keynote of Scripture

McGrath is right. When due consideration is given to the biblical values and principles that underpin genuine Christian faith, one quickly finds that

---

3. Throughout the history of the church, Christians themselves have leveled criticism at their own faith for just such a failure. The Danish philosopher and Christian writer Søren Kierkegaard is a prime example of this. As the Kierkegaard scholar Walter Lowrie has highlighted, toward the end of his life Kierkegaard made it his aim to "introduce Christianity into Christendom" by virulently attacking established Christianity in general, and more specifically as it was practiced in his own country of Denmark. See Søren Kierkegaard, *The Point of View of My Work as an Author* (San Francisco: Harper & Row, 1962), xxiv.

4. Alister E. McGrath, "Challenges from Atheism," in *Beyond Opinion: Living the Faith We Defend*, ed. Ravi Zacharias (Nashville: Thomas Nelson, 2007), 31.

Christian faith is far from being a preserver of the status quo. A biblical Christian faith is a faith that majors in change. Part of its aim is the transformation of the real into the ideal, the alteration of what is into what ought to be. And the mutation it envisages is not one-dimensional; rather, it is a multifaceted objective that embraces all the dimensions of reality. It encompasses the personal, the social, and the cosmic realm. In the vision of Christian faith, by the time the transformation project reaches its fruition, nothing will remain the same. Every aspect of reality will receive a renewed image and a total makeover: people will be changed, society will be changed, and the world and its order will be changed.

This note of transformation is not a marginal and muted chime of the Christian construct; it runs throughout the gamut of the biblical narrative and is sounded with clarity by several of its major voices. This is evident in the very theme that constitutes the thrust of the biblical narrative: redemption. Running through the biblical story is a redemptive red line that not only seeks to mitigate the adverse consequences of the fall, but aims at nothing less than the restoration of the ruined Edenic order under God's unchallenged rule. It is the freeing of the creation from its present condition so that it can be all that it was intended to be by its creator. The prophets of the Old Testament kept this hope alive by constantly directing the attention of their contemporaries toward the establishment of a future order that would be different from their own. It is an order whose main feature is shalom: peace, well-being, and prosperity.

Among these divine spokesmen, Isaiah, son of Amoz, can rightly boast of being the leading herald of the eschatological transformation being talked about here. Writing in times of political turmoil and moral and religious corruption, and envisaging God's impending judgment on the current sociopolitical order, the prophet nonetheless envisioned the dawning of a day that would be markedly different from his troubled times. With confidence, he directed the attention of his contemporaries to the ideal situation that humans will experience when that moment comes. This hopeful note is interspersed throughout his lengthy prophetic volume. Peering into the future, he saw a time marked by various felicitous elements. It is going to be a time of international peace, he tells us, "when nation will not take up sword against nation" (Isa 2:4). Additionally, he saw the dawning of an era of abundance and plenty when "water will gush forth in the wilderness" (35:6). Furthermore, the prophet viewed a time of social and economic harmony when humans, nature, and God will be reconciled (11:6–9). Moreover, proleptically, the prophet witnessed a "day of security" when infants will play near the cobra with no fear of being harmed (11:8). Above all, he saw from afar the arrival of a day when "the earth will be filled with the knowledge of the LORD as the waters cover the sea" under the leadership of a righteous person (11:1–9). To ensure that the picture of this coming era is etched into our minds, he depicts it with the vivid imagery of a host of people walking the Highway of Holiness on their way to Zion, the Holy City (35:8). As he draws the prophetic vision to a close, he broadens the scope of his transformation message by speaking of the future renewal and restoration that awaits the entire cosmic order, bluntly declaring, "See, I will create new heavens and a new earth. The former things will not be remembered, nor will they come to mind. But be glad and rejoice forever in what I will create" (65:17–18). The American missiologist Arthur Glasser states it well:

> In the study of the Old Testament, there is a longing for multiple assurances that all will be well in the end. There is hope that all creation will witness the final vindication of God, fully triumphant amid his creation, having banished from it all that was contrary to [his] will. Furthermore, the Lord will be gloriously satisfied when he receives something vastly different from the fitful obedience of a small remnant of Israel, admittedly only one small segment of the human race. He will then be loved and served by a people drawn from all nations, eager to live under his direction and for his glory.[5]

When we turn to the New Testament, we find a similar emphasis. Although several of the New Testament writers were living in situations of great distress and daunting vicissitudes, they were not bashful in their affirmation and appropriation of the biblical message of eschatological transformation. They affirmed boldly and categorically that the prevailing moment would not be the last chapter of history. Rather, they saw it as a penultimate moment which will be replaced by one that is more conducive to human flourishing. One such witness is the apostle Peter, who reportedly was crucified by the Romans for his unswerving commitment to Christ.[6] In his response to mockers and scoffers who were ridiculing God's alleged inability to bring about the promised social order, Peter confidently reassured the people of his day that "in keeping with [God's] promise we are looking forward to a new heaven and a new earth,

---

5. Arthur Glasser, *Announcing the Kingdom: The Story of God's Mission in the Bible* (Grand Rapids: Baker, 2003), 19.

6. Tertullian and Eusebius reported that Peter was crucified by Nero in Rome. Eusebius further adds that, at his request, Peter was crucified upside down. See Leon Morris, *The Gospel According to John* (Grand Rapids: Eerdmans, 1971), 876, note 52.

where righteousness dwells" (2 Pet 3:13). For him, the apparent delay in the fulfillment of the promise should not be interpreted as an indication of divine relenting. Adamantly, he argued that it is instead a sign of God's grace, patience, and forbearance (2 Pet 3:9). To his mind, the arrival of the expected righteous regime would come after the purging of the present world order of all evil and wickedness to make way for the emergence of a restored and renewed creation.[7]

In the same vein, John, who was suffering in exile on the isle of Patmos for his faith in Jesus Christ, did not despair about the future. While he spoke bluntly of the adverse circumstances that the people of God, including himself, were facing, he sought to stiffen their spines in the face of adversity by directing their gaze to a day when the situation would be reversed. Echoing both Isaiah and Peter, he speaks confidently of a time when God will make everything new. As he saw it, under the coming regime, living will no longer be a cause of dread, but a delight. It will take place in a milieu where people will not hunger, thirst, or suffer from the effects of the natural elements. Instead, they will be refreshed and will experience the consolation of God himself (Rev 7:16–17). This will be the day when God's desire and purpose to "destroy all evil and bring to an end every grief that plagues humankind" will dawn.[8]

Transformation: A Future Hope with Present Implications

Now it should not escape our attention that Scripture speaks of the establishment of this perfect shalom community in the future tense. Hence, the transformed social order that is envisaged is an eschatological hope. Currently, it exists nowhere on earth. Today, by and large, our planet is a broken place where conflicts and strife of all sorts abound. The nations of this world have yet to learn the wisdom of beating "their swords into plowshares and their spears into pruning hooks" (Isa 2:4). It is also evident that the expected order is closely associated with God and his work. What will transpire will be the work of the exalted and sovereign Lord himself who pledges to "make everything new" (Rev 21:5). All this means that what we are talking about here is not some historical and materialistic project that humans will execute by their

---

7. While he uses language that seems to suggest the complete obliteration of the creation itself, when his thought is considered in the context of the totality of Scripture, this appears unlikely. Indeed, several biblical scholars have abandoned the older interpretation of obliteration in favor of an understanding that the fire of 2 Pet 3:10 is referring to purification instead of complete destruction and obliteration. See Christopher Wright, *Old Testament Ethics for the People of God* (Downers Grove: IVP Academic, 2004), 141, particularly note 55.

8. Glasser, *Announcing the Kingdom*, 21.

own efforts. We are speaking instead of a project that God will providentially carry out on behalf of humans and for their well-being. The focus of the hope, therefore, is God, not humans.

However, while this is true, we should not form the impression that the hope is so transcendent and remote that it bears no relevance to current reality. We should not entertain such a notion for at least two fundamental reasons. First, the God of the promise is the sovereign owner of the world. Despite its present condition, the earth and all that it contains is the Lord's (Ps 24:1). While in its current state the world is not the theater where his will is fully realized, God has not abandoned it to its own devices, nor has he signed it over to the forces of evil. While he works toward its full transformation and renewal, his care for it continues.

The second reason pertains to the nature of biblical hope. Rightly understood, biblical hope does not consist merely in an encouragement for the future alone. Often, it contains features that are intended to influence the present as well. Sometimes, this takes the form of a prophetic down payment in the present.[9] At other times, it takes the form of a challenge and exhortation to the present to reflect, in some form, the reality that lies ahead. As it directs our gaze forward to encourage our hearts by what is coming, Christian hope challenges us to let our lives be impacted, in a real way, by God's promised future. Hence, John admonishes us to let the eschatological expectation serve as a moral detergent that purifies us in the here and now (1 John 3:3). Peter issues a similar admonition. Our expectation of the establishment of the glorious and righteous order should compel us to make "every effort to be found spotless, blameless and at peace with him" now (2 Pet 3:14). Paul, for his part, uses the eschatological hope for a variety of pastoral objectives. He appeals to it as a motivation for faithful engagement and service (1 Cor 15:58), for endurance in suffering (Rom 8:18), for solace in bereavement (1 Thess 4:18), for stamina in the face of suffering (Rom 8:18), and for zeal in the performance of good works (Titus 2:14). As the German theologian Jürgen Moltmann puts it, the future is not completely foreign to the present because "already [it] announces itself and exerts its influence on the present through the promise it awakens."[10]

---

9. Nathan's prophecy regarding the son of David who would build the house that the dying king wanted to construct for the Lord is an illustration of this incremental fulfillment phenomenon. The down payment took place under Solomon, David's son who built the magnificent temple in Jerusalem. But the ultimate fulfillment of the prophecy would await the arrival of Jesus, David's greater Son, who would not only build a greater temple, but would be the one to perpetuate David's rule, as promised by God (2 Sam 7:12–16; cf. Luke 1:31–33).

10. Jürgen Moltmann, *Theology of Hope* (New York: Harper & Row, 1967), 18.

Thus, far from being irrelevant for the present, biblical hope bears pertinent implications for the here and now. Indeed, through the influence it exerts on the present, eschatological hope can be said to begin to be realized. Here are just two illustrations that support this claim. While our world is beset with conflicts of all sorts, Scripture tells us that amid such strife, peace and reconciliation are possible, even among bitter enemies. Christ is our Peacemaker. In him, those "who once were far away have been brought near" (Eph 2:13). And the peace that he brokers, and the truce that he negotiates, is real, for it stems from a cessation of hostility between formerly estranged social groups. This is a ceasefire that paves the way for real brotherhood. Where Christ rules, all human-made distinctions that stand in the way of genuine fellowship, be they ethnic, religious, or cultural, are relativized. For in him, "there is no Gentile or Jew, circumcised or uncircumcised, barbarian, Scythian, slave or free" (Col 3:11). Second, while our world is the scene of horrendous acts of godlessness that cause heartrending brokenness and unbearable pain, it is not altogether bereft of righteousness. If that were the case, it would be uninhabitable, since it would be pure mayhem. Happily, the intrusion of grace in the realm of history has infused into an otherwise corrupt order a dose of wholesomeness that empowers us to reject ungodliness and embrace uprightness and godly living in this present age (Titus 2:12). That is why, every now and then, we detect signs of the righteousness that Peter longs to see dwell in the eschatological community (2 Pet 3:13), and the shalom that the Old Testament prophets talked about.

I had the privilege of a sneak preview of this new order firsthand on two different occasions. The first was in 1992 at a congress on Caribbean evangelization that was convened in the city of Santo Domingo in the Dominican Republic. The congress coincided with the 500th anniversary of the arrival of Christopher Columbus in the Caribbean region, and, understandably, it focused on the impact of Columbus's landing on the people of the regions.

One impact of the European arrival was the slicing of the Caribbean territories into minuscule pieces of land and the division of the numerous ethnic groups that were brought into the region from various parts of the globe. Haiti and the Dominican Republic are the prime examples of this geographic truncation and ethnic animosity. The two countries share the same island and have a history of conflict and animosity.

During one of the sessions of the week-long conference, a white Dominican woman went up onto the platform and apologized to the Haitian participants for the ill-treatment Haitians had received from her country. Hearing the woman's apology and request for forgiveness, a Black Haitian participant at the congress leaped onto the platform with open arms and embraced the repentant sister as a sign of his acceptance of her apology and the granting of her request for forgiveness. I know this well, because I was this Black Haitian.

The place of the second incident was Chiang Mai, Thailand, and the occasion was the 2006 triennial consultation of the International Council for Evangelical Theological Education. While the international gathering was busy discussing the implications of the emergence of global Christianity for theological education, war broke out between Israel and Hezbollah. Instinctively, we suspended the proceedings for a moment of reflection and prayer for the conflict. Among the participants were a Palestinian believer and a Jewish Christian. During the session they went to the front of the large gathering and shared a handshake and a hug to indicate their reconciliation and fraternity in Christ. I experienced that moment firsthand too, since, at the time, I was serving as Director of the Council, and was actually leading the session where it all happened.

These moments were spontaneous, unplanned, and short. Yet, they were hugely significant. This is because they were glimpses in the here and now of the brotherhood that will characterize the fully reconciled humanity that is being forged now as a result of Christ's redemptive work on the cross. That's why they were the highpoints of both gatherings. They remained memorable long after the well-crafted and polished presentations masterfully delivered from the podium had faded from memory.

But what lies behind this irruption of the future into the present? The answer is not far afield, but close at hand. It is easily surmised from what has been said thus far. In a nutshell, it is what is sometimes referred to by New Testament scholars as the Christ Event: that is, the appearance of Jesus Christ on the historical scene in the multifaceted event of the history of redemption which encompasses his birth, death, and resurrection. This is the one thing that makes possible the experience of future hope in the here and now. In that momentous event, "the culmination of the ages has come" upon us (1 Cor 10:11). Through it the "last days" have arrived (Acts 2:16–17; Joel 2:28–32). In Christ, the future casts its shadow on the present and challenges the present to align itself with what it is destined to be. As Kevin Giles puts it, in Christ, "end-times realities have broken into history."[11]

This intrusion of the future in the present is seen both in the crucifixion and in the resurrection of Jesus Christ – the two most stupendous happenings in the history of redemption. At the cross, Christ triumphed over the forces

---

11. Kevin Giles, *What on Earth Is the Church?* (Downers Grove: IVP, 1995), 131.

that opposed God and his plan for the world (Col 2:1–15), thus signaling that the future belongs to him not to them. Further, at the cross, Christ, the slain Lamb, triumphed and is acknowledged as the Conquering Lion (Rev 5:1ff.) who sealed definitively the victory over Satan, our archenemy. Although his banishment is yet to be actualized (Gen 3:15; Rev 20:1–3), his doom is sure. For its part, the resurrection accomplished two eschatological feats. It signals the conquest of death, our most dreaded foe, and it introduces a new order of life into the realm of history. As Paul states in his second letter to Timothy, already "Christ Jesus . . . has destroyed death and has brought . . . immortality to light through the gospel" (2 Tim 1:10). Through his triumphant resurrection from the dead, Christ has won a victory that accrues to the benefit of all who trust in him. For his victory over death was not his alone. His resurrection was the first fruits of the resurrection-related transformation that all who trust in him will experience (1 Cor 15:23). As the late American New Testament scholar George Eldon Ladd states: "The resurrection of Jesus means nothing less than the appearance upon the scene of the historical of something that belongs to the eternal order! . . . It is the manifestation of something utterly new. Eternal life has appeared amid mortality."[12]

Transforming Influence: God's Mandate to His People

Now if through his redemptive accomplishments Christ renders possible the beginning of God's promised transformation in the here and now, under the new covenant the responsibility to make such an experience real falls on the shoulders of the church – his chosen people. The people of God have not been brought into being only to be the beneficiaries of the blessings of God; they exist to be channels through which these same blessings flow to the rest of humanity. In the Old Testament, for instance, God made it clear that his election of Abraham and Israel was meant to redound to the blessing of the world (Gen 18:18–19; 12:3). For his part, having accomplished the mission God had entrusted to him, Jesus entrusted the continuation of the work of redemption to those who were the first beneficiaries of the fulfillment of God's plan of salvation. It is significant that Jesus made the transfer of the missional mandate a point of focus both before the cross and after the resurrection. Before the cross, he said to his Father that "just as you sent me into world, I have sent them into the world" (John 17:18). After the resurrection, he commissioned

---

12. George Eldon Ladd, *A Theology of the New Testament* (Grand Rapids: Eerdmans, 1974), 326–27.

the small band of eleven by using similar terms (John 20:21), and instructed them to "go and make disciples of all nations" (Matt 28:19).

Jesus's engagement with the society of his day was controversial; but it was also immensely beneficial. His presence was good news. This was true particularly for the poor, the oppressed, and the marginalized (Matt 11:1ff.; Luke 4:18ff.). In passing the missional mandate on to his disciples, he expected their own engagement with their context to be nothing less. In his Sermon on the Mount, he makes it clear that their ministry was to have a social dimension. Their very existence was to exert a transforming influence on their milieu. They were to accomplish this both by their being and by their actions. As to their being, they were to be salt of the earth and the light of the world (Matt 5:13–14). With respect to their witness, they were to allow their light to shine so brightly that people would see their good works and glorify God (Matt 5:16). And, more than all this, they were to aspire for nothing less than God's ideal for their context. Astonishingly, Jesus did not refrain from commanding them to pray that God's very will might be done on earth as it is in heaven (Matt 6:10)!

There is no doubt that in speaking to his disciples, Jesus had the whole church in view. This is abundantly clear from his High Priestly Prayer where he says that his intercession is not for his contemporary disciples alone, but for all who will believe in him through their ministry (John 17:20). But, if this reference to the future church was perhaps too oblique in Jesus's teaching, some of the New Testament writers make it abundantly plain later. For instance, writing to the small church at Philippi, Paul conveyed Jesus's mandate in his own words. He enjoined them to "do everything without complaining or arguing so that you may become blameless and pure, children of God without fault in a warped and crooked generation. Then you will shine among them like stars in the sky as you hold firmly to the word of life" (Phil 2:14–16a). In his first letter, Peter expresses a similar thought. Echoing Jesus's saying in the Sermon on the Mount, he adds that the Christian community's exemplary existence within a perverse culture can result in causing unbelieving members of that culture to bring glory to God (1 Pet 2:12).

If due credence is given to the scriptural testimony, therefore, it seems evident that the task of prodding the world into conformity to the will of God for life in community is a responsibility that is given to the church – the people of God. The people of God are to be a redeeming presence in the world now. As the Cuban American theologian Justo González argues, by living out the future reign of God, the church subverts the ruling and destructive powers now.[13] As we will argue in the remainder of this book, in faithfulness to the Lord the church must carry this responsibility with utmost seriousness. However, we must note an important caveat at this point. The execution of this task must be conducted humbly, without an attitude of exceptionalism and triumphalism. Exceptionalism must be avoided because, as sovereign, God can use whomever and whatever he pleases to fulfill his purpose. He who made a donkey talk and caused a pagan ruler to carry out his plan has at his disposal resources that we cannot fathom (Num 22:30; Isa 41:2). We must steer away from triumphalism because our endeavors in the here and now should never claim completeness and finality. We are the church militant waiting to become the church triumphant. Our efforts, though important, can only faintly reflect and imperfectly approximate God's ideal; they can never reach it. Such an exploit can be accomplished only by the God of the promise who in his time will "make all things new" (Rev 21:5 NET).

Admittedly, this is an uncomfortable position. We seem caught between a rock and a hard place. On the one hand, we cannot remain inactive and resign ourselves fatalistically to an order that contradicts God's design. On the other hand, we are painfully aware that our efforts to change it will always fall short of the ideal that we seek. But this is the posture of those who live in this period of redemptive history – the period that is sandwiched between Christ's two appearances or the two epiphanies. While his first appearance inaugurated the time of promised transformation and thus gives meaning to our efforts to see it reflected in the here and now, it is only at his second appearance that is yet to come that it will be consummated. The late British theologian John Stott aptly summed up our predicament. We who live in this interim period, he said, "live 'between the times,' suspended rather uncomfortably between the 'already' and the 'not yet.'"[14]

With this caveat in mind, let us go back to the burden of our task and ask ourselves how the church can best fulfill the responsibility entrusted to it by the Lord. How can the church best function as an agent of change in the here and now in anticipation of the coming new order? That's the question we will endeavor to explore in the balance of this book. As a sneak preview, we are putting forth the suggestion that the church best advances the cause of social transformation by being *authentically engaged* with the present social order. As is evident in the italicized phrase, the two key concepts that serve as a hinge for

---

13. Justo González, *Mañana: Christian Theology from a Hispanic Perspective* (Nashville: Abingdon, 1990), 166.

14. John Stott, *The Message of Timothy and Titus* (Leicester: Inter-Varsity Press, 1997), 197.

this project are *engagement* and *authenticity*. Engagement speaks of an ecclesial praxis that is multifaceted. It is a holistic posture that commits the church to recognize, support, and where possible carry out legitimate activities aimed at orienting society in the direction desired by God. As for authenticity, this speaks of a deep-seated regard for the being of the church. Here the claim is that praxis must be governed by being. Engagement is authentic when it always maintains the integrity of the church as God's alternative society within the wider society.

The Purpose of This Book

With this said, we can now briefly map out the road that lies ahead of us. The book consists of four parts. In the first section, we will review some of the major views on the role of the church in the world, and we will make a case for the concept of authentic engagement as a preferred paradigm for a robust ecclesial praxis. In the second part, we will develop the ecclesiology that informs a credible involvement by the church in the world. In keeping with this conviction, this second section of the book will go beyond a theology of the church to address its life in the world, with a stress on the church's representative role and peculiar or countercultural lifestyle. But an authentic ecclesial praxis needs more than a solid ecclesiology; it also needs an ecclesial presence that is genuine and authentic. Having laid this two-pronged foundation, the book moves, in part 3, to the specific dimension of ecclesial engagement. This section will endeavor to broach the various facets of the church's engagement with the world, encompassing its mode of life, its evangelistic and kerygmatic activity, its promotion of human well-being through its promotion and defense of human worth and dignity, and the exercise of its prophetic calling. In part 4, we will put forward a stance that we believe to be conducive to the church's transforming role in the social domain.

Part One

Models of Transforming Engagement

2

Major Views on the Church's Role in the World

In the previous chapter we argued that the people of God have a transforming call on their lives. Wherever they happen to be, their presence and actions should exert an influence that results in the alteration of the context. If this premise is valid, the question is: what posture should the people of God adopt to play such a role? What stance must they take to be of benefit to the context in which they are located? *Why* is the church on earth, and *how* should it order its life to fulfill its purpose? Our approach in this chapter is twofold. First, we will review some of the major responses which have been given to this question. Second, we will assess these responses with a view to determining their strength for the transformation of a given social order.

Mapping out the Options

In a little book titled *The Community Called Church*,[1] Juan Luis Segundo, a Latin American theologian from Uruguay, begins with just such a question. "What is the infinitesimal Christian Community supposed to do within the vast community of mankind?" he asks.[2] In an address delivered at the first International Congress on World Evangelization that was convened in Lausanne, Switzerland, in 1974, Graham made a comment that offered some insight in the direction of a response to the query that Segundo would ask two years later. In his speech to the congress, Graham listed three stances Christians tended to take on the matter of the church's role in society. "The first," he said, "is to deny that we have any social responsibility as Christians.... The

---

1. Juan Luis Segundo, S.J., *The Community Called Church* (Maryknoll: Orbis, 1976).
2. Segundo, *Community Called Church*, 9.

second . . . is to let social concern become our all-consuming mission. . . . A third is to identify the Gospel with any one particular political program." He went on to acknowledge candidly that the third option had been his danger.³

We believe that Graham's categorization is basically correct. However, when we ponder the question more deeply, we detect a need for some adjustment in his response if we are to gain a wider range of responses that Christians make to the question under discussion. We think, for instance, that there is merit in combining Graham's third point with his second point to form a single option. This seems sensible when we consider the fact that when social concern becomes the all-consuming mission of the church, the temptation is real for the church to align itself rather uncritically with the political program that seems to pursue the change it considers urgent and paramount. If our suggested amendment is correct, Graham's categorization boils down to two positions – both extreme. At the one end of the spectrum is the denial of social responsibility by the church, and at the other end, the assumption of full social responsibility by it.

This leads to a second adjustment, and this time it concerns the need to expand Graham's categorization to include other competing options.⁴ What we are saying here is that there is reason to affirm the existence of intermediary or median positions, and two of them come to mind. In the first place, there is the case where the church seeks to alleviate suffering *without seeking* necessarily to alter the socio-political order. Second, we can think of the situation where the church desires social change as the outcome of its effort but refrains from pursuing such a goal directly. Both are legitimate postures of engagement that shouldn't be ignored. Now, if we insert these two mediating positions into Graham's two polar-opposite options, and if we classify them all under the rubric of engagement, we end up with the following categorization of the church's praxiological activity in the sociopolitical realm: (1) the nonengagement posture, (2) the restrictive engagement stance, (3) the indirect engagement position, and (4) the thoroughgoing engagement stance.

---

3. Billy Graham, "Why the Berlin Congress?," in *One Race, One Gospel, One Task*, eds. Carl F. Henry and Stanley Mooneyham (Minneapolis: Worldwide Publications, 1967), 1:31–32.

4. In his book *One-Sided Christianity? Uniting the Church to Heal a Lost and Broken World* (Grand Rapids: Zondervan, 1993), Ronald Sider identifies four models which he groups roughly along the lines of religious/theological traditions. From right to left he labels the models Individualistic Evangelical, Radical Anabaptist, Dominant Ecumenical, and Secular Christian (pp. 25–44). His grouping is helpful and reflects similarities with my own categorization. There are, however, differences as well. For instance, while his construct is informed by the attitude vis-à-vis evangelism and social action, ours is shaped by a sharper focus on the church's engagement with the social order.

What are the strengths and viability of these views with respect to the church's role in the transformation of a given sociopolitical sphere? The burden of this chapter is to explore this question. It will show that the ecclesial praxis advocated by these models is either too timid or too radical for the church's authentic engagement in the social realm.

Nonengagement

We begin our examination, then, with the posture of nonengagement. Essentially, this stance argues for the withdrawal of the church from a world considered irredeemable. Within mainstream Christianity and among some fringe groups tangentially connected to it, there are those who take the position that the church and the world should be separate from each other. For them, the only appropriate stance that the church should maintain toward the social domain is one of withdrawal and avoidance of contact. It goes without saying that connected to this policy of nonengagement is the absence of any meaningful sense of responsibility on the part of the church toward the material order. This, of course, does not mean a lack of concern for the temporal domain, but instead a lack of confidence in the possibility of any change for the better of the current order.

Undergirding this posture are two theological beliefs: a pessimistic view of the world and an escapist and isolationist understanding of the church. In the perspective of nonengagement advocates, the present world was damaged beyond repair by the fall. Part of the impact of humanity's rebellion against God was the disruption of the fellowship that existed between him and humans prior to that catastrophic event. In its present condition, the world is in decay and is doomed to destruction. The world's sorry state is compounded by the fact that it is under the power of evil and under the sway of the powers of darkness. For the American pastor Greg Boyd, for instance, Christians ought to abstain from *all* political involvement because that domain has been completely surrendered to Satan. "The authority of *all* the kingdoms of the world has been given to Satan. . . . Functionally, Satan is the acting CEO of all earthly governments."[5] When all of this is considered, the world is seen as a sphere to flee rather than a domain to engage with a view to changing it.

---

5. Greg Boyd, *The Myth of a Christian Nation* (Grand Rapids: Zondervan, 2005), 21. Emphasis added. Boyd appeals to Luke 4:6 to support this claim. He makes much of the Tempter's allegation that all "authority has been delivered to him," and of Jesus's seeming acquiescence to Satan's claim.

While the church shares the same geographical space as the world, it is completely distinct from it. For the early Anabaptists who initially adopted this posture of noninvolvement, the church must maintain its distance from mainstream society even when the society in which it is located claims to be Christian. Since the fall has corrupted the material order beyond repair, the Christian is to flee that order to avoid being swept away in its coming doom and destruction. It is best to come apart and pray for the day of judgment that will come on the prevailing order. If there is something that should preoccupy the church in such a doomed world, it is the rescue of the soul which is "lost and in need of salvation."[6] As Avery Dulles argues, in this perspective the kerygmatic function of the church takes center stage. Its raison d'être in the present order is simply to herald the salvific message with a view to rescuing the maximum number of perishing souls from a world that is heading for destruction. Such a responsibility does not make room for the promotion of a divine reign that has presumably entered the historical domain with a view to altering its present configuration. The Ecuadorian theologian René Padilla offers an apt summary of this model:

> [Herein] lies a conception of salvation as only spiritual . . . or future salvation of the soul in which this life has meaning only as "preparation for the world beyond." In this case history is assimilated by a future eschatology, and religion is converted into a means of escape from present reality. The result is total misunderstanding of society's problems in the name of being separated from the world. This is distortion of the gospel that has led to Marxist criticism of Christian eschatology as "the opiate of the people."[7]

Beside this pessimistic view of the world, this posture is undergirded by an ecclesiology that has as its main features isolationism, detachment, and impermanence. In his book entitled *What on Earth Is the Church?*, Kevin Giles points out that for a wide cross section of Christians, the church is, in essence, the local assembly. The congregation is the manifestation of the church in its totality in a local setting.[8] We have here a form of congregationalism that denies the name "church" to any other entity than the local congregation. And

---

6. John Gladwin, *God's People in God's World: Biblical Motives for Social Involvement* (Leicester: Inter-Varsity Press 1979), 8.

7. Cited in Samuel Escobar, *In Search of Christ in Latin America* (Carlisle: Langham Global Library, 2019), 213.

8. Giles, *What on Earth Is the Church?*, 13–14.

because each congregation is a stand-alone and autonomous entity, the church is, in the main, a hodgepodge of disparate units which have no necessary connection between them. To the extent that the concept of "church" has a meaning broader than the local congregation, such understanding refers only to a heavenly reality which constitutes the universal church – the assembly of all believers in continuous session in heaven in which Christians on earth participate in a spiritual sense.

At the hands of theologians such as Karl Barth and Hans Küng, this congregational understanding takes on a dimension that further weakens the church's standing in the world and its ability to conduct meaningful action in the temporal domain. For in their ecclesiology, the church exists like a hermit, and its being is characterized by a lack of permanence. For both theologians, the congregation is an event that is constituted by the act of gathering. Hence, where there is no gathering there is no church because the congregation is not a permanent reality that exists by itself. For Barth, the church is the event that occurs at a particular place by the work of the Spirit. He writes:

> We believe in the existence of the Church – which means that we believe each particular congregation to be a congregation of Christ. *Credo ecclesiam* means that I believe that here, at that place, in this assembly the work of the Holy Spirit takes place. By that is not intended a deification of the creature.[9]

And for Küng,

> An *ekklesia* is not something that is formed and founded once and for all and remains unchanged; it becomes an *ekklesia* by the fact of a repeated concrete event, people coming together and congregating, in particular [gathering] for the purpose of worshipping God. The concrete congregation is the actual manifestation, the representation, indeed the realization of the New Testament community.[10]

This approach does not seem to offer a satisfactory response to the question before us. The problem with this construal lies not in what it affirms, but in what is left unsaid, and this obtains both in the realm of theology and in the area of praxis. If we consider the first domain, we note that the theology of the church and the world on which the nonengagement rests is seriously lacking.

---

9. Karl Barth, *Dogmatics in Outline* (New York: Harper Touch Books, 1959), 142–43.
10. Hans Küng, *The Church* (New York: Sheed and Ward, 1968), 84.

True, there is biblical ground for a congregational understanding of the church. In various places, the New Testament refers to the church as an assembly that meets in a given place (Rom 16:1–5). And Jesus says that where believers gather, he is in their midst (Matt 18:19–20). However, this doesn't present the whole biblical portrayal of the church. There are other places where the Bible speaks of the church in broader terms than a stand-alone and occasional entity. We find references in the New Testament to the church existing in a city and a region (1 Cor 1:2; 1 Thess 1:1–2). And there are references to fellowship and interchange among the units that constitute the wider Christian presence in these places (Rom 16:3b). Considering this, we must affirm that beside the heavenly *communio santorum* (Heb 12:22–23), there is a *communio terrena* – a *terrestrial* communion of saints. There is a horizontal relationship which entails the sharing of life, and not only a vertical and purely spiritual relationship.

If we turn to the notion of impermanence, it seems to collide with the several biblical metaphors which view the church as an enduring body. One thinks of such metaphors as the body of Christ (Col 1:18; 1 Cor 12:27), the temple of God (Eph 2:20–22), and the vine and the branches (John 15:1–3), to name just a few. These figures of speech seem to convey the idea of endurance, continuance, and permanence, rather than intermittency.

Similarly, the theology of the world that seems to provide warrant for the escapist stance of the church seems truncated. A full-orbed biblical understanding of the world cannot generate such a pessimistic attitude toward it that we are propelled to take flight from it. In his small but important book entitled *God's People in God's World*, John Gladwin argues persuasively, to our minds, that a biblical understanding of the world must make the distinction between the world as God's creation and the world as an approach to life. The first speaks of the *good* order that God brought into being, and of which he is still the owner (Gen 1–2; Ps 24:1), while the second speaks of the way in which people live in God's world in defiance of him.[11] While Scripture enjoins distancing from the latter, as for example John admonishes in 1 John 2:15–17, it sanctions engagement with the former. Indeed, the way to resist the world as an anti-God system is to engage the world as God's good creation, even in its fallen state.

This dual sense of the concept of "world" and the stance that believers are to adopt toward it are clear in Jesus's prayer for his disciples at the end of his earthly ministry. That is why the praxis that Jesus recommended to them is one of engagement, not disengagement. They were to remain *in* the world,

---

11. Gladwin, *God's People*, 29.

while not being *of* the world (John 17:11, 14–15). And, in Jesus's view, such engagement is by no means futile. For through it, even the world as a system that is raised against God *can* change. In the Sermon on the Mount, Jesus told the disciples that through their engagement, the world will observe their good works and glorify God (Matt 5:16). Considering all this, it seems reasonable to take the stance that society can in fact change for the better. And such change has always involved the engagement of the people of God – even if only a small number of them.

Restrictive Engagement

We come to the second position which we call limited or restrictive engagement. We deem this label an appropriate descriptor of this view because, unlike the first, it does not advocate a withdrawal of the church from the social sphere but instead *sets boundaries* to the function that the church is allowed to exercise in that order. It limits the church's involvement to certain areas of social life while deeming it unacceptable in others, particularly the political domain. Here the church's role is limited to clearly delineated aspects of a given society's sociopolitical life. In a nutshell, the view limits the church's engagement to the provision of social services, social assistance, and spiritual nurture.

Growing up in Haiti, we both have firsthand knowledge of this approach. I (Dieumeme) remember vividly the way a prominent church in Port-au-Prince, the country's capital, used to introduce its popular weekly radio program. With great fanfare, the introduction to the program resounded: "L'Eglise Baptiste des Cités is now on the air for the edification of believers and the spiritual salvation of the nation." For our study, the important thing to note in this statement is the goal the broadcast sought to accomplish in Haitian society: *spiritual salvation*. In the Haiti of those days, it was important for the church to make this clarification and offer such a caveat. For to leave the term "salvation" unqualified would be viewed as a criticism of the political powers. Although it was apparent to all that the country was beset with a host of social problems, in the eyes of the body politic it needed salvation in no other domain except the spiritual realm.

This focus on the spiritual domain did not mean that the church was impervious to the problems that confronted the country. By no means! Just a stone's throw from its beautiful and imposing building was a ministry connected to it entitled Aide aux Enfants (Aid to Children). That ministry provided food, clothing, shelter, and educational opportunities to countless children of the densely populated city.

And the Eglise Baptiste des Cités was not unique in this. Throughout the city of Port-au-Prince, and, indeed, the entire country, churches and mission agencies were doing all sorts of things to meet the needs of the distressed populace. These included orphanages, schools, clinics, hospitals, and other endeavors designed to alleviate the sufferings and improve the plight of the people.

Nor was Haiti the only place where this was happening. This sort of social intervention on the part of the church was taking place in various countries in what was at that time called the Third World. It was a time when, for most people, responsible ministry meant the provision of spiritual nurture and social assistance. And this kind of social engagement represented a marked shift in the attitude of the church vis-à-vis social responsibility. There was a time when such effort was viewed as falling outside the purview of legitimate Christian ministry because of its resemblance to the so-called "social gospel." The social gospel was the movement that was popular in the United States during the latter part of the nineteenth century and first quarter of the twentieth, and which focused on addressing issues of social justice and human needs. Nuñez and Taylor took note of this shift when they asserted that "it seems that most evangelical leaders in the worldwide evangelical community are not concerned anymore about the question of the validity of social assistance as a dimension of the missionary task."[12] But, in their estimation, that advance, though welcome, fell short of the kind of involvement required for the advent of meaningful social change because it remained at the level of social aid. As they saw it, something more was needed. "The greatest challenge . . . [had] to do with social responsibility *as political action to produce radical social change.*"[13] Speaking specifically of Latin America, they stated: "the big issue [was] whether or not we should get involved as church in *transforming the basic structures of society.*"[14]

If we ask what prevented the church from including that dimension in its social witness, the answer is not hard to find; it lies in the truncated vision of reality that underlies the restrictive engagement approach. Far from seeing social reality as a whole, it creates a dichotomy between the spiritual and the social, and further divides the social realm itself into two components: the social proper and the political. It sanctions the church's activity in the former

---

12. Emilio Nuñez and William Taylor, *Crisis and Hope in Latin America* (Pasadena: William Carey Library, 1996), 406. Nuñez admits that even he did not understand that the mission needed to go beyond the level of the alleviation of needs. "In those days we were not discussing yet whether political action was a duty of the Christian" (409).

13. Nuñez and Taylor, *Crisis and Hope*, 106.

14. Nuñez and Taylor, 106.

and prohibits it in the latter. In his meticulous study of Haitian Protestantism, the Haitian sociologist and theologian Charles-Poisset Romain confirmed that a major trait of the social ethics of the Haitian Protestant church is the separation of the social and the political and *the refusal of the church to be involved in the latter.*[15] The church, he argues, sees its role as embracing the spiritual domain and the social domain *minus the political realm*. This results in the adoption of an apolitical stance that ends up guaranteeing the status quo.

Romain sees two main theological bases for this ecclesial stance. The first is the doctrine of the two kingdoms championed by the German Reformer Martin Luther, and the second the ecclesiological concept of otherworldliness or *extraterritoriality*.

The doctrine of the two kingdoms, as is well known, stresses the twofold action of God in creation and redemption. This action is executed respectively through the temporal powers and the church. As the agency established by God for the fulfillment of his purpose, secular government wields near absolute power in the order of creation and is virtually immune from challenges by the church whose realm of activity is restricted to the order of redemption. It is true that Luther advocates a relationship of mutual acknowledgment, interdependence, and complementarity between the two servants of God. However, in actuality, it is clear that in that relationship the scale tips in favor of the temporal order. For while he makes allowances for the involvement of temporal authorities in ecclesiastical and even doctrinal matters, he denies the church the right to unilaterally undertake political actions aimed at transforming the social order. The Christian's sociopolitical involvement is restricted solely to the performance of vocational duties and the execution of tasks assigned by the state.

Alongside this doctrine of the division of spheres of authority is the ecclesiology of otherworldliness, or as Romain calls it, extraterritoriality. According to this view, although the church lives in the world, it doesn't consider the world its true home. The territory to which the church belongs lies beyond the temporal domain in the celestial realm. In its eyes, the temporal realm is nothing more than a place of transition to which the Christian is loosely attached, and in whose fortune the believer has a very low stake. Because of this, one's plight in the world is not a major concern because of the expectation of better things that lie ahead. Such a church behaves as a celestial entity, with no firm footing in the terrestrial.

---

15. Charles-Poisset Romain, *Le Protestantisme dans la société haïtienne* (Port au Prince: Editions Henry des Champs, 1985), 238.

We cannot fairly lay the charge of social indifference or lack of concern at the feet of this kind of ecclesial engagement. Throughout the world, the ministry of social assistance has saved millions of lives and alleviated the suffering of untold millions of others. As bad as the condition of our world is, it would be much worse without the work the church has done in areas such as health care, education, poverty alleviation, food, water, and so on. And such a ministry should not be opposed, for throughout the gospels we see the Lord Jesus meeting people's pressing needs of various kinds – healing the sick, feeding the hungry, defending the marginalized (Matt 4:23–25; John 6:1–15).

Having said that, we must express our agreement with Nuñez and Taylor that, though helpful, that kind of engagement falls short of what is needed to make a meaningful difference in the social order. Its impotence stems from several defects. To begin with, the theology of the two kingdoms which upholds it places the political domain outside the realm of redemption and shelters it from evangelical witness and prophetic challenge.[16] It vitiates the doctrine of Christ's universal lordship, which claims for him every sphere of reality. As Lord of the universe to whom all authority has been given, Christ's sovereignty knows no limits. It extends to every sphere of life: "the economic and the political, the social and the cultural, the aesthetic and the ecological, the personal and the communitarian."[17] As Abraham Kuyper famously said: "There is not a square inch in the whole domain of our human existence over which Christ, who is sovereign over all, does not cry, 'Mine.'"[18] Or in the terse wording of René Padilla: "Nothing and no one is excluded from his lordship."[19] Further, it reduces the gospel to the level of private faith, and in so doing undermines its power to challenge reality. Where a rigorous gospel critique and strong structures of accountability are absent, the ground is fertile for the exercise of absolute power, the breeding of corruption, and the stymieing of every transforming effort. By blunting the political edge of the gospel, the position nullifies its transforming potential, and, perhaps unknowingly, makes the church an accomplice of the status quo. For far from being politically neutral, the stance of apoliticism is itself a political stance.

---

16. Dieumeme Noëlliste, "Poverty and the Gospel: The Case of Haiti," *Evangelical Review of Theology* 34, no. 4 (2010): 317.

17. *La Iglesia local como agente de transformacion: una eclesiologia para la misión integral*, eds. C. René Padilla and Tetsunao Yamamori (Buenos Aires: Kairos, 2003), 21–22.

18. Abraham Kuyper, "Sphere Sovereignty," in *Abraham Kuyper: A Centennial Reader*, ed. James D. Bratt (Grand Rapids: Eerdmans, 1998), 488.

19. Padilla and Yamamori, *La Iglesia local*, 22.

Second, with respect to the ecclesiology of *extraterritoriality*, it fails to recognize that, while the people have a heavenly citizenship, their terrestrial life, no matter how short, is by no means inconsequential or irrelevant in the eyes of God. What we do at an airport terminal while we wait to board a flight to a destination may not matter much. But what we do during our earthly journey matters a great deal. Scripture makes it clear that such terrestrial activity has eternal import, since we must give an account of our lives to the Lord (Matt 25:31–46; 1 Cor 3:12–15; Rom 14:10–12). It also has temporal significance for the earthly city, as Jeremiah made clear to the Jewish exiles in Babylon (Jer 29:1–7).

Third, on the practical side, by bracketing out the political domain, the restrictive engagement approach seriously limits the scope and impact of the church's witness. As a starter, for all its desire and efforts to alleviate people's plight, there are certain social goods that are beyond the church's capacity to deliver. These can be provided only by the political powers that control society's resources. In contexts where those who wield political power are not inclined to shoulder such responsibility willingly, the common good is bound to suffer if the prophetic challenge is not uttered. More significantly, the exemption of the political realm from evangelical accountability means the confining of the church's effort to attacking the symptoms of society's ills while leaving untouched the root causes of those ills. These efforts do of course sometimes result in the improving of personal lives. But even in such cases, often the recalcitrant context, in its desire to maintain itself, pushes these persons out to other latitudes. Herein lies the main cause of the brain drain phenomenon that afflicts many a Majority World country and constitutes a major impediment to their development.

As I pen these words, Haiti, our country of origin, is going through a time of deep insecurity. Violent gangs kidnap people at will with impunity. They render life literally unlivable. They're allowed to unleash such mayhem on the society, including the church, because of a near total vacuum of adequate political power. This is a problem that no sector of society can solve except the political.

Indirect Engagement

There are persons who are genuinely concerned with social change, and who sincerely believe that the church has a role to play in the transformation of the social order, but who can't countenance the notion that the church itself must be directly involved in the execution of that task. Rather, they construe the church's input as an *indirect* contribution. The church pushes society toward God's ideal for communal life via the persons it brings into its fold.

According to this view, the world consists of lost people who stand in need of salvation. The primary responsibility of the church in such a world is the proclamation of the message of spiritual and eternal salvation with the hope that people who respond to the message will become agents of change. In this theory, as the number of converts increases, society will experience changes for the better. In any society, the existence of an army of transformed people will result in the transformation of that society. "The greater the number of converts to the gospel, the greater the changes" that society will experience.[20]

This position enjoys the endorsement of several influential evangelical leaders. The late Billy Graham, for instance, whom we referenced earlier, was convinced that "if we want moral reform, the quickest and surest way is by evangelism."[21] According to him, "the transforming Gospel of Jesus Christ is the only way to reverse the moral trends of the present hour."[22] To those who long for the transformation of society, therefore, Graham confidently recommends evangelism as the surest method to accomplish such a goal. "Do we want social reform?" he asks rhetorically, and without missing a beat he answers: "The preaching of the Cross could do more to bring social change than any other method."[23] The same thinking was reflected in the first Lausanne Congress which is often regarded as a turning point in the thinking of evangelicals on the question of the church's involvement in social change. There, the church's praxiological engagement was placed on a rung lower in its ladder of activities than its evangelistic responsibility. Graham was clear on this. He declared categorically that social responsibility "is not our priority mission. After all, humanists may heal, feed, and help, but social presence isn't Gospel proclamation. . . . Evangelism and the salvation of souls is the vital mission of the Church."[24]

Now the Lausanne Covenant, which came out of that historic Congress, *did* advance the thinking of evangelicals on the matter significantly. It clearly affirmed that "evangelism and socio-political involvement are both part of

---

20. Nuñez and Taylor, *Crisis and Hope*, 406.

21. Carl F. Henry and Stanley Mooneyham, eds., *One Race, One Gospel, One Task* (Minneapolis: Worldwide Publications, 1967), 1:31–32.

22. Henry and Mooneyham, *One Race, One Gospel, One Task*, 1:31–32.

23. Henry and Mooneyham, 1:31–32.

24. Billy Graham, "Why Lausanne?," in *Let the Earth Hear His Voice*, ed. J. D. Douglas (Minneapolis: Worldwide Publications, 1975), 29–31.

our Christian duty."[25] However, the Covenant goes on to nuance that stance by clarifying that "in the church's mission of sacrificial service, evangelism is *primary*."[26] If we ask the framers of the document to say which of these two activities comes first, John Stott, who was one of the drafters of the Covenant, responds: "normally, the church will not have to choose between evangelism and social action since both are included in its mission. [However], if a choice has to be made, then evangelism is primary."[27] Here, we clearly have a hierarchical ordering of the two functions. "The church is in the world for the primary purpose of announcing the kerygma."[28] Its diaconic function is secondary. While the "performance of social service is an outcome of the new birth," the proper priority must be maintained.[29]

Armed with this conviction, proponents of this position are convinced that the church must give priority attention to the preaching of the gospel. In this respect, the American theologian Carl F. Henry asserts: "We repudiate the inversion of the New Testament by current emphases on the revolutionizing of social structures. . . . Outside a rediscovery of the Gospel of grace, there now remains no long-range prospect for the survival of modern civilization, but only a guarantee of its utter collapse."[30] Perhaps the renowned American author and prison reformer Charles Colson provides the most apt summary of this position. In his magisterial work *How Now Shall We Live?*, Colson argues that the transformation of society is contingent upon the transformation of people – the change of their hearts and wills by the gospel.[31]

What should we make of this stance? If we examine history carefully, we cannot fairly deny that the proclamation of the gospel has been beneficial to society. Many a struggle to root out evil from the social realm was led by persons who were transformed by the gospel and who were convinced that the gospel that transformed their personal lives could also transform their societies. The activities of freedom fighters such as Bartolomé de las Casas, William Wilberforce, Frederick Douglass, Martin Luther King Jr., and Desmond Tutu, to name only a few, amply illustrate this point.

---

25. Douglas, *Let the Earth Hear His Voice*, 4–5.
26. Douglas, 4–5. Emphasis added.
27. Douglas, 4–5.
28. C. Peter Wagner, *Latin American Theology: Radical or Evangelical? The Struggle for the Faith in a Young Church* (Grand Rapids: Eerdmans, 1970), 106.
29. Wagner, *Latin American Theology*, 106.
30. Henry and Mooneyham, *One Race, One Gospel, One Task*, 1:16–17.
31. Charles Colson, *How Now Shall We Live?* (Wheaton: Tyndale House, 1999), 381.

Having said that, we must admit that the examples cited above represent more the exception than the rule. If we are to judge this position by its transformational impact, we must confess that, overall, its track record is not sterling. As Nuñez and Taylor remark, the spread of the gospel and the church growth that accompanied it has not necessarily "meant a radical change in the attitude of the church toward social issues and social transformation."[32] We must admit that this is a frustrating reality for those of us who believe with all our hearts in the transforming power of the gospel.

Two features seem to weaken the transforming potential of this approach. The first is its apparent temporal prioritization of the task of verbal proclamation over social involvement. Evangelism is primary, the Lausanne Covenant declares. But what is meant by primary? As the story of the good Samaritan shows, when this policy is rigidly applied, there is the likelihood that critical social needs can go unmet. As presented in the gospels, Jesus's ministry seems to reflect a sensitivity and flexibility that avoids such rigidity. While his ultimate concern was always with meeting the spiritual need of humans, on several occasions he did not shirk from first addressing the urgent material situation that was before him. His handling of the case of the woman caught in adultery is a case in point (John 8:1–11). He spared her life *first* before dismissing her with the admonition to "go, and . . . sin no more" (8:11 ESV).

Perhaps a better way to understand the concept of priority might be to construe it in *logical* rather than temporal terms. I am using the term "logical" here to mean the motivation and objective that lies behind all that we do as disciples of Christ – our actions as well as our words. The reason or logic behind all we do is to point people to the God who is revealed in Christ. In this sense, evangelism does indeed have priority since in this understanding all that is done (word and action) is *motivated* by the gospel, *for the purpose* of attracting people to God, to the end that they may *glorify him* (2 Cor 5:14–15; Matt 5:16).

The other debilitating feature of the approach is the loose connection it makes between the church as an entity and social engagement. In this construal, the function of social witness is outsourced to individual members of the church. But the embrace of such a responsibility by individual Christians is by no means guaranteed. Christians may or may not do it. Further, even when Christians do answer that call, history has shown that individual Christians engaged in the struggle for social change do not automatically enjoy the approval and support of the corporate church. The church did not at first rally round transformational leaders such as Martin Luther King Jr., Dietrich

---

32. Nuñez and Taylor, *Crisis and Hope*, 406.

Bonhoeffer, and so on. Here, the effort of transformation can easily become a *happenstance* that is carried out in a *trickle-down* fashion rather than with purpose and intentionality. We cannot help wondering if this approach to social engagement doesn't provide part of the explanation for the coexistence in the world of such a vast number of Christians along with so much social evil.

Unbridled or Thoroughgoing Engagement

We come now to a position which is the opposite of the first. We dub it unbridled and thoroughgoing because it makes the project of transformation the overriding task of the church. In this position, the church's transformational responsibility is paramount and trumps everything else. The church's involvement in the world becomes all-consuming and takes center stage. Those who embrace this approach are of the view that, in contexts ridden with socio-structural problems, it is not enough for the church to engage in the mere description and analysis of the prevailing reality; it must seek to change it by all means possible. The proponents of this position take seriously the words of Karl Marx, who said, in his eleventh thesis on Feuerbach, that "the philosophers have only *interpreted* the world . . . the point, however, is to change it."[33] The urgency of the situation makes it imperative for the church to participate in the birth of a new order. And, further, as the church pursues this objective, its participation need not be stymied by limiting constraints and inhibiting conditions which were established prior to its engagement in the struggle for change. If there is an a priori condition, it is the commitment to carry out the project of transformation to a successful end.

The underlying premise that undergirds this ecclesial praxis is the conviction that the church exists for others. As such, the church is, at core, a *servant* whose very being is tied to what it does for the well-being of the world. Thus, in this construal, mission determines essence.

This understanding of the church's role in the world enjoys the support of several prominent theologians. The German theologian Dietrich Bonhoeffer seemed to set the stage for it. In his *Letters and Papers from Prison* he writes, "The church is only the church when it exists for others. To make a start it should give away all its property to those in need. The clergy must live solely on the free-will offerings of their congregations, or possibly engage in some

---

33. Karl Marx, "Eleven Theses on Feuerbach," in *The Marx-Engels Reader*, ed. Robert C. Tucker, 2nd ed. (New York: Norton & Co., 1978), 145.

secular calling."[34] As is well known, Bonhoeffer gave credence to this belief by joining the plot to assassinate Adolf Hitler to rid German society of the threat that the despotic leader posed. Similarly, the American theologian and Harvard University professor Harvey Cox is clear about the church's role in the secular city. For him, "the church's task in the secular city is to be the *diakonos* of the city, the servant who bends himself to struggle for its wholeness and health."[35] If we ask what that "bending" entails, others of similar persuasion come with ready answers. Among them, we can name Leonardo Boff of Brazil and Juan Luis Segundo of Uruguay whom we referenced earlier. According to them, the church's "bending" can take the form of the endorsement of elements of a non-Christian ideology, or the active cooperation with non-Christian actors and movements that are working for change, or even the use of violent means if the situation requires it.[36] Further, for a theologian like Boff, the permission for such unrestrained engagement is not to be sought from an external authority; rather, it emanates from within the agents themselves. For him, "active resistance [is] a dictate of conscience."[37]

If we wonder whether such a bold move by the church for the betterment of the world is in keeping with its nature, the proponents of the unbridled position have no trouble answering in the affirmative. This is because, in their view, church and world aren't fundamentally different. As they see it, there exists a close correlation between the two that blurs the boundaries between them and removes any hindrance to cooperation between them in the execution of the transformation project. For a theologian like Segundo, for instance, the only thing that sets the church apart from the world is the knowledge it possesses of what God is doing in the world. The belief and involvement of the church have only "objective importance."[38] They make us aware that God's dealing with the Christian community is essentially the same as his dealing with the universal community. While the non-Christian participates in God's plan spontaneously and unconsciously, the Christian does so consciously because he or she is the

---

34. Dietrich Bonhoeffer, *Letters and Papers from Prison*, rev. ed. (New York: Macmillan, 1963), 203.

35. Harvey Cox, *The Secular City* (New York: Macmillan, 1965), 134.

36. Leonardo Boff, *Salvation and Liberation* (Maryknoll: Orbis, 1984), 10–11; Juan Luis Segundo, S.J., *The Liberation of Theology*, trans. John Drury (Maryknoll: Orbis, 1974).

37. Leonardo Boff, "La Iglesia es una Casta Meretriz," *Cristianismo y Sociedad* 84 (1985): 120.

38. Segundo, *Community Called Church*, 11.

one who "already knows," and such knowledge is "what distinguishes and defines him [or her]."[39]

Boff is of the same view, except that he makes his argument for the close connection between the church and the world by appealing to such universal values as love, fellowship, and community. He is convinced that wherever these values are on display, *there* is the church, whether we realize it or not. Hence, according to him, "Christianity could exist before Christianity. . . . It is as extensive as the human world. It could exist before Christ and can still exist today outside of Christian limits where the word Christianity is neither used nor known."[40]

In the heyday of the theology of revolution movement in the 1960s, the push for this kind of thoroughgoing engagement by the church was intense in places where the revolutionary ferment was strong. In Latin America, for instance, an organization known as Iglesia y Sociedad in America Latina (ISAL), which had close connections with the World Council of Churches, was a staunch promotor of this approach. ISAL went so far as to advise the churches in the region to boldly embrace the project of transformation by aligning themselves ideologically and praxiologically with those who were committed to overturning the current status quo. ISAL boldly asked churches to serve as

> task fronts, whether as centres of support, or as means for promotion and political recruitment, and also as places of ideological struggle in which an effort is made to set free the Christian's conscience in order that it may respond to the option [for], and to militancy in support of, the popular masses.[41]

Since, in those days, some of those who were engaged in the pursuit of sociostructural change tended to lean toward the left, the admonition was clearly an appeal for alignment with the Marxist ideology and the endorsement of the revolutionary activism it inspired.

One might think that the stance being discussed here is a thing of the past, or that it is an option advocated only by left-leaning activists. Surprise! This is certainly not the case. The push for the church to throw itself unreservedly into the pursuit of a cause that it deems urgent and necessary can happen

---

39. Segundo, 11.

40. Leonardo Boff, *Jesus Christ Liberator* (Maryknoll: Orbis, 1979), 250.

41. Rafael Tomas Carvajal, Filemon Escobar, et al., *America Latina: Movilización popular y fe Cristiana* (Montevideo: ISAL, 1971), 148. My translation.

in any age and can be made by those on the right as well as the left of the ideological spectrum. As I write these words, we are witnessing just such a stance in two places. In Ukraine, Vladimir Putin, president of the Russian Federation, is waging an unprovoked war against the people of that land with the full support of the Russian Orthodox Church led by Patriarch Kirill. A close ally of the Russian leader, Kirill has led the church to buy into Putin's expansionist ideology whereby he has abrogated to himself the right to lay claim to territory that used to be part of the former Russian empire and the old Soviet Union, and to incorporate it into the current Russian state.[42] As was the case with the Confessing Church during the Nazi regime in Germany, a small group of Russian priests, among them eighty-nine-year-old Father Georgy Edelshtein, have denounced the war. Sadly, such a stance has come at the cost of persecution by the state, including fines and imprisonment.[43]

In the United States, a version of the unbridled engagement was clear in the presidency of Donald Trump, and in the popularity he continued to enjoy among a good swath of the population after demitting office. Following the presidency of Barack Obama, some on the religious right were so convinced that American society needed to change according to conservative values that they entered into an alliance with President Trump whereby they followed wholesale and religiously all that the Trumpian regime demanded. They toed the Trumpian line even when that entailed condoning behaviors that were contrary to their own time-honored ideological commitments and moral values.[44]

In this perspective, it is impossible to doubt the commitment of the church to the transformation of a given social order. Where the church has this understanding of its reason for being, the status quo cannot be at ease. The position of taking off the table all pretense to a neutral and apolitical posture must be commended.

---

42. Ina Merdjanova, "Russia's War in Ukraine and the Limits of Religious Diplomacy," *Occasional Papers on Religion in Eastern Europe* 42, no. 4 (2022).

43. Agence France Presse, "Risking Jail and Church Ire, Russian Priests Condemn Ukraine Conflict," France24, 1 May 2022, https://www.france24.com/en/live-news/20220501-risking-jail-and-church-ire-russian-priests-condemn-ukraine-conflict. On a trip to Russia in the spring of 2018 to take part in a mission conference at the Kostroma Theological Seminary, my wife and I had the privilege of meeting Father Edelshtein in his parish located just outside the city of Kostroma. While a committed Russian Orthodox churchman, he displayed an incredible irenic spirit and an avidity for Protestant-Orthodox dialogue.

44. James W. Skillen and James R. Skillen, "Evangelical Double-Mindedness in Support of Donald Trump," in *The Spiritual Danger of Donald Trump: 30 Evangelical Christians on Justice, Truth, and Moral Integrity*, ed. Ronald J. Sider and Bandy Lee (Eugene: Cascade, 2020), 164–68.

Yet, this positive appraisal notwithstanding, we cannot overlook the issues that bedevil this understanding of the church's role in the world. First, it is an overstatement to reduce the church's mission in the world to that of servant only. True, the church's mission is directed externally for the benefit of others, but it also has other dimensions that should not be set aside. One such is the inward aspect of its work by which it attends to its own health through nurture and edification (2 Pet 3:18; Eph 4:11–16). A weak and feeble church cannot exert the sort of influence that will redound to the world's good. Besides this, its function includes an upward direction which points to its service to God. The church's reason for being is doxological: it exists to bring glory and praise to God (Col 3:17). In this regard, Graham's warning against reducing the church's role to activism for the transformation of the social order is in order. Perhaps there is a fourth danger for us, and this is the danger of trying to make all Christians act alike, regardless of where God may have placed them.[45]

Besides our concern with the reductionist tendency of the thoroughgoing approach, we see problems with its openness and carte blanche approach to a particular political and ideological perspective. A realignment of the sort it advocates could stifle the church's ability to exercise a credible critical function in the event of the degeneration of what may currently appear to be a progressive political option. The church's involvement must always be carried out in a way that safeguards its freedom and its ability to credibly raise a critical voice whenever the need arises, regardless of who occupies the seat of power. And, as the Peruvian evangelical theologian Samuel Escobar urges, this requires an attitude of suspicion both "toward the pretensions of those who exercise power in society" and toward the "ideological constructions of those who try to gain power."[46] Unless such care is exercised, the church runs the risk of becoming the religious servant of yet another political master, and thereby renders itself useless to the very cause of change.

We detect a similar difficulty regarding the matter of the use of ways and means. Because of the church's nature, there are certain means which are beyond the purview of the church to employ in its pursuit of change despite their usefulness and legitimacy. Violence is one such means. The use of these means by the church injures the cause by the question it raises regarding the character and integrity of the agent.

Furthermore, the ecclesiology which serves as the theological underpinning of the thoroughgoing position is flawed. In their desire to take the world

---

45. Graham, "Why Lausanne?," 29–30.
46. Escobar, *In Search of Christ*, 188.

seriously, the proponents of this view overstep the theological bounds when they insist that church and world share the same ontological status. Certainly, the church and world are related, but they are distinct and distinguishable entities. The boundaries between them aren't as blurred as Segundo and Boff contend.

For all these reasons, it seems that the praxis of thoroughgoing engagement is way too radical; it needs to be tempered by the adoption of a more cautious stance vis-à-vis ecclesial participation in social change.

If the analysis we've conducted in this chapter has merit, we can conclude that the ecclesial praxes advocated by the views we've explored suffer from two deficiencies that chip away at the potency of the church to exert a transforming influence on the social domain. The debilitating feature of the first three modes of engagement is their timidity. For different reasons they display a hesitancy to adequately engage the social domain. By contrast, the weakness of the fourth model is the opposite. In its zeal to enact change, it overshoots the limits and overcommits the church. Considering the weaknesses that beset these models, there is a need for a stance that mediates between them and overcomes their weaknesses. We suggest authentic engagement as such a model.

3

Authentic Engagement

In the previous chapter, we concluded that the models of church-world relation on offer fall short of what is needed for the church to engage society in a way that is likely to result in the latter's meaningful transformation. If that conclusion is valid, the search for a more effective model of the relationship between the church and the world must continue. We therefore remain haunted by the need to lay hands on a modus operandi that can avoid the timidity of the first three of the approaches analyzed above and the radicalness of the fourth. In its endeavor to exert a salutary and transforming influence on the social domain, can the church find such a modus operandi? In other words, can the church find a way to engage the world in a manner that is trenchant enough to move society in the direction of the will of God for life in community, without at the same time impugning its integrity? We believe such a model, in fact, exists, and we label it *authentic engagement*. The task of this chapter is to make the case for this approach.

Meaning

What do we mean by "authentic engagement"? In the construal we're putting forth, we conceive "engagement" as firmness of commitment for the realization of a given aim. Engagement, in our view, begins with the conviction that a certain envisioned aim is desirable and worthy of actualization. It is a mental decision to pursue a coveted objective with passion and resoluteness. At this stage, engagement can be likened to a potentiality that longs for, and eagerly awaits, actualization. But such firmness of mind and longing of heart are likely to fall short of the targeted aim if they aren't accompanied by intentionality. Hence, to be efficacious, engagement must be intentional. It needs intentionality if it is to be carried out with direction, purpose, and determination. The engaged agent is not a person who adopts a cavalier, lackadaisical, nonchalant, lukewarm, and laissez-faire attitude toward the pursuit of the desired objective. Rather, it is someone who, being cognizant of the importance of the stakes, displays ownership and zeal in the pursuit of the coveted goal.

But important though they are, if engagement is to be effective it cannot stop with the aforementioned features. We know of numerous projects that met their death at the level of desire and intention. In addition to cognitive resolve and intentionality, there must be active involvement. At this point, engagement takes the form of the expenditure of energy. To become real, the inspiration that gives rise to it and that drives the process at the cognitive and affective levels must be complemented by perspiration – the exertion of effort. To paraphrase the eighteenth-century French playwright Boileau, nothing beautiful, noble, and worthy can be achieved without sweat and exertion. Regardless of the strength of conviction and the power of intention, no aim will be achieved if the agent adopts an inactive posture – that is, if he or she acts as a spectator who sits on the sidelines with crossed arms and legs. At some point in the process, activism must enter the picture. To use an odd concept that has gained currency and acceptance in recent times, engagement must propel us to get in "good trouble, necessary trouble."[1] Activism is essential because it is like a midwife who attends to the delivery of a baby. It is activism that attends to the delivery of the envisioned reality. Without it, the most promising and achievable vision is condemned to remain in the womb or be stillborn.

If such is engagement, what then can be said of the qualifier "authentic"? What conditions must be satisfied for engagement to qualify as authentic? A moment's thought leads us to offer the suggestion that authenticity speaks of the quality of a thing that reflects factuality. It denotes that which displays conformity to reality. Such conformity imparts to the thing in question the character of genuineness and veracity. Where there is correspondence between what the thing appears to be and what it is in fact, there one finds solid ground for unquestioned trustworthiness, and, therefore, the removal of any basis for suspicion or accusation of phoniness and unreality. The authentic thing, thus, is a thing that enjoys authority, integrity, and credibility.

Putting the two concepts together, we can define "authentic engagement" as active involvement that doesn't jeopardize integrity. It is acting with integrity.

---

1. The phrase "good trouble, necessary trouble" was uttered by the late American civil rights icon John Lewis to describe his own involvement in the struggle for civil rights on behalf of fellow Black people in the United States. Lewis used the phrase in response to the concern of his mother who admonished him against getting involved in political activities likely to get him into trouble – that is, to result in physical harm to his person.

Put another way, authentic engagement is *involvement within bounds*. Crucial to authentic engagement is the avoidance of two dangers: the danger of passivity on the one hand, and the danger of untamed exuberance on the other. On one pole, authentic engagement avoids a posture of inaction because it wants to avoid raising questions about the seriousness of its commitment. On the other pole, it shuns exuberance because it wants to avoid being pushed beyond allowable limits and, in so doing, compromise the legitimacy of its activity.

When applied to the church, authentic engagement is the approach which advocates the direct involvement of the church in the social order but always in a way that doesn't compromise its nature and character or impugn the credibility of its witness. As we've shown in the previous chapter, the other approaches can reach useful outcomes, but, except for the unbridled model, they are unlikely to result in the transformation of the structures that impede the flourishing of life, because they exempt these very structures from the critique of the gospel. Yet, in the absence of a change of these systems, any transformation of the social order runs the risk of being superficial. If the gospel has any chance of exerting a transforming influence on any social order, its presentation cannot avoid confronting the life-inhibiting realities of that order – whatever they may be. When the destructive realities of the context aren't considered, "the Gospel is distorted and the Christian life impoverished."[2] The aim of such engagement is to challenge the social order to conform itself as much as possible to the values of the reign of God that has entered the realm of history in the person and work of Jesus Christ. The gospel is a vertical and transcultural message which contains a word from beyond for the human predicament.[3] This doesn't mean the establishment of a utopian society in the here and now. We grant that such a goal can only be reached by God at the consummation of his redemptive plan at the return of Christ and the complete elimination of evil and renewal of creation that will ensue (Rev 21:1–4). But, if the prayer that the Lord taught us to pray has any meaning, it must be possible to steer the prevailing order in the direction of the will of God that is done in heaven. Authentic engagement, therefore, insists on the obligation of the people of God to hold up before society, in words and deeds, God's ideal for a healthy community life. For while "men cannot build by themselves the kingdom of God on earth . . . evangelical social action will

---

2. Nuñez and Taylor, *Crisis and Hope*, 414.

3. Archibald M. Hunter, *Introducing the New Testament* (Philadelphia: Westminster Press, 1957), 14. Hunter was echoing Karl Barth in this statement.

contribute to create a better world, as an anticipation of the one for which Christians pray daily."[4]

Because the reality that needs transformation is total, any engagement that seeks to bring it in tune with the will of God must be holistic. This means that, *in appropriate ways*, the praxis of the people of God must seek to engage a given context at the *various* levels of its existence. As Stephen Mott states, "the battle for change must be fought on a variety of fronts."[5] In the pursuit of that task, one should not rule a priori as inadmissible ways and means that are commensurate with the nature and identity of the people of God, and which conform to God's will.

But the argument for the meaningful involvement of the church in the social arena mustn't be construed as advocacy of indiscriminate participation by the church. The approach of authentic engagement does not advocate the church's blind participation in *all and sundry* endeavors undertaken in the pursuit of the transformation project. Nor does it support the endorsement by the church of the posture of ideological/political alignment – be it to the right or the left. To the contrary, it argues that if its engagement is to be authentic, the church must guard against committing acts that are inimical to its identity; it must protect its credibility by maintaining a clear distance from the powers that be. As we argued in the previous chapter, this is the major weakness of the unbridled approach. In its eagerness to bring about the transformation of the prevailing order, it displays an inclination to overstep the boundaries. In contradistinction, authentic engagement is contingent on the erection of firm guardrails and clear boundaries between the church and the holders of political power. It does not do so in a spirit of self-righteousness, contempt, and cynicism toward the temporal order, or in denial of the usefulness and legitimacy of certain activities of the temporal order to the transformation project. Indeed, we agree, once more, with Mott that, in the pursuit of change, "the necessity of one campaign does not negate that of another."[6] What drives us to sound this alarm is the conviction that if the church is to guard against the danger of politicizing the gospel for the benefit of a given political system and thus render it useless for the society at large, this principle of ideological distancing must be maintained. "The church as church is not supposed to be naïve, allowing itself to be manipulated by a particular ideology, whether of the

---

4. Nuñez and Taylor, *Crisis and Hope*, 414.

5. Stephen Charles Mott, *Biblical Ethics and Social Change* (New York: Oxford University Press, 1982), 140.

6. Mott, *Biblical Ethics*, 140.

political left or of the political right."[7] Similarly, if the church is to protect its identity as a community for which certain values are considered nonnegotiable, there are activities it cannot engage in, and there are certain attitudes it cannot endorse, without injury or harm. Here expediency and pragmatism cannot be elevated to the level of determinant guidelines and decisive criteria. As René Padilla warned several years ago: "If there is no possibility of evaluating praxis [and expediency] based on a guideline that is over and above [them], the way is open to justify *any* praxis as long as it works, with the ends justifying the means 'philosophy.'"[8]

Foundations

Being biblical is a quality that most Christians claim to cherish. This is in keeping with their basic commitment to the authority of Scripture and their avowed submission to it as the ultimate canon for faith and practice. Taking this as a litmus test, we must ask ourselves if there is biblical and theological warrant for the view we've put forward. Can the notion of authentic engagement hold under the searchlight of Scripture? We believe it can. Indeed, there is good warrant for it both in the Old and in the New Testament.

As we open the Old Testament, we come face to face with God's disclosure of his decision to choose a people for himself to be a conduit of his blessings for the world. To Abraham who was living in Ur of the Chaldees, God gave the following promise: "I will make you into a great nation, and I will bless you; I will make your name great, and you will be a blessing . . . and *all peoples on earth will be blessed through you*" (Gen 12:2–3; emphasis added). Following that watershed declaration, in response to rampant moral and social degeneration, God enunciated his mission for the people-to-be, and the way in which they were to carry it out. Beside its missional and soteriological dimension that would find its fulfillment in the seed of Abraham,[9] the promised blessing would come to the rest of humankind by means of moral influence that the chosen people would exert in their capacity as a distinctive ethical community. Israel was chosen by God not just for its own benefit but to be a light to the nations (Isa 42:6; 49:6). After revealing the promise, God clarified further the purpose that lay behind his choice. About Abraham who was living in corrupt

---

7. Nuñez and Taylor, *Crisis and Hope*, 423.

8. C. René Padilla, "La teología de la liberación: una evaluación critica," *Misión* 2, no. 2 (March–June 1982): 20. Emphasis added. My translation.

9. See Gal 3:15–17.

Sodom and Gomorrah, God said: "I have chosen him, so that he will direct his children and his household after him to keep the way of the LORD by doing what is right and just, so that the LORD will bring about for Abraham what he has promised him" (Gen 18:19). The choice was not an end in itself; it was a means to a much greater end. As Christopher Wright states in his commentary on this passage: "Election means *election to an ethical agenda*. The distinctive quality of the people of God *committed to righteousness and justice* stands as the purpose of election on the one hand and the means to mission on the other."[10]

Centuries later, when the original Abrahamic clan was large enough to become a more expansive and cohesive community, and eventually a nation, God made it clear that the new ethnic entity would have a unique relationship with him. To the Israelites, fresh out of Egyptian bondage through the grand act of redemption that God had wrought on their behalf, and who were encamped in front of Mount Sinai, God said: "If you obey me fully and keep my covenant, then out of all nations you will be my treasured possession. Although the whole earth is mine, you will be for me a kingdom of priests and a holy nation" (Exod 19:5–6). As God's chosen people, they were to display a character that reflected holistic holiness as the hallmark of their uniqueness. They were to be holy as he is holy (Lev 19:2). But the holiness in question was no ghettoized piety practiced on the margins of society by a group of hermits who had taken flight from the world. No. It was a world-engaging and full-orbed holiness which was to permeate the national life of the chosen people. And that permeation was to happen through the moral influence the people were to exert upon the society as a whole. As is clear from the Holiness Code (Lev 19), that God-mandated holiness was the organizing principle that was meant to govern the nation's social life. Wright's explanation of the breadth of holiness in question here is worth citing at length:

> Holiness affected more than the ritual area of life. Holiness dictated generosity with agricultural produce (Lev 19:9–10); fair treatment and payment of employees (19:13); practical compassion for the disabled, and respect for the elderly (19:14, 32); the integrity of the judicial process (19:15); safety precautions (19:16b); ecological sensitivity (19:23ff.); equality before the law for ethnic minorities (19:33–34); honesty in trade and business (19:35–36).[11]

---

10. Wright, *Old Testament Ethics*, 50–51.
11. Wright, 50–51.

Beside the comprehensive holiness outlined in the Holiness Code, a host of other texts in the Torah embody provisions designed to foster a just, humane, and gentle society. For instance, on the negative side, we find legislation against oppression of the weak and vulnerable, against corrupt behaviors, against injustice toward the poor, and against sexual impurity. On the positive side, there are laws that require generosity toward the destitute, sensitivity to debtors, care and concern for aliens and strangers, and so on. Here is no fragmented ethics concerned only with the personal and spiritual dimensions of life. Rather, here is an ethic that is far-reaching and all-embracing. And the people of God were mandated to lead the world in its implementation.

Crossing over into the New Testament, we notice that the status of chosenness attributed to ancient Israel is also ascribed to the church. Using language that clearly echoes the Sinai covenant (Exod 19:4–5), Peter describes the diasporic community scattered throughout western Asia as "chosen according to the foreknowledge of God the Father, through the sanctifying work of the Spirit" (1 Pet 1:1–2). He goes on to highlight the peculiarity and uniqueness that comes with the privilege of election. Like Israel of old, he describes the fledgling Christian community, who were facing all sorts of persecution, as "a chosen people, a royal priesthood, a holy nation, [and] God's special possession" (1 Pet 1:1; 2:9–10). And he admonished them to emulate God's holiness just as Israel was charged to do, by repeating the formula: "Be holy, because I am holy" (1 Pet 1:16).

To this new people of God, a socio-ethical task akin to the one entrusted to the old is given. Echoes of that mandate can be heard in various places in the New Testament (Phil 2:13–18; Titus 2:11–14). But we find it stated with clarity and force in the portion of Scripture commonly known as the Sermon on the Mount (Matt 5–7), one of the five discourses delivered by Jesus according to the Gospel of Matthew.

The Sermon on the Mount is considered "the main example of Jesus' ethical teaching."[12] Some scholars even view it as a sort of manifesto of the kingdom which made its appearance in the world in the person and work of Jesus.[13] It embodies an ethic which, in many ways, is continuous with that of the Old Testament (though surpassing it), proclaiming the righteousness of the newly arrived kingdom. It lays out for those who belong to the new order a threefold ethical teaching. First, it spells out who the followers of Jesus are. Second, it

---

12. Donald Hagner, *Matthew 1–13*, Word Biblical Commentary 33 (Dallas: Word, 1993), 82.

13. John R. W. Stott, *Christian Counter-Culture: The Message of the Sermon on the Mount* (Downers Grove: IVP, 1978), 15.

distills what their conduct should be. Lastly, it says how they are to witness to the world. One may call the Sermon a statement on being, mission, and engagement, or alternatively, a charter of identity, conduct, and action.

Of particular importance for our purpose here is the pericope in Matthew 5:13–16, which lies within the main body of the Sermon but toward its beginning. In it, Jesus tells his disciples in clear and emphatic terms how they are to engage their environment:

> You are the salt of the earth. But if the salt loses its saltiness, how can it be made salty again? It is no longer good for anything, except to be thrown out and trampled underfoot.
>
> You are the light of the world. A town built on a hill cannot be hidden. Neither do people light a lamp and put it under a bowl. Instead they put it on its stand, and it gives light to everyone in the house. In the same way, let your light shine before others, that they may see your good deeds and glorify your Father in heaven.

The strategic location of this statement should not be missed. Jesus nestles it between his description of the character of those who claim to be his disciples (5:1–12), and his wide-ranging instructions on how they are to live as members of the new order (5:17 – 7:27). In other words, the statement is sandwiched between Jesus's discourse on character and his treatise on conduct. This positioning of the text seems to convey the thought that these things – character and conduct – are not just matters of private or personal import. The spirituality they are meant to foster is not self-absorbed and convent-like. It is a spirituality that is meant to prepare members of the kingdom to engage the world in a potent and authentic way for its betterment and well-being. While the disciples of Jesus, like Israel, are a peculiar bunch, they are not hermits whose existence is of no importance to the world. Far from it. Their presence is relevant to the well-being of the world. By referring to his followers as "salt of the earth" and "light of the world," Jesus intends to say, in a pithy way, that they are to be a unique people with a widespread transforming ethical impact designed to be a means of blessing to the world.

Jesus's use of the salt and light metaphors is hugely important for the approach we're commending. These metaphors clearly convey the thought that engagement that would be culture-impacting and society-transforming must be integral and all-encompassing. Together, they convey the thought that the church has a moral responsibility toward the world, and that responsibility extends to the entire social domain: its moral influence must penetrate and permeate the entire fabric of society.

The precise meaning of the salt metaphor is not easy to pin down. Scholars of the New Testament give various interpretations of what may have been in the mind of the Lord when he used that imagery.[14] There is, however, broad agreement on the recognition of the ability of salt to have a transforming impact on a substance with which it comes into contact. It does so through its preserving, purifying, seasoning, and fertilizing qualities. But, to exercise that power, it must come into close contact with the substance needing protection, savor, or productivity. Despite its great qualities, salt is of no use if it is not rubbed into the substance or sprinkled out from the saltshaker. To be of use, salt must give itself away. Jesus is saying that to protect, sanitize, or fertilize the moral ecology of a given context, the church, as salt, must spend itself and penetrate the entire fabric of that context.

A similar observation can be made with respect to the light metaphor. Jesus calls his disciples "light of the *world*." This means that their presence is to be conspicuous and visible to the world. Perhaps taking his cue from Jesus, Paul will later make a similar assertion, likening the members of the small church in Philippi to "stars in the sky" charged with the duty to shine in the midst of a "warped and crooked generation" (Phil 2:14–15). In both cases the metaphors speak of the comprehensive nature of the moral influence of the people of God although their number would have been minuscule when these declarations were made. Whether it is the sun projecting its rays, or a lamp which is lit in a given area, or a star appearing in the open sky, selectivity of coverage is not an option. In each case, they invade the area indiscriminately. In the same way, Jesus is saying that, as light, the church must venture out and endeavor to illumine all aspects of life. If its moral influence is to be felt in the entire fabric of society, its ethical witness must cover the whole social domain. It must broaden its ethical agenda. If the church's witness is confined to its four walls, if it is limited to only one dimension, then the ethical mandate given by the Lord is not adequately carried out. Light spares nothing that comes into contact with its revealing power.

It is worth noting that there seems to be a level of necessity attached to the sort of social engagement that Jesus is commending. We surmise it in the emphatic way in which Jesus states the disciples' identity. In the Greek, the text doesn't just say "you are the salt," but "*you yourselves* are the salt of the earth . . . *you yourselves* are the light of the world." This seems to suggest that the kind of ethical influence Jesus is thinking about is intended to be exerted,

---

14. Scholars disagree on what exactly Jesus intended to convey by his use of the salt metaphor. Hence, they offer various suggestions for its meaning. See Hagner, *Matthew 1–13*, 99.

at least primarily, by his disciples.[15] This seems clear from the fact that the light that defines them, and which they are to project to the world, does not originate in themselves but finds its source in the Father and the Son who are both said to be light (1 John 1:5; John 1:4). The implication is that if they fail to carry it out, the mandate runs the risk of being left unattended to. Beside this, the necessity also seems inherent in the very meaning of the metaphors themselves. In the world of Jesus, as, indeed, in today's world, salt and light were commodities that were essential to the maintenance of life itself. As Hagner comments, just as these items are vitally important for everyday life, so the "disciples are vitally significant and necessary to the world in their witness to God and his kingdom."[16]

Criteria

Now, if the affirmative declarations of the pericope spell out the identity of the disciples, and in so doing suggest the need for their full-orbed engagement in the social order, the remainder of that passage (the bulk of it) sounds a loud alarm concerning the danger of the uselessness of their witness. In the rest of his statement, Jesus makes it abundantly clear that despite its transforming qualities, salt can become worthless, and as such be thrown out, trampled over, and despised by people (Matt 5:13). Similarly, despite its capacity to illuminate, light can be kept from shining and thus be prevented from dispelling darkness (5:14c–15). The point of this stern warning is to underscore with red ink the truth that if their moral influence is to be beneficial to the world, the disciples must engage the world *correctly*. In other words, *mere engagement doesn't suffice; to be transforming, engagement must be authentic.*

In Jesus's warning, we detect two problems that impugn the authenticity of the engagement of a transforming agent. The first is the problem of *misuse*. Speaking of the light, Jesus warns against the silliness of lighting a lamp and then placing it under a bowl. The act of hiding a light is a blatant misuse because it impedes the agent from fulfilling its intended purpose. Instead, proper use of the agent requires a deliberate exposure that gives it the opportunity to fulfill its intended purpose to the maximum. Rather than being hidden under a bowl, the light is to be placed on full display on a lampstand where it can give light to everyone in the house (5:15). This handling of the moral agent accomplishes both an ethical function and a missional objective. In illuminating everyone's

---

15. See Stott, *Christian Counter-Culture*, 65.
16. Hagner, *Matthew 1–13*, 99.

way, it dissipates the darkness that engulfs them and shows them where to walk. It performs, then, a paradigmatic role. But this ethical outcome is only a penultimate goal; the ultimate objective is missional and spiritual: that the observation by a watching world of such engagement may result in the praise of God (5:16).

Here, the deficiency and ineptness of the first three modes of engagement analyzed in our previous chapter become evident. True, it may be too harsh to level against them the charge of misuse, but the charge of inadequate use of the transforming agent seems fair. The extent and severity of their inadequacy varies according to the way they place their lid on the light and thus prevent it from shining. In the case of the nonengagement approach, the lid is so tightly placed that it seems to allow only a minimum of light to escape, if any at all. Admittedly, the restrictive and indirect approaches position the lid in a manner that allows the light to shine more broadly, and with greater force; however, the light shines *only in a given direction*. So, in both instances, the agent is prevented from making its full impact.

In ethics, there is a principle called "supererogation." This simply means that a moral agent is not blameworthy for what he or she is unable to do.[17] In French the principle is expressed in the saying "*À l'impossible nul n'est tenu*," meaning, "No one can be held accountable for that which it is impossible to do." But the reverse is also true. If the agent has the capacity and ability to do something and yet fails to do it, his or her conduct is deemed morally blameworthy. Applying this principle to the issue at hand, we can say that to the extent that the stances we've reviewed hold back the church from casting its full light onto the entirety of the social landscape, they render its engagement deficient because they keep it from acting in a manner that is commensurate with its being and identity. Such engagement is lacking in authenticity since it fails to comport fully with the being and identity of the church.

The second problem highlighted by Jesus is the *loss of identity*. Jesus says that the function of salt is to exert a wholesome influence on the substance with which it comes into contact. But the execution of that function is contingent on the *salt remaining salt*. In other words, it depends on the salt maintaining its identity. If the salt loses its saltiness, it becomes useless, and is, therefore, held in contempt (5:13).

There is something striking to observe and ponder deeply in this warning. It is the oddity and the counterintuitiveness of the notion of salt losing its

---

17. John Feinberg and Paul Feinberg, *Ethics in a Brave New World*, 2nd ed. (Wheaton: Crossway, 2010), 24–25.

saltiness. If the problem with the light is a problem of *inappropriate use* of the transforming agent, the issue with the salt is much more severe: it is the *defect in the very being of the agent*. This is sobering. Jesus is in effect saying that the disciples can lose their identity completely and thus become something else. Is it farfetched to deduce from this that Jesus is suggesting that the church can look like church and yet cease to be church because it loses its moral and ethical edge?

How can such a thing happen? The answer seems to lie in the main message that the Sermon seeks to convey. The imperative that the Sermon seeks to impress upon the disciples is this: that belonging to the kingdom requires that one reflects its light through one's mode of being and behavior. In other words, belonging to the kingdom requires conformity to its values and norms as Jesus lays them out in his discourse on character and treatise on conduct. The loss of saltiness or compromise of identity that Jesus warns against occurs when the disciples engage the world in a manner that vitiates the norms and values enunciated in the Sermon. Acting in a manner that contradicts the ideals of the kingdom is tantamount to acting like the world. When this happens, they lose their distinctiveness; they emulate the surrounding culture and thus nullify Jesus's call to be different (Matt 6:8), which is the main theme of the Sermon.[18]

Jesus's sobering caution seems to suggest that in its engagement, the church must always remain true to itself. Genuine salt is always different from the substance to which it is applied. To maintain its integrity, the church's mode of relating to the world must be *contact without confusion, engagement without alignment, participation without absorption, attentiveness without conformity.* To discharge the function of preservative in the world, it is imperative that the church retain the virtues that the kingdom deems essential, and abide by its norms. Herein lies the deficiency of the unbridled approach. In its eagerness to change the world, it seems open to putting on the line the integrity of the agent by failing to erect clear lines of demarcation between the church and the world. This blurring of the boundaries can cloud its identity and compromise its witness.

We began this exploration with an examination of the socio-ethical call placed upon Israel as God's people. Midway through our journey, we turned our attention to the church, the new people of God, and we have remained

---

18. Stott, *Sermon on the Mount*, 18–19. Stott states this with great force: "There is no single paragraph of the Sermon on the Mount in which this contrast between Christian and non-Christian standards is not drawn. It is the underlying theme of the Sermon; everything else is a variation of it" (19).

exclusively with it since. This approach may give the reader the impression that the criteria of authenticity that we glean from Jesus's warning to his disciples weren't relevant to his old covenant people. This would be incorrect. For both the church and Israel, the authenticity of their social witness depends on the maintenance of their distinctiveness and integrity as God's chosen people. John Stott makes this point with force and clarity:

> The essential theme of the whole Bible from beginning to end is that God's historical purpose is to call out a people for himself; that this people is a "holy" people, set apart from the world to belong to him and to obey; and this vocation is to be true to its identity, that is, to be "holy" or "different" in all its outlook and behaviour.[19]

Indeed, the history of Israel provides a vivid illustration of the harm that can be done to the social witness of the people of God when they fail to "be true to [their] identity." The people who were chosen to be a blessing to the world and a light to the nations became itself subject to the nations (2 Kgs 17). This forfeiture of their calling and God-assigned purpose occurred through a lifestyle that mirrored the ways of the surrounding nations. There are things you cannot do if you are to remain who you are. The African theologian and churchman David Zac Niringiye puts it well:

> Instead of embodying God's reign of justice, mercy and the fear of the Lord, corruption and injustice held sway. They fashioned themselves according to the life and worship of their neighbours and did the things God had forbidden them to do. . . . "They followed worthless idols and themselves became worthless" (2 Kings 17:15). They were no longer one nation, God's people.[20]

Here is a warning that the modern church everywhere needs to heed less it suffer a similar fate.

---

19. Stott, 17.
20. David Zac Niringiye, *The Church: God's Pilgrim People* (Carlisle: Langham Global Library, 2014), 71.

Part Two

Ecclesial Consciousness for Transforming Engagement

4

Society of the Triune God

The longing for the transformation of the world into a better place is a commonly held sentiment. Our argument in this book is that the people of God are not inconsequential to the pursuit and satisfaction of that desire. In the previous chapter, we set forth a concept that should guide the legitimate involvement of the people of God in the pursuit of such an objective. The question that begs for a response at this juncture is this: What sort of people can shoulder such a responsibility? What view must they have of themselves to answer the call to engage in the daunting task of social change? This chapter will seek to answer this question by searching for an understanding of the nature of the church, known in theology as ecclesiology. The chapter's burden, then, is to provide a doctrinal substantiation and foundation for the church's engagement in the social domain for the enhancement of the common good.

Identity and Engagement

The search for identity is a shared human experience. Our sense of purpose is intricately connected to our awareness of who we are. Knowing and understanding our identity precedes knowing, appropriating, and manifesting why we exist – our raison d'être. Similarly, our conviction about the nature of the Christian community is important for our understanding of the way in which it should engage the world. As the mind naturally moves the human body, so the thoughts of the members of the church will determine and direct its actions or lack thereof. Scripture says that as people think in their hearts, so they are (Prov 23:7).[1] Paul makes the claim that the *knowledge* that our bodies are the temples of the Holy Spirit should inform our *use* of them (1 Cor 6:19).

---

1. New King James Version. The Bible emphasizes a connection between one's thoughts or heart posture/condition and one's actions. See Rom 12:1–2; Mark 7:21–22.

In searching for identity, the person who looks inwards rather than upwards runs the risk of faltering. This is because the design reflects the Designer and the creation's identity is entrenched in its Creator. Correspondingly, a view of the church that centers on humanity rather than on God falls short of accurately capturing the true essence of the community of faith, and of its mission in the world. Considering this, we will argue for an ecclesiology that is consciously God-centered as the basis for the authentic engagement that we advocated in the previous chapter. Because our understanding of God is avowedly Trinitarian, when we say "God-centered," we mean a view of the church that links it to all three members of the Godhead rather than to one member alone. A Trinitarian ecclesiology views the church as a community with an identity firmly anchored in the one God who exists in the persons of the Father, the Son, and the Holy Spirit.

Trinitarian Ecclesiology in History

Early Christian literature did not contain an abundance of writings on the doctrine of the church. Among the few most noted works in the field of ecclesiology is Cyprian's *The Unity of the Catholic Church* which documents his understanding of the nature and operation of the church. In this work, Cyprian makes a strong case for the unity of the church around the leadership of Peter, stresses the essentiality of the church for salvation, and puts forth the view that the church was an empirical and geographically extended institution which was essentially the spiritual equivalent of the Roman state under one ruler – the bishop.[2] Further, he likens those involved in Christian ministry to the Aaronic priesthood which was hierarchically ordered. For centuries, his perspective served as the reigning ecclesiological model.

Cyprian's Aaron-like mediatorial priesthood would lose traction in the Reformation era. This was due in part to the Reformers' doctrine of justification by faith and their belief in the universal priesthood of all believers, which sought to level the ground for all as far as access to God is concerned. Reformation ecclesiology stressed the fact that both laity and clergy experience the salvific grace of God and can access God directly. With this new perspective, the hierarchical ordering of the church was challenged, resulting in a lasting and

---

2. Excerpts from Cyprian ecclesiology are found in Henry Bettenson, *Documents of the Christian Church*, 2nd ed. (Oxford: Oxford University Press, 1963), 71–73. For helpful summaries of his view of the church, see J. N. D. Kelly, *Early Christian Doctrines* (New York: Harper & Row, 1978), 203–207; Giles, *What on Earth Is the Church?*, 213–14; and Colin Gunton and Daniel W. Hardy, *On Being the Church: Essays on the Christian Community* (Edinburgh: T&T Clark, 1989).

unbridgeable gulf in ecclesiological understanding. On the one side were the Reformers who shrugged off their excommunication by the pope with the retort that they were the one true church, with all members having equal access to God. On the other side were the Counter-Reformers who continued to hold firmly to the Cyprianic ecclesiology, stressing that the church is a visible, institutional, and hierarchical society similar to any earthly kingdom.[3]

The term "Trinity" entered Christian theology early in the history of Christian thought. This occurred in the seminal work of North African theologian Tertullian. A neologist with a brilliant legal mind, Tertullian is credited with coining the verbiage *una substantia, tres personae* that we use to this day. Admittedly, the term is not found in Scripture, but the concept of "three persons sharing one substance" *does* have biblical support.[4] It was this conviction that informed the affirmation and enunciation of the doctrine by the early thinkers in the church, both in the East and in the West, even if their explanations of it varied.[5]

Yet, despite the early consensus on the triune nature of God, the doctrine of the church remained, for the most part, unaffected by it. While there were occasional statements connecting the church to the Trinity, for most of Christian history the church has been described largely in Christological terms. Among the members of the Trinity, the church's relationship to the Son received priority attention. But the hegemony of this Christological ecclesiology would not last forever. In the aftermath of the Second World War, a theological reflection emerged that showed a shift away from the traditional Christological understanding of church to a Trinitarian understanding of its nature and life. In various ways, theologians of differing stripes have sought to relate the church intimately to the triune God, not just to one member of

---

3. This Counter-Reformation ecclesiology was articulated with particular force by Robert Bellarmine, the staunch defender of the Roman Catholic position. See Avery Dulles, *Models of the Church* (Garden City: Doubleday, 1978), 20.

4. In the Old Testament, many passages address God as at the same time being distinct from God, such as Yahweh and the Messiah (Pss 45:6–7; 110:1; Isa 9:6; Dan 7:13–14). Moreover, the implication of three divine persons can be found in the Trisagion ("Holy, holy, holy," Isa 6:3).

5. The Western theologians, for instance, focused on the unity of essence of the Godhead and moved to speak of the three persons or hypostases. In contradistinction, the Eastern theologians, also called the Cappadocian fathers, focused on the threeness of the Godhead, based on their contention that the divine being is three in essence. James R. White, *The Forgotten Trinity* (Minneapolis: Bethany House, 1998), 178. White articulates that as persecution ended, the church focused its attention on the issues of the deity of Christ and the Trinity. Emperor Constantine called for a major council of the church, known as the Council of Nicaea, to address the nature of Christ in AD 325.

the Godhead.[6] The Orthodox theologian George Dion Dragas expresses this shift well when he states that "the nature of the Church is to be understood as the Church of the Triune God. The Holy Trinity is the ultimate basis and source of the Church's existence and, as such, the Church is in the image and likeness of God."[7] We believe that there is much to commend this way of conceiving the church. Scripture seems to contain compelling evidence in support of a close connection between the triune God and the ecclesial community. Consequently, the view of the church that we will articulate as the ground for the praxis of authentic engagement will follow broadly similar lines.

The Church as the People of God the Father

Perhaps the clearest connection of the church to God the Father is the New Testament's portrayal of the Christian community as the *people of God*. This description is made by both Peter who ministered among the church of the Jewish diaspora (1 Pet 1:1–2), and Paul who labored among the gentile churches (Eph 3:8), and it is alluded to by John (Rev 1:6; 21:3). Addressing the church in the Dispersion, Peter says: "you are a chosen race, a royal priesthood, a holy nation, a people for [God's] own possession" (1 Pet 2:9 ESV). Peter's addressees were Jews; it is not farfetched to think that to some of them, his declaration may have been seen as a reminder of their relationship with Yahweh, the God of the old covenant (Exod 19:5). In Paul, however, the application is broadened and extended to those who were previously "without God" – literally the atheists, Greek *atheoi* (Eph 2:12). Paul boldly calls the churches in the gentile community "the Israel of God" (Gal 6:16), the household of God, and the church of God (1 Tim 3:15; Eph 2:19). In 2 Corinthians 6:16, he makes it clear that his attribution of peoplehood to the Gentiles is not fanciful. For in this text, Paul extends to the church writ large the declaration of peoplehood that God himself made with respect to Israel. Addressing the Corinthians,

---

6. See, for instance, John Zizioulas, *Being as Communion: Studies in Personhood and the Church* (Crestwood: St. Vladimir's Seminary Press, 1985), who argues that "ecclesial being is bound to the very being of God" (15); Robert Jenson, "The Church," in Carl E. Braaten and Robert W. Jenson, eds., *Christian Dogmatics*, vol. 1 (Philadelphia: Fortress, 1984), who contends that the Christian community is the actualization of, and the explicit witness to, the being of God (189); Catherine LaCugna, *God for Us: The Trinity and the Christian Life* (New York: HarperCollins, 1991); Miroslav Volf, *After Our Likeness: The Church as the Image of the Trinity* (Grand Rapids: Eerdmans, 1998).

7. Father George Dragas, "Orthodox Ecclesiology in Outline," *The Greek Orthodox Theological Review* 26, no. 3 (1981). The statement also appears in Alister E. McGrath, *Christian Theology: An Introduction*, 6th ed. (Oxford: Blackwell, 2016), 325.

he says: "We are the temple of the living God; as God said: 'I will make my dwelling among them, and walk among them and I will be their God and they *shall be my people.*'" (ESV, emphasis added). Moved by love and mercy, God the Father chose a people for himself and set them apart to take part in the fulfillment of his plan in the present age.[8] Like the Israelites, the Corinthian believers were God's people, although their community was plagued with internal divisions, sexual immorality, and interpersonal conflict. While Paul was the human instrument that God used for the establishment of the church in Corinth (Acts 18:1–11; 1 Cor 3:5–11), he emphasized that their existence came by *divine choice* – they were "the church *of God* in Corinth" (1 Cor 1:2; emphasis added). Several assertions can be drawn from this basic claim, but we will mention just two.

Chosen by God

The Old Testament quotation that Paul cites in 2 Corinthians 6:16 invites us to backpedal to the historic Israelite community he is alluding to in this text. Over four centuries had elapsed since God chose Abraham to be the means by which he would bring into being a peculiar people who would become a blessing to all the nations of the earth (Gen 12:1–3; Exod 15:13, 16; Deut 14:2; 32:9–10; Isa 62:4; Jer 12:7–10). Now, while they were under the heavy yoke of Egyptian bondage, God sent Moses to deliver them, promising to take them as his own people to the land that he had sworn to give to their patriarchal ancestors. A wilderness journey ensued, during which Yahweh's loyal kindness and compassion (*hesed*) was displayed in his protection and provision for a people that would repeatedly slip into idolatry, even after their establishment in the promised land as a sovereign nation. Their disobedience eventually led to their decline and fall. But even during this era of waywardness, Yahweh's love stood firm as he repeated his commitment to consider the nation of Israel as his people. He tells the prophet Hosea, "I will plant her as my own in the land. I will have pity on 'No Pity' (Lo-Ruhamah). I will say to 'Not My People' (Lo-Ammi), 'You are my people!' And he will say, 'You are my God!'" (Hos 2:23 NET). To those who would speculate that this appellation was due to Israel's goodness, the twists and turns of their story demonstrate that it was Yahweh's love that dictated his choice, as he stated (Deut 7:6–11; 9:1–6). So, when the apostle to the Gentiles uses the phrase "my people" to refer to the Christian community, he is saying that, like Israel of old, the church exists

---

8. Exod 6:7; Lev 26:11–12.

by *divine choice*, rooted in divine love because of a divine eternal plan. As God the Father took the initiative to graciously choose Israel to be a people for himself amid all the peoples of the world, so he called "not only from the Jews but also from the Gentiles" a people to be the objects of his mercy (Rom 9:24–26). The African theologian David Zac Niringiye sees a common thread between the two groups, and argues for a continuity of existence between the two communities of faith, because they share the covenantal promises that God made to Abraham:

> Although the Bible gives specific accounts of diverse communities and their encounters with God in different times and places, and could therefore be characterized as many stories, it is also one story and one community, the story of the community of faith both in ancient times and in succeeding generations, who are all united in Christ.[9]

Similarly, Alister McGrath highlights this continuity by pointing out the element of faith that is common to both Israel and the church, and the notion of divine choice that characterizes the origins of both.[10] Indeed, like Israel, the church exists by divine choice. The Catholic theologian Paul Minear, in his seminal work *Images of the Church in the New Testament*, explains that the term "race" that Peter uses in the passage referred to above (1 Pet 2:9) depicts the identity of the Christian community by virtue of its divine election.[11] So, the church is "the chosen" race which includes diverse ethnic groups and races, male and female, young and old, rich and poor.

Owned by God

The appellation "people of God" also conveys the theological reality of *divine ownership*. The emphasis of the prepositional phrase lies in the genitive possessive. The statement "I will be *their* God and they will be *my* people" indicates that the church belongs to God.[12] And this statement should not be

---

9. Niringiye, *The Church*, 27.

10. McGrath, *Christian Theology* (6th ed.), 355.

11. Paul Minear, *Images of the Church in the New Testament* (Philadelphia: Westminster Press, 1960), 72.

12. Daniel B. Wallace, *Greek Grammar: Beyond the Basics* (Grand Rapids: Zondervan, 1997), 82. Expressions such as "My Lord and my God" are not to be considered as meaning that the subject owns God fully but rather broadly. Thus, God belongs to his people in the sense that he is the one they worship and submit to.

taken lightly because, as Peter explains in his letter to the diasporic community, the price that was paid for this acquisition was not gold, nor silver, nor an exorbitant amount of money, nor the blood of goats and calves used in the Levitical system, but the very blood of his Son (1 Pet 1:18–19; Heb 9:12). And that blood, while shed by the incarnate Son, somehow implicates the Father. It is interesting that in Paul's farewell address to the elders of the church of Ephesus, he begs them to monitor themselves and to handle with care the flock of which the Holy Spirit has made them overseers, and clarifies that he is talking about "the church of God" that was purchased with *God's* "own blood" (Acts 20:28).[13] This divine ownership of the church is reiterated at the beginning of several of Paul's epistles. He takes pains to stress the connection between the church and God the Father by stating that those who belong to the Christian community are the "church *of* God in Corinth" (1 Cor 1:2; 2 Cor 1:1), "*God's* holy people in Ephesus" (Eph 1:1), "*all God's holy people* in Christ Jesus at Philippi" (Phil 1:1), and "*God's* holy people in Colossae" (Col 1:2). Undeniably, the geographical location of the local churches might be different, but regardless of where they were situated, they were all seen as under divine proprietorship. The church, wherever it is located, is God's own possession.

The Church as the Community of God the Son

But, in the perspective of the New Testament, the appellation "people of God," while important, doesn't provide a complete picture of what the church is. An essential facet of the church's identity is the tie it maintains with Jesus the incarnate Son. The New Testament underscores the church's closeness to Jesus by means of categorical assertions and a series of colorful imagery.

Let's consider some of the Lord's declarations first. In Acts, Luke presents Jesus as boldly standing for the church when he told Paul that by persecuting the church, Paul was persecuting him: "I am Jesus whom you are persecuting," he astonishingly declared (Acts 9:5). And he intervened to protect the nascent and fledgling church from the attacks of the merciless pharisee, and went on to enlist him as one of the church's staunchest and most fearless promoters. Another assertion is Jesus's pledge of his perpetual presence with the church by promising that wherever two or three gather in his name, he will be in their midst because he will be with them until the end of the age (Matt 18:20; 28:20).

---

13. In the Greek, the genitive here can be taken as an attributive genitive, which means "his own blood," or a possessive genitive, "with the blood of his own." Since the referent is the Son, the NET Bible adds it for clarity.

But arguably, the most significant statement of the Lord about the church is his response to Peter in Matthew 16:16–19 following the latter's confession of him as the Son of God:

> You are blessed, Simon, son of Jonah, because flesh and blood did not reveal this to you, but my Father in heaven! And I tell you that you are Peter, and on this rock *I will build my church*, and the gates of Hades will not overpower it. I will give you the keys of the kingdom of heaven. Whatever you bind on earth will have been bound in heaven, and whatever you release on earth will have been released in heaven. [NET, emphasis added]

Belonging Also to the Son

These are remarkable words. They contain important ecclesiological themes that are echoed in the rest of the New Testament. First, Jesus is here claiming the church as *his own*. "I will build *my church* [Gk: *mou ecclesia*]," he flatly says (Matt 16:18). This indicates that, just as the Father has ownership of the church, so does the Son. In their own way, some New Testament writers echo this note of Christological ownership. Paul, for instance, after asking the members of the church of Rome to greet one another with a holy kiss, concludes with a salutation to them from "the churches *of* Christ" (Rom 16:16). Similarly, John in exile on Patmos portrays the risen Christ, "clothed with a long robe and with a golden sash around his chest," walking among the local churches, commanding their good works and perseverance, pointing to where they have fallen, and demanding their repentance (Rev 1:12–13 ESV).

Founded by, and upon, the Son

Second, Jesus declares himself to be *the builder* of the church: "I will build my church," he says. In saying this, we can reasonably infer that he is claiming to be both the founder and the foundation of the universal church – the global messianic community.[14] As *founder*, he set the stage for its establishment. He took the initiative to prepare for the launching of the new ecclesial community. He selected the core group of twelve who formed the nucleus of the new movement, trained and equipped them, prayed for them, commissioned them

---

14. As several scholars have argued, *ecclesia* here refers to the church writ large, not just a local entity.

(Matt 28:20; Acts 1:8), and commended them to his Father (John 17:9–17). Jesus's careful preparation for the launch of the Christian community is clearly seen in the lengthy discourse he delivered to the Twelve prior to going to the cross (John 13–17), his delicate handling of Peter (John 21:15ff.), and his confrontation of Saul who was bent on stopping the nascent and fledgling movement from its beginning (Acts 9:3–9).

As *foundation*, Christ is the infrastructure upon which the church rests. That infrastructure is the solid complex which consists of his person, his work, and the faith that is placed in him. True, when Jesus told Peter that he would build the church upon "this rock," we join the group of scholars who believe that he was probably referring to Peter. But we nuance this interpretation with the caveat that the reference was most likely not to Peter qua Peter, but to Peter the confessing disciple who had just been given the divinely inspired revelation that Jesus was the Son of God.[15] From that point on, all who would become part of the ecclesial community everywhere must make a confession like the one Peter made. For the experience of salvation that provides entry into the ecclesial community comes by confessing that Jesus is Lord and the risen Christ (Rom 10:9). The establishment and expansion of the ecclesial community is predicated upon the proclamation of that Christ-centered salvific message everywhere (Luke 24:45–47).

Besides all this, the work of Christ, particularly the cross, imparts a uniqueness to the new community that elevates it to a much higher dimension than the original people of God. In his letter to the Ephesians, Paul tells us that through the cross, Christ dismantled the barriers that kept the various ethnic groups apart, thus paving the way for the coming into being of an ethnically and socially diverse community. From that point on, the people of God would no longer consist of one particular ethnic group, but would form a cosmopolitan and inclusive community in which the socio-historical differentiations are all relativized (Gal 3:28; 1 Cor 12:13).

Paul emphasizes this truth in his letter to the gentile members of the church in Ephesians 2:19: "You are no longer foreigners and strangers, but fellow citizens with God's people and also members of his household." Amazingly, the wall of hostility that existed between them and the Jewish people has been broken down, abolished, or rendered inoperative in the flesh of Jesus Christ, resulting in a unity that transcends religious backgrounds, cultural differences, earthly nationalities, political polarizations, geographical locations, and skin pigmentations. This new race of a kind that is unprecedented, highlighted in

---

15. Donald Hagner, *Matthew 14–28*, Word Biblical Commentary (Dallas: Word, 1995), 470.

the Petrine writings, can be perfectly juxtaposed with the concept of the new humanity created by Christ in the Pauline account (Eph 2:15). Both writers boldly proclaim the supernatural existence of a corporate entity, where our spiritual identity supersedes our national one, where Gentiles and Jews become fellow members of the family of God, and where a brother/sisterhood is created anew, giving the church a unique calling and a distinct role in the fulfillment of the purposes of God. Clement of Alexandria, one of the church fathers of the second century, aptly commented, "We who worship God in a new way, as the third race, are Christians."[16] As Augustine expressed it, "His whole church, which is diffused everywhere, is his body, of which he is also the Head; however, not only believers of this present time, but also they who were before, and who will be after us even to the end of the world."[17] The concept of catholicity is one of the unique features of the church, for in the company of the redeemed, there is neither Greek nor Jew, circumcision nor uncircumcision, barbarian, Scythian, slave or free.[18]

This mark of inclusion is so significant for the church's identity that Paul labels the community a new humanity, a mystery that was formerly hidden but is now revealed thanks to Christ's redemptive accomplishment (Eph 3:6). But this new humanity, this third race, is a community in the making. The mystery that was unveiled through Christ's work has only begun to be unfolded. The fullness of the Gentiles that will signal the end of the hardening of Israel, the original people of God, is yet to come in (Rom 11:25–26). The assembling of the numberless, pan-national, multilingual, ecclesial throng at worship before the Lamb is yet to be completed (Rev 7:9–13).

All this means that the new community that Christ's cross made possible is eschatological in nature. While its existence is a matter of history, its full realization lies in the future. As Harper and Metzger explain: "The church is a community both of fulfilment and of hope, realizing the blessings of the future while yet awaiting the fullness of these blessings to be revealed at Christ's second coming."[19]

---

16. Clement of Alexandria, *Stromateis* (*Miscellanies*), and Epistle to Diognetus, cited in F. F. Bruce, *The Epistles to the Colossians, to Philemon, and to the Ephesians* (Grand Rapids: Eerdmans, 1984), 296.

17. Augustine, "Sermon 71.32" in *Works of Saint Augustine: A Translation for the 21st Century* (Hyde Park, NY: New York City Press, 1997), 3/3:265–66.

18. Col 3:11.

19. Brad Harper and Paul Louis Metzger, *Exploring Ecclesiology: An Evangelical and Ecumenical Introduction* (Grand Rapids: Baker, 2009), 48.

That is why Paul emphatically declares that "no one can lay any foundation other than the one already laid, which is Jesus Christ" (1 Cor 3:11). In Ephesians 2:20, he refers to Christ as the chief cornerstone, the first and principal solid stone usually placed at the corner of an edifice to determine every other measurement in the construction. This pivotal role that Christ plays in his church is the fulfillment of one among the many messianic prophecies uttered in the Old Testament: "So this is what the sovereign LORD says: 'See, I lay a stone in Zion, a tested stone, a precious cornerstone for a sure foundation; the one who relies on it will never be dismayed. I will make justice the measuring line and righteousness the plumb line'" (Isa 28:16–17). Jesus identified himself as the stone that the builders rejected that has become the cornerstone (Mark 12:10). It is into him that the building is to grow in every way (Eph 4:15).

Maintained and Sustained by the Son

If we now turn to the imagery, we find a rich collection of metaphors that depict the relationship of Christ and the church. The relationship is described in terms of Shepherd and sheep (John 10:1–21; Heb 13:20), Vine and branches (John 15:1–5), Bridegroom and bride (Eph 5:25–27; Rev 19:7), and body and Head (Col 1:18). Each one of these images by itself sufficiently communicates the importance of Christ for the life of the church. But the depiction of Christ as the Head of the church, and the church as the body of Christ, is particularly striking. Found only in the Pauline corpus, this physiological imagery depicts the *union* of the church and Christ. Just as the body and the head of a person form one organism, so Christ and his church cannot be separated. The symbolism also speaks of a connection that is vital to the existence and growth of the church.[20] Life, direction, protection, and nourishment flow from the head to the body. A beheaded body has no life. The church is thus permeated with the life received from Christ. Thus, Paul bluntly states that the life of the members of the ecclesial community is not only hidden in Christ, but that Christ *is* their life (Col 3:3–4).

Instituted and Empowered by God the Spirit

If the original people of God could exist without a permanent and ongoing relationship with the Spirit, according to the New Testament such cannot be the case for the people of God who have become the community of the Son.

---

20. Col 1:15, 18.

Both the emergence of the new community and its ongoing life are attributable to the operation of the Spirit. It is thus not farfetched to assert that without the work of the Holy Spirit there would be no church.

Born by, and of, the Spirit

It took the work of the Spirit to bring the preparation that Jesus made and the foundation he laid to its intended fruition – the establishment of an ecclesial body. And this is true historically, spiritually, and corporately.

Historically, it was the Spirit who struck the match that caused fire to spark from the fuel-soaked wood that Jesus had assembled. And this was by design. On several occasions before going to the cross, Jesus promised his small band of disciples that he would send them the Holy Spirit (John 7:37; 14:20ff.). Further, he stressed that they should not venture out and attempt anything before that promise had been fulfilled (Acts 1:8). And as he had said, so it happened. The obedience of the disciples to the Lord's command and the faithfulness of the Lord to his promise produced the unprecedented Pentecost event that resulted in the birth of the ecclesial community (Acts 2). We should not fail to note that while Jesus's three-year ministry resulted in a following of 120, the Spirit's one-day action produced a big ecclesiastical bang that brought in a harvest of 3,000! And from that point, the Spirit assumed the leadership of the Christian mission that resulted in astronomical numeral growth and wide geographical expansion (Acts 5:14; 8:1; 13:1ff.).

Besides being the agent who brought the church into existence, the Spirit is the agent who made its members fit for participation in the ecclesial community. For, to become part of the new humanity made possible by Christ's redemptive work, one must go through a metamorphosis, which is called the new birth or regeneration. As John put it, one has to be "born of God" (John 3:3). To use a modern scientific concept, this involves a change in the DNA that we all inherit from Adam (Rom 5:12; Eph 2:1–4). But this work is not done by God the Father, nor by God the Son, but by God the Spirit. Jesus explained it with great clarity to the Jewish scholar Nicodemus, and Paul declares it without ambiguity in his letter to the young pastor Titus (John 3; Titus 3:3–5). The divine birth gives the members of the new community a place in the divine family and makes them "partakers of the divine nature" (John 1:11–12; Rom 8; Gal 4:4–6; 1 Pet 1:4). It also transfers them into a different domain (Col 1:13). As Paul asserts, "If anyone is in Christ, he is a new creation. The old has passed away; behold, the new has come" (2 Cor 5:17 ESV). As Lewis Sperry Chafer states, "Regeneration is a most essential step in that preparation which must be made if individuals from this fallen race are to be constituted worthy dwellers within that highest of all spheres and made associates there with the Father, the Son, and the Holy Spirit."[21]

And there is more to it than that. Besides his historical and spiritual work, the Spirit exercised a corporate function in the establishment of the ecclesial community. It is he who inducted (and continues to induct) those born of God into the ecclesial community. "For we were all baptized by one Spirit so as to form one body – whether Jews or Gentiles, slave or free – and we were all given the one Spirit to drink" (1 Cor 12:13). That's why Paul boldly declares that "if anyone does not have the Spirit of Christ, they do not belong to Christ" (Rom 8:9). Furthermore, he seals them, marking as his heirs those whom God chose in Christ before the world was created.[22] Without a doubt, the constitution of the church is predicated upon the work of the Holy Spirit. The Spirit is the glue that brings and holds the Christian community together. The American theologian Edmund Clowney further explains the role of the Spirit thus:

> The Spirit comes to realize God's promises. He makes the church the people of God as the prophets predicted, giving them new hearts in the New Covenant (Ezek 36:25–28). He joins them to Jesus Christ, for no-one can say "Jesus is Lord!" apart from the Spirit (1 Cor 12:3). The church is therefore the people of God and the assembly of Christ because it is the fellowship of the Spirit. The Spirit fulfils; he does not obliterate membership in God's people or discipleship in following Christ.[23]

Empowered by the Spirit

We have established that the coming of the Spirit was (and continues to be) of prime importance to the constitution of the church. But the involvement of the third member of the Trinity did not (and does not) stop there. At the conclusion of that initial work, he did not sign off, turn over the keys, and leave. No. He continues to be intimately implicated in the life of the community. As a starter, he takes residence within the community by inhabiting its members individually and the body corporately (John 14:16–17; 1 Cor 6:19; 3:16).

---

21. Lewis Sperry Chafer, *Systematic Theology*, ed. John F. Walvoord (Wheaton: Victor, 1988), 115.
22. Edmund Clowney, *The Church* (Downers Grove: IVP, 1996), 50.
23. Clowney, *The Church*, 51.

Further, he supplies the community with what it needs to function properly and effectively (1 Cor 12; Rom 12:3–10). Moreover, he is ever present to reassure the members of the community of their status and privilege with God the Father (Gal 4:6; Rom 8:15–17), to intercede on their behalf (Rom 8:26), and to enable them to discern his will (1 Cor 2:10ff.). Finally, he gives all the members of the community the ability to cultivate and manifest the qualities that are "utterly foreign to the natural [person]"; he gives "new capacities for joy and sorrow, love, peace, guidance, and all the host of realities in the spiritual world."[24] Considering this intricate and thoroughgoing involvement of the Spirit in the life of the ecclesial community, we can safely say that the fulfillment of the promise made long ago, and subsequently relayed by Jesus, ushered in an age during which the existence of the people of God is conceivable only as they live in the Spirit (Gal 5:25; Rom 8:6–11).

And this function of the Spirit in the life of the ecclesial community should not be received with a yawn – something we acknowledge but consider inconsequential. This would be to misunderstand the biblical portrayal of the Spirit. Throughout, Scripture consistently presents the Spirit as the power that originates from beyond the created order to empower people to do extraordinary things. In the words of Anthony Thiselton, he is the Beyond who is Within,[25] meaning the transcendent power of God who resides in and amid his people. And the purpose of that residence is not just to accompany but to empower. Thus, the American New Testament scholar Gordon Fee is correct when he speaks of the Spirit as the empowering presence of God.[26]

Holistic Trinitarian Connection

Now the Trinity is not a divided entity. While it consists of three distinct persons, all three members share the same essence. It is this sharing of essence that constitutes their fundamental unity. Besides this, their lives comingle and interpenetrate.[27] Long ago, Augustine of Hippo stated this principle of mutual

---

24. Clowney, 121.

25. Anthony Thiselton, *The Hermeneutics of Doctrine* (Grand Rapids: Eerdmans, 2007), 416.

26. Gordon Fee, *God's Empowering Presence* (Peabody: Hendrickson, 1994).

27. Theologians use the technical term *perichoresis* to refer to this. In his depiction of the mutual permeation of God the Father and God the Son, Gregory of Nyssa in the fourth century used the infinitive *perichorein* to argue for the divinity of Jesus. The term was further propagated by John of Damascus in the eighth century to speak of the coinherence or the moving (Latin *circumincessio*) of the members of the Godhead around each other.

interpenetration thus: "Each is in each; all are in each; each is in all; all are in all; and all are in one."[28] Jesus gives us a glimpse of this mystery when he says that he is in the Father, and the Father is in him (John 17:21). The point of this for our discussion is that while we focus on the importance of each member for the church, this is not intended to convey the idea that the church relates to them separately. While each member of the Godhead plays a distinctive role in the church's life, as shown in the foregoing analysis, the church relates to the Trinity *as Trinity*, not piecemeal. The New Testament gives several hints of this. For instance, in his commissioning of the disciples to make disciples of all nations, the risen Christ commanded them to baptize in the name of the triune God: Father, Son, and Holy Spirit (Matt 28:20). The point of this command is that the pan-national church that Jesus envisaged was to be identified with the triune God. Another example is Paul's threefold benediction formula of 2 Corinthians 13:14, where he prays for the blessing of all three members of the Godhead to be showered on the Corinthian believers: "the grace of the Lord Jesus Christ, and the love of God, and the fellowship of the Holy Spirit." A last example worth mentioning here is the shared ownership of the church by the Father and Jesus. As indicated earlier, the church is said to be owned by the Father, and by Jesus. And if we wonder how, Jesus explains. Praying to the Father for the disciples, he says: "I am praying . . . for those whom *you* have given me, for they are yours. *All [that are mine] are yours, and yours are mine*" (John 17:9–10 ESV, emphasis added).

Trinitarian Theology and Authentic Engagement

The point of this chapter-long exposition of the nature of the church is to lay bare the identity of the community that is called to engage society with a view to exerting a transforming influence for good upon it. If our analysis is correct, that community is not a mere social gathering of like-minded people. It is not an architectural structure regardless of how impressive that is. It doesn't belong to any nation or society, though it is embedded, in this sense, as part of a nation or society. Its definition does not stem first and foremost from its connection to a particular ethnicity, a specific tradition, or a given communion. It is first and foremost a *theo*logical community. It is theological because its identity comes from its relationship with and connection to the triune God. The other relationships aren't unimportant, but they are not determinative.

---

28. Augustine, *The Trinity*. Trans. Edmond Hill. Edited by John E. Rotelle (New York: New York City Press, 1991), V. 8. 9.

The church is the people of God, constituted into the community of Christ by the power of the Spirit. Its birth, life, sustenance, and engagement in the world must reflect this bedrock self-understanding. The American theologian Stanley Grenz says it well:

> We are one people of God . . . because we are the company of those whom the Spirit has already brought to share in the love between the Father and the Son. . . . As these people, we are called to reflect in the present the eternal dynamic of the triune God, that community which we will enjoy in the great eschatological fellowship on the renewed earth. Only our primary identity as participants in the fellowship of the triune God forms the ultimate foundation for the various other facets of our doctrine of the church. Our participation in the divine life provides the basis for the ministry of the church in the world.[29]

The church then is a unique community within the wider society. To be authentically engaged in the social order, and thus influence that order for good, it must be conscious of its attachment to its Creator, Sustainer, and Empowerer: the Father, Son, and Holy Spirit. The specific ways to live out this authentic engagement based on the Trinitarian ecclesiology just described will be delineated in the following chapters.

---

29. Stanley Grenz, *Theology for the Community of God* (Grand Rapids: Eerdmans, 2000), 484–85.

5

Ambassador of Heaven

God did not bring the church into being to be an end in itself.[1] The reason for its existence goes beyond its self-perpetuation. While the church has an obligation to attend to its own health, its aim is to fulfill a purpose much greater and broader than that. As the Finnish theologian Veli-Matti Kärkkäinen puts it, the church exists to "participate in the wider salvific purposes of God."[2] Considering this, having articulated a theological understanding of the church, we must now endeavor to determine the significance of the view we set forth for the issue at hand. What does this view suggest for the role of the church in the temporal domain? What contribution can a Trinitarian entity with a spiritual, eschatological, and social dimension make to the transformation of the milieu in which it is embodied?

Differentiating Activities from Role

To be sure, the question regarding the church's role in the world is not a novel one, nor have answers to it been lacking. Throughout history, ecclesiastical practices as well as theological reflection have revealed a variety of ways in which the church's role and mission have been understood. In his book *The Essence of the Church*, Craig Van Gelder provides a helpful survey of some of these historical views. For most of the church's first 1,500 years, he argues, the focus was on the church as an institution that existed primarily to maintain and project to the world apostolic authority, mainly through the

---

1. Millard Erickson, *Christian Theology* (Grand Rapids: Baker Academic, [2nd ed.] 1998; [3rd ed.] 2013), 1060.
2. Veli-Matti Kärkkäinen, "Ecclesiology and the Church in Christian Tradition and Western Theology," in Gene L. Green, Stephen T. Pardue, and K. K. Yeo, eds., *The Church from Every Tribe and Tongue: Ecclesiology in the Majority World* (Carlisle: Langham Global Library, 2018), 27–28.

office of the papacy.³ During the Reformation era, the focus shifted in two directions. The Magisterial Reformers understood the role of the church to consist primarily in the dual task of preaching and teaching the word (which was considered the locus of authority), and the correct administration of the sacraments.⁴ For their part, the Radical Reformers directed the spotlight primarily on the need for the church to foster fellowship among believers.⁵ With the rise of denominationalism from the eighteenth century onward, the focus shifted again, but this time in the direction of conceiving the church as a voluntary organization that existed essentially to meet the personal needs of its members.⁶

But not everyone embraces the approach of identifying a single activity as the paramount function of the church. There are thinkers who prefer a more eclectic approach that incorporates several ecclesial functions under one overarching theme. An example of this is the noted American Baptist theologian Millard J. Erickson. In his major work *Christian Theology*, Erickson lists several activities (such as evangelism, worship, social concern, and edification) as legitimate functions that the church should carry out. However, he insists that the church's execution of these tasks should be shaped by the gospel, which he considers to be the factor which lies at the heart of everything that the church does.⁷ The Australian theologian Michael Bird seems to concur with this sentiment. In his magisterial work *Evangelical Theology*, Bird refers approvingly to the British missiologist Lesslie Newbigin's six characteristics of the church,⁸ and proceeds to ground them in the gospel. He writes:

> An evangelical ecclesiology is . . . the attempt to be a gospel driven-church. We are the community of the gospelized: the company of the gospel, the public face of the gospel, the hermeneutic of the gospel. The worship, mission, ethics, symbols, testimony, and spirituality of the church are shaped by what it thinks of and does with the gospel of Jesus Christ.⁹

---

3. Craig Van Gelder, *The Essence of the Church: A Community Created by the Spirit* (Grand Rapids: Baker, 2000), 55.
4. Van Gelder, *Essence of the Church*, 57.
5. Van Gelder, 60.
6. Van Gelder, 67.
7. Erickson, *Christian Theology* (2nd ed.), 1069.
8. Michael Bird, *Evangelical Theology* (Grand Rapids: Zondervan, 2013), 706.
9. Bird, *Evangelical Theology*, 707.

In our estimation, the eclectic approach has much to commend it. Even a cursory reading of the New Testament shows that much more is expected of the church than the execution of just one function. In its pages, we find calls to the church to fulfill a variety of functions including proclamation, edification, fellowship, worship, mutual help, and attention to social concern. In his seminal study of the New Testament's view of the church, *The Images of the Church*, the Catholic theologian Paul Minear identifies over ninety images that are used by its different authors to refer to the church.[10] Indeed, it is doubtful whether those who advocate a single function in actuality limit the scope of the church's endeavor to the carrying out of that activity alone.

We deem it also correct to anchor these activities in a foundational principle that provides a rationale, grounding, logical coherence, and direction to the execution of these functions. And on this, Erickson and Bird are right to look to the gospel as best suited for this role. But, in our estimation, we think that in the search for an overarching role of the church in the world, we need to go beyond identifying a principle and provide a list of functions that fall under its purview. And, in this regard, as we will demonstrate below, we think that Bird seems more helpful than Erickson. Besides identifying the principle that gives shape to the things that the church does, we need to find a descriptor that states the capacity in which the church does these things. In our view it is preferable to view the gospel as the substance of what God wishes to accomplish in the world and the church as the agent that puts that substance to work. In the words of Gene L. Green, "the church's existence is instrumental in God's mission."[11] While Bird does not put it in these terms, he seems to allude to this understanding when he says that the activities that the church conducts are to be shaped by what the "church thinks of, and what it does with, the gospel." This suggests that church and gospel carry out two distinct although related functions: the gospel is the tool, the asset, the material, or the stuff given to the church for the conduct of its work, while the church is the agent that wields that tool.

The Church as God's Representative

If this is true, the question we must then ask is: How should we name the capacity in which the church carries out the action that it does? The answer, to our mind, lies in a simple but apt concept: *representation*. We contend

---

10. Minear, *Images of the Church*.
11. Green, Pardue, and Yeo, *Church from Every Tribe*, 4.

that the consciousness of being the representative of the triune God within a given social domain, and the resolve to act in a manner congruent with that representational function, is key to the church's authentic engagement in the transformation of that order for the better. In a succinct statement, Bird brings together the Trinitarian identity of the church that we spelled out in the previous chapter and the representational mandate that we are suggesting. He writes: "What appears to be the unifying element of [the biblical portrayal of the church] is that the one God of creation has one people, sharing in one Spirit, and united to one Lord Jesus; they *represent* God in the world, to the world, and for the world."[12]

A representative is an official authorized agent. Representatives are emissaries or envoys who are empowered by others to stand in their place. Their induction to that role empowers them to act and speak authoritatively on behalf of the commissioning or sending agent.

Genuine representatives do not behave as rogue agents. As emissaries, they do not view their status as the freedom to act and to speak any way they like. Their appointment and commissioning are always accompanied by marching orders, a message, a code of conduct that governs the way they carry out their work. The authenticity and legitimacy of their pronouncements and actions are contingent upon the conformity they bear to the instrument or protocol that sets the parameters of their appointment. That's why careful representatives are always mindful of the parameters within which their mandate is to be exercised.

The mechanism of representation is used in various areas of life. In the realm of politics, for instance, it is at the heart of the democratic system of government – be it parliamentarian or republican. Citizens who cannot attend personally to their interests authorize and empower others to do so on their behalf by voting them into office. We also find it in the domain of international relations. Throughout the world leaders of governments authorize and empower persons to represent their governments to other governments. They are emissaries who are empowered to act and speak on their behalf. At any given time, a government typically has several envoys deployed in various places around the world to represent it. However, regardless of the country to which those envoys are sent, the actions they carry out and the words they speak reflect the position of their government.

To our mind, the notion of representation, particularly as it is used in the field of diplomacy, is an apt descriptor of the church's overarching role in the world. The similarities are instructive. Just as a head of government sovereignly

---

12. Bird, *Evangelical Theology*, 718. Emphasis added.

chooses and sends ambassadors to various parts of the world to represent him or her, so the triune God deploys his church to various corners of the globe to be his representative. Just as the various envoys of a head of government are given one overall message to share, so the church of the triune God, wherever it is embedded, is entrusted with one message: the gospel of the kingdom. Just as the emissaries of a government must return to their home country to give an account of their work abroad, so the church of the triune God must return to its heavenly sender regardless of its place of deployment, to give an account of the work accomplished on his behalf.

Biblical and Theological Grounding

The concept of representation as a general descriptor of the overarching role of the church in the world can claim solid biblical and theological support. Among the many examples that we could cite to buttress this claim, the following seem most compelling.

First, we mention the concept of *divine presence*. God, as is well known, is a transcendent being, but his transcendence does not preclude him from being present everywhere in his world. In Psalm 139, the psalmist tells us that it is not possible for anyone to escape God's presence; wherever one goes, God is there (139:7–12). Since his presence pervades the entire universe, we can refer to this as the *cosmic* presence of God. Besides this general presence, Scripture speaks of the fact that God is present with each one of us. A constant refrain of Holy Writ is the assurance that God will never leave us nor forsake his own (Isa 41:10; Matt 28:20; Heb 13:5). Since this experience is specific to the individual believer, we can call this the *personal* presence of God.

More germane to our purpose here, however, is Scripture's assertion that God is present in the world through his people, the church. Both Jesus and Paul concur with this. Speaking to his disciples, Jesus gave the assurance that wherever his people gather in his name, he is in their midst (Matt 18:20). In giving this promise, Jesus is saying that the mere gathering of the people of God constitutes a sanctuary where God's special presence manifests itself. This thought leads us to conclude that the more numerous and the more frequent are the gatherings of the people of God, the more saturated is the world with God's special manifestation. But, as significant as it is, Jesus's pronouncement seems to suggest that the presence he promises is occasional and purely spiritual. Happily, Paul adds a dimension to the discussion that keeps us from drawing that mistaken conclusion. In his first letter to the Corinthian Christians, he informs them that they embody the presence of God by virtue of the Holy

Spirit who dwells in them both individually and corporately (1 Cor 6:19; 3:17). Since the indwelling of the Spirit is a permanent reality, the people of God in Corinth constituted a permanent and continuous presence of God in that locality. Wherever the church is, it constitutes *God's presence in that place*.

The next argument that buttresses our case is the use of the *temple* metaphor to refer to the church. Veli-Matti Kärkkäinen calls the temple a determinative symbol of the church.[13] We find this designation for the ecclesial community in several places in the Pauline letters, but it is its use in the Corinthian correspondence, particularly 1 Corinthians 3:16–17, that is of special interest to us. In this text, Paul refers to the church as the temple of God four times, and he makes it clear that he is not talking about something abstract, but that the reference is to the Corinthian Christians themselves: "*You yourselves* are God's temple . . . *you together* are that temple," he insists. As the people of God, regardless of their number, they were *corporately God's temple in that city* because of the Spirit of God who indwelled them as a corporate community. This presence has a level of concreteness and visibility to it. Many commentators see this in Paul's use of the Greek word *naos* instead of *ieron*. Whereas *ieron* speaks of the inner temple, *naos* denotes the temple building itself.[14] By referring to the Corinthian Christians as a temple, Paul is saying that their role can be likened to the role that the tabernacle and the temple played in the history of ancient Israel. They were the loci of God's *shekinah* glory. In his massive commentary on First Corinthians, the British theologian Anthony Thiselton writes: "In the Jewish and Christian apocalyptic, the sacredness of the temple as *radiating God's presence* is . . . axiomatic."[15] For Paul, "the Corinthians [were] God's sanctuary in which the Holy Spirit dwells."[16] They were the shrine of God.

The reference to the people of God as *priests* is the third line of argument that supports the case for the church's representational role. Among many things, the New Testament refers to Christians as "a kingdom and priests" (Rev 1:6; 5:10) and "a royal priesthood" (1 Pet 2:9). This language, as is well known, harks back to the pronouncement God made at Mount Sinai where he designated the recently redeemed Israel from Egyptian bondage as his "treasured possession . . . a *kingdom of priests* and a holy nation" (Exod 19:5–6;

---

13. Kärkkäinen, "Ecclesiology and the Church," 17.

14. Anthony Thiselton, *The First Epistle to the Corinthians: A Commentary on the Greek Text*, The New International Greek New Testament (Grand Rapids: Eerdmans, 2000), 315.

15. Thiselton, *Corinthians*, 316. Emphasis mine.

16. Thiselton, 316.

emphasis added). By carrying over this designation to the church, Scripture intends to make the point that both Israel and the church are called to carry out a universal priesthood. This universal priesthood entails the exercise of a mediatorial function. They are to represent the people before God, and God before the people. Just as the status of priesthood laid upon Israel the responsibility to "represent God and mediate for him with the nations," so ecclesiastical priesthood makes it incumbent on the church to represent God before the world.[17]

The fourth consideration in our construal is inherent in the *approach* the Lord has recommended to the church in its endeavor to engage the world. Unlike Israel, the approach the Lord requires is not primarily centripetal, but centrifugal. Its method of engagement is not to be primarily attraction but invasion. Theirs was to be an outgoing methodology. This modality is already insinuated in the giving of what is commonly referred to as the Great Commission (Matt 28:19), but it is made explicit in the Gospel of John. There, Jesus bluntly says that the church's mode of engagement must be missional. He not only specifies that the locus of the disciples' ministry is the world itself, but he also *sends* them on a mission into the world! And what is more, the pattern of their missional dispatch is none other than the pattern used by the Father himself with Jesus: "As the Father has sent me, I am sending you" (John 20:21). Once they were joined to the Lord, they automatically joined his missionary society. As they go, "they receive power and authority as accredited representatives of Christ's kingdom. . . . They live in the world as his embassy proclaiming his reconciliation, entrusted with the authority of his commission."[18] That mission doesn't come with only the prestige and honor of representatives, however. At times, it attracts suffering and even the paying of the ultimate sacrifice.

That Jesus's mission to the world entailed his representation of the Father is abundantly clear from the testimony of the evangelists. Matthew tells us that Jesus came with the authority of the Father. He presents him as Immanuel to whom "all authority . . . has been given" (Matt 28:18). The use of the passive voice in this verse suggests that the authority was granted to him by God himself. Further, John tells us that Jesus came to reveal the Father and to show us what he is like. The Fourth Evangelist is emphatic that before Jesus's coming, "no one [had] ever seen God" (John 1:18). His arrival changed that situation

---

17. The quote is from Charles Briggs, quoted in Walter C. Kaiser, *The Promise-Plan of God: A Biblical Theology of the Old and New Testaments* (Grand Rapids: Zondervan, 2008), 75.

18. Minear, *Images of the Church*, 63.

of ignorance, since he has made the Father known – he has explained him. That's why he could say confidently that to see him was tantamount to seeing the Father himself (14:9). Jesus also asserted that he came to do the works of the Father, that is, to carry out his mission in the world (17:4). All this suggests that in passing on the missional torch to his disciples, and, through them, to the church, he intended them and the future church also to represent God in the arena of the world. As Paul Minear aptly puts it: "God sent the Messiah, the Messiah sent his apostles, and all whom they called were also sent."[19] With this sending, the commission has been universalized. From that point on, "every Christian is called to live in God and to speak for God in every culture."[20]

When ambassadors travel to foreign lands to represent their governments, they go with the awareness that the success of their mission requires their entrenchment in the places to which they are sent. Ambassadors aren't tourists who travel for the fun of it or for the purpose of sightseeing. Rather, they travel with a view to becoming residents; and as such they understand that their work requires thorough knowledge of the peculiarities and intricacies of their places of deployment. This remains a *sine qua non* for the success of the mission of any envoy – whether diplomat or missionary. Yet, regardless of how deep and how profound their embeddedness, the residency of the diplomatic corps is never considered permanent. This is because of the temporary nature of their mission. When the mandate ends, they must return home. The end of the mission itself says that their stay was representational; they were there as representatives of their countries, not in their capacities as private citizens.

The New Testament puts the church in a similar situation. On the one hand, it portrays the church as being commissioned and dispatched by God into the world to represent him in that arena. Following the model left by Christ, the church's work in the world must be done incarnationally, not remotely. Just as it was necessary for the incarnate Logos to become immersed in the life situation of the people of his time, so the fulfillment of the mission he entrusted to his church can be fulfilled only at close range, not from a distance.[21] On the other hand, Scripture portrays the stay of the people of God in the temporal domain as transient and temporary. With respect to the world, the status of the church is like that of exiles, sojourners, and strangers (1 Pet 1:1; 2:11; Heb 11:13). While here, they live with the awareness that they belong to another city,

---

19. Minear, 63.

20. W. Ross Hastings, *Theological Ethics: The Moral Life of the Gospel in Contemporary Context* (Grand Rapids: Zondervan, 2021), 19.

21. Escobar, *In Search of Christ*, 276.

and with the keen sense that they share another citizenship (Heb 11:13; Phil 3:20). As important as their journey in the temporal domain is, it is nonetheless provisional; it will end when the mandate expires – when the representational assignment is completed.

At this juncture, we must guard against allowing the language of sending that we've been using throughout this section to create confusion in our minds regarding the places where the representational task is to be executed. The places to which we are "sent" are primarily our countries of origin! Christians are called to be ambassadors of Christ in the countries of their biological birth. They represent the kingdom of God – the transcendent realm of their new life – to the domain of their continued earthly existence. Their lives thus embody a dual relationship, which calls for keen awareness of their primary allegiance lest the ambassadorial role is vitiated and compromised.

Praxiological Implications

It is common knowledge that the reason a country establishes a diplomatic mission in a foreign land is to defend its interests in that land. This objective is usually pursued through the influence that the representatives of the sending country exert on the host country. The more effective the influence, the greater the impact it is likely to have. Now, if it's true that the people of God exist to serve him, one can say that God's purpose in establishing ecclesial communities throughout the world is similar. God's intention is that these divine signposts will promote his ideals, defend his interests, and uphold his values in the places where they are implanted. Jesus's instruction to us to pray for the Lord's will to be done on earth as it is in heaven clearly supports this judgment (Matt 6:10).

Ecclesial communities accomplish this mission by exerting an influence that is designed to bend their places of deployment in the direction of God's will for community life. In their capacity as God's representatives, their mission is to prod, woo, and nudge the contexts in which they are embedded to align themselves with the design, plan, and purpose of God for their lives. This seems to be what Jesus had in mind when he said that his disciples are to let their light shine before others so that they may see their good works and glorify their Father in heaven (Matt 5:16).

If this is the case, we submit that, from the perspective of the representational model, the very presence of ecclesial communities is a ferment of transformation. Their existence presents a challenge to the status quo that prevails in their environment. As is the case with an embassy, an ecclesial community, when correctly understood, is a sign of the presence of a "foreign" power in the locality where it is situated. Just as the sight of an embassy suggests the political position of the country it represents, so the sight of an ecclesial community in any milieu should bring to awareness God's political vision and ideals for that context. For its presence signifies the existence of an alternative regime that is different from the one that the milieu knows and is accustomed to. In so far as an ecclesial community claims to represent something better than the reigning system, its very presence constitutes a critique of that order. Perhaps more significant than all this is the message the presence of the ecclesial community communicates about the future of the current order: *Ecclesial communities signal the eventual end of the system that prevails where they are embedded.* This stems from the fact that if they are genuine representatives of God, their "arrival" anywhere simultaneously signals the commencement of the new order that God is fashioning *and* the beginning of the end of the current order. For, inasmuch as they are Christ's communities, they are closely related to the kingdom that Jesus introduced to the temporal domain and that he pledges to consummate. This makes them harbingers of what is to come. It makes them signs of the arrival of the transformation that will eventually come upon the creation and humanity. Of first importance, then, we submit that the church represents God by living as an authentic symbol of the new order that God pledges to bring about. Amid the old order, it is the sign or anticipation of the new order that God is fashioning. It is the foretaste of what the social order will be like under the unchallenged rule of God. As Van Gelder puts it:

> This new community is to live as a sign to the world that the full redemptive reign of God is present in the world. Being a sign means that the very presence of the church in the world is a missionary statement by God. This new community is to live as a foretaste of this new redemption. . . . And this new community is to serve as an instrument . . . [of] good news to others. It expresses this both in what it is and in what it does, both through its presence and intentional acts.[22]

But as is well known, influence is not something that happens automatically. To become efficacious and impactful, an influence requires the exertion of effort, the expenditure of energy, and the employment of diplomatic skills. This is true of the church as well. If ecclesial communities are to exert an influence that will result in the transformation of the contexts in which they are embedded, their presence must be accompanied by what Van Gelder calls

---

22. Van Gelder, *Essence of the Church*, 99.

in the above quotation "intentional acts." First, their mode of life must be reflective of the values of the divine order they purport to represent. Second, as with all ambassadors, besides modeling they must communicate the positions and perspective of the government they represent. Third, when necessary, they must actively defend and promote the order they represent. Fourth, again as true ambassadors, they must keep alive the confidence in the eventual triumph of the order they represent. The balance of this book will be devoted to fleshing out what it means for the church to discharge these representational functions.

Part Three

Acts of Transforming Engagement

6

Exemplar of a New Order

There are experiences one never forgets regardless of the amount of time that has elapsed since they occurred. For me, one such experience happened in seminary decades ago in a class on Christianity and Marxism. The remark I heard was so striking that, as I write this sentence, I can visualize myself in the classroom along with my classmates when the revered professor uttered the words. While delivering a lecture on Marxist ideology, our professor said that Karl Marx, after reading the gospels, reportedly concluded that if Christians had followed the teaching of Jesus, Marxism would be made redundant. I said to myself then, and it has stayed with me until now: "What a challenge we Christians have."

We ended the previous chapter with the claim that the presence of the ecclesial community is by itself, in some sense, transforming. If the church really represents an alternative to the prevailing order, then its mere presence should be unsettling to the status quo. This, however, is only the beginning of the transformation process. Important though it is, the influence that the ecclesial community exerts by its mere presence can only be passive, and, by that token, incidental. To be efficacious, and to result in impactful change, the ecclesial presence needs to be reinforced and enhanced by "intentional acts," to repeat the happy phrase of Van Gelder. The goal of these acts is to bring to the surface what lies latent in the ecclesial presence. Their aim is to make clear its meaning, substance, purpose, and intention. By making these features evident, the influence of the ecclesial community gains in strength and is rendered compelling.

What we are about to say may not receive the approval of all, but we believe it is true. The first intentional act that the church should carry out in its endeavor to impact any context is paradigmatic in nature. We are using "paradigm" in the sense of a model that provides a demonstration of something.

It is a sample that provides a picture of the bigger thing. If you see the paradigm, you can be sure that you have seen the thing.

If we turn to the realm of diplomacy once again, we know that embassies aren't merely buildings with the names of their countries of origin affixed on them. They are more than that; they are extensions of the territories of the countries whose names they bear. And their claims to be the authoritative symbols of, and proxies for, their countries receive credence and weight not just because of their mere presence but because of the way the members of diplomatic missions live their lives both inside and outside their compounds. Similarly, if the church is to exert a credible and authentic influence on any milieu, it cannot be content with being a mere presence; it must move from being a presence to being a *showcase*. That is, it must be a demonstration of the order that it claims to represent in the context where it is embedded. In other words, the church must be the exemplar of the social order that its presence advertises, and that it claims is more conducive to human flourishing than the order within which it exists.

Some thirty years ago, the South African missiologist David Bosch published a groundbreaking book in the field of missiology entitled *Transforming Mission*. In his treatment of Paul's theology of mission in this massive work, Bosch found that the paradigmatic approach we are advocating here was a key feature in Paul's approach to the church's witness to the world as well. Bosch writes:

> In Paul's understanding, the church is "the world in obedience to God." . . . Its primary mission in the world is to *be* new creation. Its very existence should be for the sake of the glory of God. Yet precisely this influences the outsiders. Through their conduct, believers attract "outsiders" or put them off. . . . Their lifestyle is either attractive or offensive. Where it is attractive, people are drawn to the church, even if the church does not actively go out to evangelize them. . . . The church is not otherworldly. . . . It is involved in the world. . . . Christians are called *to practice a messianic lifestyle within the church but also to exercise a revolutionary impact on the values of the world.*[1]

This paradigmatic or modeling function is essential to the church's exercise of its transforming influence regardless of the setting and the time in which

---

1. David Bosch, *Transforming Mission: Paradigm Shifts in Theology of Mission* (Maryknoll: Orbis, 1991), 167–68. Emphasis added.

the church lives. Writing two thousand years after Paul and thirty years after Bosch, in a vastly different context, the African American theologian Frederick Ware says something similar with respect to the role of the Black church in the United States. "When African American churches truly function as the church," he says, "they are the people of God, proclaiming the gospel, working for the liberation of the oppressed, and *being a model and manifestation of the new humanity in Christ.*"[2]

But what kind of ecclesial existence fulfills the requirements of this paradigmatic function? What must an ecclesial community exhibit to be a model, in the "here" and "now," of the order that God intends for human life as a whole? And what contribution does the Trinitarian ecclesiology articulated in chapter 4 make to this desired outcome? The balance of this chapter will be devoted to an exploration of these questions.

Ecclesial Life as a Reflection of the Life of the Triune God

The burden of our argument in chapter 4 was that the church bears a close relationship to the Trinity. Throughout the history of the church, judgments of varying sorts have been made about the meaning and relevance of the Trinity for the life of the church, understood both individually and collectively. For some, it is a matter of indifference whether Christians adhere to the doctrine of the Trinity or not. Sallie MacFague, for instance, flatly asserts that the Trinity is not a "necessary" doctrine.[3] The famed German theologian Friedrich Schleiermacher, known as the father of modern theology, treats the doctrine as a postscript in his epoch-making book *The Christian Faith*. German philosopher Immanuel Kant dismissed it as devoid of existential relevance and practical cash value. Due to the difficulty involved in fully understanding it, others treat the Trinity perfunctorily, with sleight of hand. It is a box to be checked to maintain one's orthodox credentials, but quickly set aside as soon as the verbal confession is made. That's why it has been said that many Christians are Trinitarian in theory but Unitarian or tri-theists in practice.[4]

Recently, however, there has been a marked change in attitude. For Protestantism the change began in earnest with the Swiss theologian Karl

---

2. Frederick L. Ware, *African American Theology: An Introduction* (Louisville: Westminster John Knox, 2016), 164. Emphasis added.

3. Sallie McFague, *Models of God: Theology for an Ecological, Nuclear Age* (Philadelphia: Fortress, 1987), 182.

4. Gerald Bray, "One God in Trinity and Trinity in Unity," in *Trinity among the Nations*, eds. Gene Green, Stephen Pardue, and K. Yeo (Grand Rapids: Eerdmans, 2015), 32.

Barth who sparked the renaissance of Trinitarian theology through his unashamed embrace of the neglected doctrine in his massive magnum opus *Church Dogmatics*. Since then, theologians of various stripes have stressed the relevance of the Trinity for the believer's spiritual life, the ordering of community life, and the life of the church itself.[5] For our purposes in this chapter, it is the last of these issues which is our focus.

With respect to the being and life of the church, many have argued that the Trinity is hugely important. For example, in his book *After Our Likeness*, the Croatian theologian Miroslav Volf sets forth the thesis that the church, however small numerically, is the image and likeness of the Trinity, and, based on this understanding, there is a fundamental correspondence between the divine/Trinitarian communion and ecclesial fellowship.[6] Because of this correlation, Volf (along with others) argues that the structure of relations within the ecclesial community should correspond to the structure of relationship among the divine persons. According to the Brazilian theologian Leonardo Boff, for instance, "the community of the Father, Son, and Holy Spirit becomes the prototype of the human [and church] community."[7]

Questions have, however, been raised about the wisdom of drawing such a seemingly close ontological parallel between the Trinity and the church.[8] Thinkers who raise these concerns typically base their discomfort on the fact that the two entities belong to two qualitatively different orders of being: the Trinity is a divine society, the church a human community. They warn that, unless one exercises care, talk of correspondence between them can be misplaced and overdrawn. Such concern mustn't be dismissed summarily. Centuries ago, a group of theologians known as the Cappadocian Fathers warned against too great a confidence when speaking of God, and suggested

---

5. Karl Barth declared his hand confidently at the opening of his massive *Church Dogmatics*. See *Church Dogmatics. Vol I/1, The Doctrine of the Word of God*. Edited by G. W. Bromiley and T. F. Torrance (Edinburgh: T&T Clark, 1975), xiii. For a sampling of those who followed suit, see, for example, Fred Sanders, *The Deep Things of God: How the Trinity Changes Everything* (Wheaton: Crossway, 2010); John Feinberg, *No One Like Him* (Wheaton: Crossway, 2001).

6. Volf, *After Our Likeness*, 197, 194. A similar concept is found in some form in other theologians who predated Volf's own contribution, among them his teacher Jürgen Moltmann, in his *Trinity and the Kingdom: The Doctrine of God* (Minneapolis: Fortress, 1981); and Zizioulas, *Being as Communion*.

7. Leonardo Boff, *Trinity and Society* (Maryknoll: Orbis, 1988), 6–7; Volf, *After Our Likeness*, 236.

8. See, for example, Andy Hay's fine study entitled *God's Shining Light: A Trinitarian Theology of Divine Light* (Eugene: Pickwick, 2017).

that when engaging in talk about God, we can never speak fluently, but can only speak in *epinoia* – stammering speech.⁹

Yet, while exercising caution, it doesn't seem inappropriate to assert that the life of the triune God is relevant for the life of the ecclesial community. In our view, it couldn't be otherwise. The goal of Christian faith is not just the acquisition of cognitive understanding; it also includes the experience of personal transformation. Biblical truths are intended to form and transform us (2 Tim 3:13–17; Rom 12:1–2). Inasmuch as the doctrine of the Trinity is a biblically rooted belief, and thus part of the divine revelation, it cannot be inconsequential to the life of the people of God. It is part of the body of revealed scriptural truths which are useful and profitable for our instruction, formation, and equipping (2 Tim 3:16–17).

Having said that, however, it doesn't seem necessary to conceive of the relevance of the Trinity to the church in terms of the church's participation in the being of God, as some proposals seem to suggest.¹⁰ It is possible to derive substantial existential and practical cash value from the relationship between the church and the Trinity without erasing the ontological distance between them. To do this, we deem it helpful to construe the correlation by using the imagery of projector and receptor. The metaphor of a shining object that projects its rays onto another object provides a helpful way to explain the relationship. The receptor receives the rays projected by the projector and transmits them to other objects in its surroundings. The Trinity can be likened to the projecting object and the church the receiving object. The Trinity casts its rays onto the church, and the light the church receives from the Trinity is refracted onto the places that surround it. As the American theologian Andrew Hay puts it, "the life and work of the church are visible insofar as they have within themselves the primary . . . reflection of the work and word of God."¹¹ As a representative of God, the ecclesial community is tasked to exhibit a mode of life that reflects the life of the triune God. To be sure, such a reflection will

---

9. See Stephen R. Holmes, "Divine Attributes," in *Mapping Modern Theology: A Thematic and Historical Introduction*, eds. Kelly M. Kapic and Bruce L. McCormack (Grand Rapids: Baker, 2012), 62. To be fair, Volf acknowledges the limitations of the correspondence thesis that he sets forth, thus agreeing with the caution that the Cappadocians sounded. He writes: "Trinitarian models bring God to expression in the same way all language about God does, namely, as a God who is revealed anthropomorphically, who always remains hidden, '*in the light of his own being*' because God dwells in '*unapproachable light*' (1 Tim 6:16)."

10. Here I am thinking particularly of Zizioulas' assertion that "ecclesial being is bound to the very being of God," and Robert Jenson's notion that the church is the actualization of the being. See above chapter 4 note 6.

11. Hay, *God's Shining Light*, 94.

always be dim and imperfect. Yet, it is the medium whereby society can have a glimpse of the new order that church represents.

If one asks how the church receives and reflects the life of the Trinity, we respond by saying that the ecclesial community's ability to reflect the life of the triune God depends upon its emulation of the character, attitude, and outlook of the members of the triune community. This is borne out by the motif and language of imitation that runs through Scripture. Concerning the Father, we are admonished to mimic his holiness, to demonstrate his love, and to adopt his forgiving spirit (Lev 19:2; Matt 5:44–45; 1 John 2:7–12; Matt 6:12). Regarding the Son, we are exhorted to imitate his humility, and to follow his self-giving and servant spirit, and his compassion (Phil 2:5–8; Mark 10:45). With respect to the Holy Spirit, we are commanded to surrender the reins of our lives to him – to allow ourselves to be governed by him (Gal 5; Eph 5:18ff.). The believer's life is bound up with Christ's life, and it is lived in the Spirit (Col 3:1–4; Gal 2:20; 5:22; Rom 8:9–11). Related to this is the biblical expectation that believers will exhibit some of God's own attributes in their lives. It is by virtue of this sharing that these attributes are called "communicable," in contradistinction to those which are the province of God alone, hence the designation "incommunicable." A faithful emulation of God by the church translates into a strong reflection of the triune life onto the ecclesial community which, in turn, results in a stronger projection of that life onto the society.

All this, of course, is not meant to convey the idea that the ecclesial community is a perfect entity. Not at all! There is no triumphalism here. The claim to perfection can be made only for the Trinity to which the church is connected, and upon whom its life depends. The church itself remains an imperfect society both qualitatively and quantitatively. Its fullness and maturity are yet to be realized (Rom 11:25; 1 John 3:1–3). In the words of the Reformers, the church is, and always will be, *ecclesia semper reformanda*, an entity in the making, a building under construction, a new humanity in perpetual process of transformation (2 Cor 3:18; Eph 4:15–16). This will remain the case until the consummation of the redemptive process, when the church will attain the fullness of what God intends it to be (1 John 3:1–3).

Ecclesial Life as the Space for Showcasing the New Order

The very fact that the church is called to function as both a receptor and a conveyor of the triune life is an index of its uniqueness and an indication of the distinctiveness of the mode of life that it is called to display. This follows logically, doesn't it? Besides the church, there is no other entity in any socio-historical context for which such an astounding claim can be made! But there is more support for the church's call to an exemplary modus vivendi. Additional warrants are found in the redemptive events that set the stage for the coming into being of the ecclesial community. We are speaking of the crucifixion and resurrection of Jesus Christ, and the unleashing of the Holy Spirit – the cluster of historical happenings known as the Christ Event. Let us explain.

While the church appeared rather late in the history of redemption, it was not an afterthought in God's mind; it was part of his eternal plan all along. Paul tells us that God "chose us in Christ before the foundation of the world" (Eph 1:4 NET). And, as God's people, the ecclesial community shares with ancient Israel a special status and unique identity that God himself confers. Yet, despite this pedigree, the church was not to become a concrete reality until the appearance of God's incarnate Son on the scene of history to inaugurate his kingdom and bring to fruition his redemptive plan, and along with this, the subsequent outpouring of the Holy Spirit in fulfillment of his promise (Acts 2:1–13; Joel 2:29). The community is thus divine, messianic, and pneumatic. It is God's people, built on Christ, constituted and maintained by the Holy Spirit (Matt 16:17–20; 1 Cor 12:13). It represents, therefore, a *new development* in the history of salvation. Indeed, Paul sees it as a mystery that was hidden in times past but now been revealed (Eph 3:1–6).

Sometimes, we seem to miss this. But the events connected with Christ's redemptive work and the outpouring of the Holy Spirit were not ordinary and trivial happenings. They were God's earth-shaking, liberating, and transforming intervention in the cosmic domain. They were historical happenings with cosmic repercussions. They were acts by which God invaded the world, and subjugated and defeated the oppressive powers that held sway in it. Scripture highlights this in several ways. Jesus himself said that by his coming, he invaded the house of the strong man and plundered it (Matt 12:28–29). Paul asserts that through the cross, Christ disarmed the powers and triumphed over them (Col 2:15). He further claims that by his resurrection and ascension, Christ filled the universe, took captive the cosmic forces that dominated it, and forever conquered death by plucking off its sting[12] (1 Cor 15:55–57). Throughout, the New Testament gives a cosmic and universal dimension to the work of Christ

---

12. I owe this happy expression to the President of Denver Seminary who used it in a chapel message on 1 Cor 15.

that encompasses his "victory over all spiritual powers of this world and the redemption . . . [of] all creation and humanity."[13]

These stupendous works of Christ created an escape route for those who were held captive by the enslaving powers. They effected a change in the world order that made possible a mode of life that is vastly different from the pattern of existence that prevails within that order. Drawing from the work of the American ethicist Stanley Hauerwas, New Testament scholar Douglas Harink provides a helpful elucidation of what we're trying to communicate here. He says: "the decisive and invasive action of God through the Son opens a *new space* in the world – *new creation space*."[14] In that space, he continues, "the Christians' own faithful action is called forth and becomes concretely possible."[15] Paul uses the phrase "in Christ" to refer to that space. "The new creation is the cosmos delivered of enslaving powers through the crucifixion."[16]

Hauerwas's fellow American ethicist John Howard Yoder joins him in stressing the idea that the new space that the Christ Event brought into being is not a mere spiritual phenomenon. The community which gathers in that newly created space is also a new sociopolitical order which has been implanted amid the existing body politic. Its political character stems from the fact that, within it, a different regime is in force. Those who make it up are people who have been rescued from the realm where the forces of enslavement operated untamed and without restraint. Their deliverance was made possible through the triumph that Christ won on the cross over the powers that keep people in bondage and impede their flourishing. They thus constitute a different *polis*.

This is so because, in agreement with other New Testament scholars, Yoder sees the powers in more than purely spiritual terms. Besides their spiritual nature, they take on socio-structural forms. They manifest themselves in all areas of human life – the economic, cultural, intellectual, social, political, and religious systems. And their influence on these areas of social life is not for good. The good news is that "they have been defeated by the concreteness of the Cross."[17] As was predicted in the *proto-evangelion*, the seed of the woman has crushed the head of the serpent (Gen 3:15). While the defeat inflicted by

---

13. Timoteo Gener, "Divine Revelation and the Practice of Asian Theology," in *Asian Christian Theology: Evangelical Perspectives*, eds. Timoteo Gener and Stephen Pardue (Carlisle: Langham Global Library, 2019), 23.

14. Douglas Harink, *Paul among the Postliberals* (Grand Rapids: Brazos, 2003), 80.

15. Harink, *Paul among the Postliberals*, 80.

16. Harink, 80.

17. John Howard Yoder, *The Politics of Jesus, Vicit Agnus Noster*. 2nd ed. (Grand Rapids: Eerdmans, 1994), 158.

Christ doesn't mean the disappearance of these powers from the creation, it *does* mean their redemption or reordering. And here is what is astounding: *the domain where such a reordering is visible is the ecclesial community*. In that community, the manifestation of the powers takes new shape – a reshaping that sets the community apart from the world around it. The church, therefore, is the primary locus of God's new creation; it is the new sociopolitical order that God is creating in Jesus Christ. In it, because of Christ's victory over the powers and the unleashing of the Spirit, people are enabled to *receive* the mode of life of the triune God and *transmit* it to their environs.

But the work that God is doing in the church is not intended to be limited to the ecclesial domain. God's redemptive sight has the entire creation in view. God wants to see the reordering of the powers in society at large. What takes place in "the community of Christ and the Spirit [is] the embodiment of *part* of the creation – the new creation – which knows the reality of its redemption."[18] In the space where the powers have been subjugated, "the will of God for human socialness as a whole is prefigured by the shape of which the Body of Christ is called."[19] Hence, the ecclesial community is a paradigmatic entity. "The people of God is called to be today what the world is called to be ultimately."[20] In other words, "God is remaking the cosmos and humanity in Christ and the Holy Spirit, and human beings are . . . invited to participate in that triune remaking through the *ecclesia*."[21]

The church fulfills its representational role by living as a counter-community, an alternative society with a culture of its own that is markedly different from the dominant culture. While the church is part of the broader social milieu, it is nonetheless called to a specific form of life or countercultural existence that cannot be simply superimposed upon the existing form of life or culture of any society. It is not merely the religious coating of a particular social system. Rather, it is a subversive presence which seeks "the transformation of the prevailing system according to the way of Christ."[22] And this transforming role is performed, first, when the church is *itself* – that is, when it behaves in a manner congruent with its triune identity. Yoder writes:

---

18. Yoder, *Politics of Jesus*, 158. Emphasis added.
19. Yoder, *Body Politics: Five Practices of the Christian Community before the Watching World* (Nashville: Discipleship Resources, 1992), viii–ix.
20. Yoder, *Body Politics*, viii–ix.
21. Harink, *Paul among the Postliberals*, 81.
22. Harink, 133.

> *The order of the faith community constitutes a public offer to the entire society. . . .* It is not that first we set about a proper church and then in a later move go about deciding to care prophetically for the rest of the world. To participate in the transforming process of becoming the faith community *is itself* to speak the prophetic word, is itself the beginning of the transformation of the cosmos.[23]

Displaying the Life of the Triune God before the World

What does it mean concretely for the church to model the triune life and, in so doing, participate authentically in the transformation of its social milieu? Admittedly, it is not possible to offer in the scope of one chapter an exhaustive account of all that this implies. But based on our limited knowledge of the life of the triune God, we select the following two characteristics as a sampling of what such a life should endeavor to be.

Unity

Given the fact that unity is a dominant feature of the triune life, it should not be surprising that it is mentioned first. This requirement is not a deduction of speculative reasoning but a call from God himself as is evident from the appeal for ecclesial harmony that is sounded repeatedly in the New Testament. In his letters, Paul stresses the necessity for ecclesial togetherness both pastorally and doctrinally. Repeatedly, he admonishes communities of believers to do their utmost to be at peace among themselves. He tells them to spare no effort to keep the unity of the Spirit, to be one in mind and thought, and to avoid division at all costs (1 Thess 5:13; Eph 4:3–7; Rom 12:16; 1 Cor 3:1ff.).

But it is in the sacerdotal prayer that Jesus prayed to the Father before his death on the cross that we find the strongest statement of the necessity of ecclesial unity. In the prayer, Jesus made it abundantly clear that the band of envoys he was about to dispatch into the world as God's representatives needed to go as one. Praying first for his contemporary disciples, he asks for God's protection on them "so that they may be one *as we are one*" (John 17:11; emphasis added). He then proceeds to make a similar request of the Father for all future believers who will join their ranks (17:20–23):

---

23. Yoder, *For the Nations: Essays Evangelical and Public* (Grand Rapids: Eerdmans, 1997), 28–29. Emphasis original.

> My prayer is not for them alone. I pray also for those who will believe in me through their message, that *all* of them may be one, Father, just as you are in me and I am in you. May they also be in us so that the world may believe that you have sent me. I have given them the glory that you gave me, that they may be one as we are one – I in them and you in me – so that they may be brought to *complete unity*. Then the world will know that you sent me and have loved them even as you have loved me. (Emphasis added)

The unity the Lord desires for his church is neither superficial nor inconsequential. Its importance is evident in the emphatic force of his request, the importance he vested in ecclesial unity for the effectiveness of his mission, and the deeply theological character of the oneness that should bind believers. Besides its being inclusive, visible, and expansive, Jesus makes the bold claim that the unity he envisages for the church is to resemble the unity that exists within the Trinity itself. This is expressed through the language of mutual indwelling that permeates the prayer. He prays that all of them may be one "just as you are in me and I am in you . . . I in them and you in me . . . may they also be in us." In other words, "the unity to be enjoyed by Christ's disciples is a unity based on a mutual indwelling: the indwelling of the Spirit in each of them, and their living in God."[24] B. F. Westcott captures well the theological depth of the Lord's statement when he says that, in essence, Christian unity involves

> the interchange of the energy of the divine life . . . which finds a counterpart in harmonious relations of the members of the Church. The true unity of believers, like the Unity of the persons of the Trinity, with which it is compared, is offered as something far more than a mere moral unity of purpose, feeling, affection; it is in some mysterious [way] a vital unity . . . a symbol of a higher type of life.[25]

Few would disagree that modeling a "higher type of life" before the world would redound to its good. The world needs a demonstration of real unity. Yet, with due allowance for some faint signs of interest in bridging ecclesial divides at sporadic times in Christian history, in the main the ideal of ecclesial

---

24. D. A. Carson, *Showing the Spirit: The Farewell Discourse and Final Prayer of Jesus* (Grand Rapids: Baker, 1980), 198.

25. B. F. Westcott, *The Gospel According to St. John* (repr., Grand Rapids: Eerdmans, 1973), 246.

oneness remains elusive.[26] Sadly, amid our hopelessly divided world stands an equally divided church. The disjunctions take on different shapes and forms in different parts of the world, but no place seems to be spared it. For instance, in parts of the Caribbean where we are from, the dominant factor in separation is social status. The social polarities are mostly the elite versus the masses, uptown versus downtown, peasant versus urban, the haves versus the have-nots.[27] In other settings, such as parts of Africa, the divide is tribal. The bloodbath that took place among the Hutus and Tutsis in Christian Rwanda toward the end of the twentieth century was a painful illustration of this inconvenient truth.[28] In still other places, such as the United States, two seemingly unsurmountable roadblocks are erected to Christian unity: race and politics. Here, race and ethnicity function as conveyors of ecclesial identity, and political/ideological affiliation is, for many, the mark of genuine faith. In the hotly contested 2020 presidential election, some Christians went so far as to say on social media that genuine Christians could not be members of a certain political party!

The prevalence of these divisive elements that keep the church from modeling unity before a world rent asunder by divisions of all sorts is due, in large measure, to the downplaying or perhaps complete disregard of a key feature of the ecclesial community, namely, reconciliation. When it functions well, the church is a reconciled community where distinctives, while not erased, are relativized. In his letter to the Ephesians, Paul underlines this with red ink. He explains that the new humanity that God is making consists of people who were formerly alienated from one another. In the past they were kept apart by sundry segregations. But now the alienating factors have been canceled, and their removal constitutes the hallmark of the new society! In Christ, a rapprochement occurred between those who were far away and those who were considered near, making them one united body. Through the cross, Christ served as an effective peacemaker who brought down the barriers that kept people apart and annulled the hostility that nourished their resentment. In the words of Kevin Giles "the concept of the church is a 'third race,' a *tertium genus*, neither Jewish nor gentile."[29]

---

26. See Ronald Sider and Ben Lowe, *The Future of Our Faith* (Grand Rapids: Brazos, 2016), chapter 8.

27. Dieumeme Noëlliste, "Enlisting Theology in the Project of Human Reconciliation," in *Confronting the Legacy of Racism*, ed. Dieumeme Noëlliste (Denver Seminary: Vernon Grounds Institute of Public Ethics, 2016), 2.

28. Niringiye, *The Church*, 3–4.

29. Giles, *What on Earth Is the Church?*, 138.

Because the breaking down of the walls that separated people was one of the accomplishments of the cross, in a real sense unity is a gift. In his person and work, Christ has accomplished it for the church. But considering Christ's High Priestly Prayer, the unity that is a theological truth needs to become a practical reality. The church everywhere needs to strive toward practical reconciliation. The unity that is given must be actualized by the church in its corporate life.[30] This requires intentional action and conscious effort on the part of the members of the new humanity. It is in keeping with these considerations that Chadian theologian Abel Ndjerareou asks African Christians who live in countries rent asunder by tribal divisions to consciously privilege their Christ-centered identity over all others in the effort to combat tribal warfare. In his book *De quelle tribu es-tu?*, he writes:

> I encourage Christians individually and the church collectively to learn and privilege in their relationships, first, their new identity in Christ . . . then their identity that flows from being created in the image of God, and lastly, respect for their specific tribal identities. To reverse this order is to create confusion and division within the new community of the people of God.[31]

Christians in other parts of the world will need to determine what, in their context, needs to be reordered and relativized to allow unity to prevail. For example, in the United States, where we live, we see the opportunity to model unity and reconciliation and, in so doing, contribute to the healing of the country. However, if African Christians need to de-absolutize their tribal identities, for American Christians this task demands the relativization of their *political and ideological alignments*. At this point in the country's history, the church is called to represent God in a society with deep and wide *political* chasms. Politics permeates everything and fuels sharp disagreements on every issue imaginable: mask wearing, vaccination, climate change, the economy, race relations, voting rights, historical monuments, immigration, and so on. Not even the heavy death toll caused by the COVID-19 pandemic and the violent attack on the country's much cherished democratic system were able to bring its people together. Alas, in an age of cable news, where people tend to retreat to their preferred echo chambers, positions very quickly become entrenched, hardened, and ironclad. Dialogue and civil discourse have become a lost art; discourse degenerates into vociferous, demonizing, and

---

30. Giles, 140.
31. Abel Ndjerareou, *De quelle tribu es-tu?* (Abijan: Editions PBA, 2007), 8.

know-it-all monologues and abusive harangues. On the rare occasions when an opposing view is voiced and heard by the other party, often it is summarily and arrogantly dismissed as "fake news" – a worthless and baseless opinion unworthy of consideration.

It is not God's practice to require of us things that aren't possible, or things for which he doesn't give us the means for their accomplishment. If Scripture demands that the church maintain unity within itself, it is because such a task is possible and feasible. Here is the point: given that the political views that pull apart the American nation are held by Christians and non-Christians alike, the church has the opportunity to show mainstream society that people with differing perspectives *can* share the same space; they need *not* inhabit parallel universes; they *can* engage in dialogue with civility and respect; and even when conversation must end in disagreement, demonization and tearing down need *not* be part of the dialogical process. But for this to happen we need to enlist the use of a key Christian virtue: humility.

Here, God's word to King Solomon is instructive. Following the inauguration of the temple, God told the praying king that when the nation was afflicted by different kinds of ills, the road to national health would depend, among other things, upon an attitude of *humility* on the part of the people of God.

> When I shut up the heavens so that there is no rain, or command locusts to devour the land, or send a plague among my people, if my people, who are called by my name, will *humble themselves* and pray and seek my face and turn from their wicked ways, then I will hear from heaven . . . and will heal their land. (2 Chr 7:13–14; emphasis added)

In our context, the self-abasement that is highlighted here as part of the prescription for national healing must include a gracious attitude toward the "other." And this isn't hard to see. Unless unity is mistaken for forced compliance, it will require humility. In a contentious context such as ours, unity can be achieved only when, at a minimum, the contending parties are willing to suspend for a time (however short) their cherished and deeply held convictions in order to listen to the "other" with respect. It also requires a posture of openness to the possibility that the views we have grown accustomed to regard as false may contain a grain of truth. And when we acknowledge the truth as such, we are duty bound to embrace it, since if it is truth it has one source: God.

Additionally, the humility that is a necessary building block for unity is not only cognitive; it is also existential. To grow in rapprochement with the other, we must not only appreciate his or her thought; we must also share his or her world. Unity requires empathy – a mutual condescension that propels us from our world into the world of the other so that, in so doing, we experience life as they do. Imagine for a moment the impact on society of churches becoming centers of such grace-filled conversations!

Holiness

Holiness is the second characteristic we've chosen to highlight. We looked at this briefly in chapter 3. The term "Trinity" is often qualified by the adjective "holy," hence the nomenclature "Holy Trinity." This is correct since each member of the divine triumvirate is indeed holy. In the Old Testament, Isaiah is particularly known for extolling the holiness of Yahweh. Following his opening declaration of God's thrice-holiness in chapter 6, the expression "Holy One of Israel" becomes a constant refrain of his (Isa 12:6; 40:25; 43:3; 54:5). John will pick up the threefold formula in his vision of the heavenly chorus in worship before the throne of God (Rev 4:8). As for the Spirit, after a few attributions of the epithet to him in the Old Testament (Ps 51:11; Isa 63:10), the adjective will serve practically as his first name in the New Testament, where he is known as the Holy Spirit – *Pneuma Hagios*. While occurrences of the qualifier are not as numerous with respect to the Son, it is nonetheless applied to him in several places in the gospels and Acts, and by different speakers, including demons (Mark 1:24; Luke 1:35; 4:34; John 6:69; Acts 2:27).

"A holy God requires a holy people," writes Dean Fleming.[32] As a community intimately related to the triune God, the church is impelled to display holiness if it is to model the life of God. As in the case of unity, such a requirement is not derived from speculative reason; it is an injunction issued by God himself. The privilege of being associated with God carries with it the obligation to show forth the holiness that is germane to his life. Hence, we are called to be holy as God is holy (1 Pet 1:16; Lev 19:2), because we were "created to be like God in true righteousness and holiness" (Eph 4:24). Based on this, the Eastern Orthodox Church, a main Christian tradition, makes the concept of divinization – *theosis* – a key feature of its understanding of the salvation experience. Jesus himself asks his disciples to be perfect as their

---

32. Dean Fleming, "On Earth As It Is in Heaven," in *Holiness and Ecclesiology in the New Testament*, eds. Kent Brower and Andy Johnson (Grand Rapids: Eerdmans, 2007), 347.

Father in heaven is perfect (Matt 5:48). The likeness to God being spoken of here is fleshed out in the community's display of a mode of life that reflects the character of God and, in so doing, marks itself out as unique and distinctive.

God's call to the church to embody and reflect his life in each context means that its modus vivendi must evidence certain fundamental characteristics. In both Hebrew and Greek, the notion of holiness connotes the idea of being set apart. As a starter, then, true holiness speaks of a mode of life that is noticeably different from the life of the surrounding environment. Without using the term "holiness," Paul makes the case for its countercultural aspect when he admonishes Christians not to be conformed to the world but to be transformed by the renewing of their minds (Rom 12:1–2). Another way of saying it is that holy living is a sort of living that goes against the cultural grain. In noticeable ways, it is countercultural. Yet, such countercultural-ness must not be mistaken for disengagement. As Joel B. Green remarks, far from being a call to retreat from the world, biblical holiness is a call to identify with God's character *within* the world with a view to making a difference in the world.[33]

Second, while such a life must, perforce, be lived at an individual and personal level, it cannot remain there. To be socially impactful, holiness must include a corporate dimension. In both the Old and the New Testament, the call to holiness is issued to the people of God as a whole (Lev 19:1ff.; 1 Pet 1:16). Holiness, then, is a communal thing.

Third, closely related to its collective character is its public nature. To have a chance to impact the environment, the alternative mode of life that holiness calls for must be visible to all. Here, Christopher Wright's comment with respect to Israel applies with equal aptness to the church. The only way Israel could make a difference in the world around it, Wright argues, was to be different "recognizably, visibly, and substantively . . . as the people belonging uniquely to Yahweh and therefore representing his character and ways."[34]

Fourth, the holiness that God asks his people to reflect is holistic in character. Often when we speak of holiness, our minds tend to turn to the spiritual domain. While it certainly includes that dimension, biblical holiness, rightly understood, is far from being a truncated concept; it is meant to cover all the dimensions of our existence. This is clear from Leviticus 19, which is the classic Old Testament text on the topic. This is the text that Peter used to admonish the diasporic church of his time to live a holy life.

---

33. Joel B. Green, "Living as Exiles: The Church in the Diaspora in 1 Peter," in Brower and Johnson, *Holiness and Ecclesiology*, 322.

34. Christopher J. H. Wright, cited by Green, "Living as Exiles," 322.

Leviticus 19 opens with God's clarion call to holiness: "Be holy because I, the LORD your God, am holy" (19:2). What is often overlooked is that following this opening salvo, the author proceeds to list several areas where holiness is to be manifested. And after elaborating on each area, he repeats the refrain: "I am the LORD." In chapter 3 we quoted Christopher Wright's list of these different areas. Wright summarizes:

> The bulk of the chapter shows us that the kind of holiness that reflects God's own holiness is thoroughly practical. It includes generosity to the poor at harvest time, justice for workers, integrity in judicial processes, considerate behavior to other people (especially the disabled), equality before the law for immigrants, honest trading, and other very "earthy" social matters. And all throughout the chapter runs the refrain "I am the LORD," as if to say, "*Your* quality of life must reflect the very heart of *my* character. This is what I require of *you* because this is what I myself would do." Holiness is the biblical "shorthand" for the very essence of God.[35]

Here is another opportunity that is afforded the church to model the divine life in the temporal domain. Admittedly, the bar that is set here is a high one. And the degree to which it can be achieved in the "here" and "now" is a matter of debate. But all agree that the ideal that God sets before us is one that Christians should always strive to approximate,[36] and that if that effort is made, the effect on any context where the church is situated is bound to be salutary.

One need not be an extreme social critic or an unrepentant cynic to recognize that we live in a world that is groaning under the pressure of a malignant moral and ethical ulcer. Those who make it their business to take the pulse of the social environment do not mince words in their description of its moral condition. They describe the moral predicament as an ethical mess, a moral collapse, a disarray.[37] And just a glimpse at the global landscape justifies this pejorative assessment; it shows that the symptoms of moral sickness can be seen everywhere. A full list of the unethical travails that beset the world would be far too long to present here, but a cursory look shows a world that is groaning under the weight of violent genocide, blatant racism, systemic economic oppression, political corruption, sexual perversion, sexual abuse,

---

35. Wright, *Old Testament Ethics*, 19; emphasis added.
36. Brower and Johnson, *Holiness and Ecclesiology*, xvii.
37. See, for example, Scott Rae, *Doing the Right Thing* (Grand Rapids: Zondervan, 2008).

domestic violence, contempt for the vulnerable, greed, the normalization of lying, disregard for the truth, cheating, denigration of people, grinding poverty, drug abuse, and the propagation of conspiracy theories, to name just a few egregious woes. The American philosopher Dallas Willard offers this sobering account of the ethical malaise that afflicts the global village:

> Societies the world around are currently in desperate straits trying to produce people who are merely capable of coping with their life on earth in a nondestructive manner. This is as true of North America and Europe as it is of the rest of the world, though the struggle takes superficially different forms in various areas. *In spiritual matters there really is no "Third World." It's all Third World.*[38]

Given the vocation of the people of God to reflect the life of the triune God, the present ethical disarray presents the church with the opportunity to reflect the holiness of God in their context, and, in so doing, display before the world a modus vivendi that eschews the anti-life features highlighted in the previous paragraph. The thicker the darkness, the more noticeable the brightness of a shining object. We will suggest how this might be done in chapter 8 of this book. But, as Paul admonishes the Philippians, the strength of a public witness is contingent upon the quality of life of the ecclesial community. To shine as lights amid "a crooked and twisted generation," the small band of Philippian Christians had to be "blameless and innocent, children of God without blemish" in their morally decadent context (Phil 2:14–16 ESV). This condition remains. But since the ills that afflict the world may not be manifested in every context with the same intensity, the church in each milieu may want to identify the particular issue(s) that plagues its society with the sharpest acuity and intentionally order its life, by the power of the Spirit, in a way that runs counter to it.

History has recorded several examples of the impact of such a witness. One instance was the compassion the early church showed toward those who were suffering. Early church historian Eusebius reported that, though small in number and lacking in material resources, the early Christians rose up to respond to the needs of their fellow humans – Christians and non-Christians alike – when the situation required it. In acting this way, Eusebius says, "they showed themselves *to the heathen in the clearest light*. . . . [They] were the

---

38. Dallas Willard, *Renovation of the Heart: Putting on the Character of Christ* (Colorado Springs: NavPress, 2002), 20. Emphasis added.

only people who amid such terrible ills showed . . . their humanity in their actions."[39]

More recently, we have seen the example of Mother Emanuel Church in Charleston, South Carolina, USA. At the church's regular weekly Bible study, a white supremacist by the name of Dylann Roof showed up as if he were a participant. Toward the end of the meeting, he opened fire and killed nine of the attendees, including the church's senior pastor. Despite the tragedy that Dylann unleashed upon the church, and his utter lack of remorse, the members extended forgiveness unconditionally to the mass murderer. The church's display of Christlikeness did not escape the attention of the American public and, indeed, the world.

Such modeling of holy living, of course, necessitates a conscious effort to resist the pressure to conform to the ethical zeitgeist that dominates a given context. We take no pleasure in saying it, but if truth be told, the allure to conformity has been the bane of Christian witness in every place and every generation. It is not breaking news to say that, the world over, many of the life-destroying ills that run rampant in our societies are also present in many an ecclesial community itself, and they are ruining its soul. Such inconsistency results in an erosion of credibility that causes many to give up on the church.[40] All too often, far from being a reason for the uplifting of God's reputation, his own people cause his name to be blasphemed and mocked by those who don't know him. Yet, particularly at this moment, it is upon such a countercultural ethical stance, made possible by the power of the Holy Spirit, that the transforming efficacy of the praxis of the people of God, and the credibility of the Christian faith itself, rests. As Robin Gill states: "If a previous generation of skeptics and academics was inclined to dismiss Christianity on logical or theoretical grounds, . . . today it is moral grounds for dismissing Christianity that are frequently used."[41]

As lamentable as this situation is, it need not lead us to despair; it is rather a wake-up call for repentance, which is part of God's prescription for social and national health. "If my people, who are called by my name, will humble themselves and pray and seek my face and turn from their wicked ways, then I will hear from heaven, and I will forgive their sin and will heal their land."[42]

---

39. Quoted by J. Herbert Kane, *A Global View of Christian Missions* (Grand Rapids: Baker, 1977), 25.

40. Willard, *Renovation of the Heart*, 48.

41. Robin Gill, *A Textbook of Christian Ethics* (London: Bloomsbury, 2014), 345.

42. 2 Chr 7:14.

7

Herald of Transforming News

The case has been made that to engage any culture in a way that is authentic, the church must project a lifestyle that reflects, in some real way, the life of the triune God. But while necessary, this is not sufficient. In addition, the proper discharge of the mandate requires the proclamation of the message of the triune God. This follows logically from the role of the church as the representative of God in the world. Just as an ambassador does not limit her or his activity in the country of assignment to merely living in a way that reflects the mode of life of the country of origin, so the church cannot limit its work in the world to which it is assigned to that of an exemplar. Inherent in the ambassador's responsibility is the articulation for the host country of the policy of the country it represents. But what is the divine policy or divine political platform the church needs to keep before the world? And how is it to be presented in such a way that it can have a transforming impact? This chapter will address these questions after a brief word on the proclamatory injunction laid out in Scripture.

The Mandate to Proclaim

To herald is to announce or proclaim important news. A herald is a messenger entrusted with the task of heralding. This note is sounded throughout Scripture. In the Old Testament, Isaiah sounds it several times. In his message of encouragement to Israel who was on the verge of undergoing the pain of captivity, he opens with an emphatic proclamation of comfort: "Comfort, comfort my people, says your God" (Isa 40:1–2). Following his lengthy exposition of the work of the Suffering Servant, he proclaims a passionate invitation to the people to avail themselves of the gracious and gratuitous provision that has been made for them (55:1ff.). And for him, this task is a noble one: "How beautiful on the mountains are the feet of those who bring good news, who proclaim peace, who bring good tidings, who proclaim salvation, who say to Zion, 'Your God reigns!'" he exclaims (52:7; cf. 40:9).

Crossing over to the New Testament, we hear it from the lips of both John the Baptist and Jesus (Matt 3:1–3; Luke 3:3; Mark 1:15–16). A quick reading of the Synoptics shows that a significant portion of Jesus's ministry was devoted to proclamation. All the Synoptic evangelists have him open his ministry with the activity of proclaiming the good news (Mark 1:15–16; Matt 4:23; Luke 4:18). And Jesus did not limit the ministry of proclamation to himself; he shared it with, and entrusted it to, the disciples. Mark tells us explicitly that the reason behind his choice and appointment of the Twelve was "that they might be with him and that he might send them out to *preach*" (Mark 3:14; emphasis added). And this reason was by no means theoretical. For part of Jesus's method of training the disciples involved sending them out "to *proclaim* [the] message" of the kingdom (Matt 10:7). Lest they forget that mandate with the passing of time, Jesus took advantage of important opportunities to remind them of the mandate to proclaim the good news. In his famous Olivet Discourse, he told them that, as a precursor to the coming of the end, "this gospel of the kingdom will be *proclaimed* throughout the whole world as a testimony to all nations" (Matt 24:14 ESV, emphasis added). Then, following his resurrection and shortly before his ascension, he appeared to them with the explanation of the significance of the events of that Easter Weekend, and ended with a reiteration of the proclamatory mandate:

> This is what I told you while I was still with you: Everything must be fulfilled that is written about me in the Law of Moses, the Prophets and the Psalms. . . . This is what is written: The Messiah will suffer and rise from the dead on the third day, and repentance for the forgiveness of sins will be *preached* in his name to all nations. (Luke 24:44–47; emphasis added)

Following the departure of the risen Christ from the world, the execution of the kerygmatic mandate was not left to chance. In the person of Paul, formerly Saul the persecutor, God himself chose and appointed an indefatigable agent to carry out the task of proclamation beyond the shores of Israel to the gentile world (Gal 1:15–16; Eph 3:8). And Paul, fully cognizant that the execution of that task couldn't stop with him, revealed that the proclamation of God's reconciling work in Christ has been entrusted to all those who have been the beneficiaries of that great work of redemption. He writes:

> If anyone is in Christ, the new creation has come: The old has gone, the new is here! All this is from God, who reconciled us to himself through Christ and *gave us the ministry of reconciliation*: that God was reconciling the world to himself in Christ, not counting people's sins against them. And *he has committed to us the message of reconciliation*. We are therefore Christ's ambassadors, as though God *were making his appeal through us*. We implore you on Christ's behalf: Be reconciled to God. (2 Cor 5:17–20; emphasis added)

Now the history of the fulfillment of this kerygmatic task has not been free of problems. At times, proclamation has been put to the service of powers, causes, and interests that had little to do with God. As an example, think of the "evangelization" campaign that accompanied the conquest of the Americas by the European powers. At other times, the content of the proclamation has been so adulterated by the inclusion of culturally and politically laden elements that the proclamation was tantamount to enculturation and the promotion of a human-made ideology. Over time, problems such as these prompted some to call for the soft-pedaling of the task of proclamation by the people of God.

In recent times, this call has been voiced most loudly by the proponents of religious pluralism. According to the pluralist ideology, which enjoys considerable appeal in our postmodern world, there is basic equality of truth and salvific efficacy among the religions of the world. This parity is supposedly based on the notion that all religions are the culturally conditioned expressions of the same transcendent reality or religious ultimate object.[1] On this view, the sort of global, pan-national, and transcultural proclamation that is commanded in Scripture is out of place. What we see instead is the prevalence of a relativistic posture which pressures the people of God to abandon the message of the exclusivity of the person of Christ and the indispensability of his atoning sacrifice for the experience of salvation. And some have succumbed to the pressure by conceding the salvific import of other faiths, or by diluting the soteriological significance of Christ, or by adopting a timid posture toward commending him to people for their salvation.

---

1. Among the best-known proponents of pluralism are John Hick, *God Has Many Names* (Philadelphia: Westminster, 1980); and Raimundo Panikkar, *The Trinity and the Religious Experience of Man* (New York: Orbis, 1973).

Evangelical pushback against the pluralist perspective has not been lacking.[2] A recent rebuttal is found in a contribution by Ivan Satyavrata to a recent book on Asian theology. In his chapter, Satyavrata points out that pluralism demands concessions that the biblically committed Christian cannot make. Among these are the relinquishing of the Bible's unique authority as the source of divine revelation and the uniqueness of Jesus Christ as the decisive revelation of God.[3] We agree with Satyavrata. If the body of biblical teaching we've summarized all too briefly is given any credence, no community that is conscious of its identity as the people of God can shrug off the mandate to be the herald of this God.

The Message to Be Proclaimed

In his book *Models of the Church*, the Roman Catholic theologian Avery Dulles reviews a variety of approaches to the doctrine of the church. One of the approaches he examines is the view of the church as herald, and in his treatment of that approach he offers the following summation: "The 'job description' of the church as herald is clear: to evangelize, that is, to receive the good news and to pass it on."[4] From what we've said in the previous section, it is clear that we agree with those who view proclamation as germane to the role of the church in the world, even if we don't join them in reducing the church's role to just that activity. The question is, what is the good news the church is called to herald?

It's a Message about the Kingdom of God

If we turn our focus once again to the New Testament, we find there not only the mandate to proclaim, but also the content of the message to be proclaimed. According to the testimony of the newer testament, the message that the ecclesial community is mandated to herald is intimately related to *the kingdom of God*. By none of the early proclaimers is the message left undefined. John's wilderness proclamation, for instance, was a clarion call

---

2. See, for instance, Vinoth Ramachandra, *The Recovery of Mission: Beyond the Pluralist Paradigm* (Grand Rapids: Eerdmans, 1996); and Christopher Wright, *Thinking Clearly about the Uniqueness of Jesus* (Crowborough: Monarch, 1997).

3. Ivan Satyavrata, "Jesus and Other Religions," in *Asian Christian Theology: Evangelical Perspectives*, eds. Timoteo Gener and Stephen Pardue (Carlisle: Langham Global Library, 2019), 225.

4. Dulles, *Models of the Church*, 3.

to his contemporaries to repent in light of the *nearness of the kingdom* (Matt 3:1–2). When Jesus picked up the baton of proclamation following John's imprisonment, his message was similar: "The time has come.... *The kingdom of God has come near. Repent and believe the good news!*" he urged (Mark 1:14–16). Furthermore, the message that is to be preached to the whole world as a precursor to the end of the age is none other than the *gospel of the kingdom* (Matt 24:14). Indeed, the concept of "kingdom" is found so frequently on the lips of Jesus that it is now recognized that the kingdom of God was the central theme of his teaching and preaching.[5]

But what is this kingdom with which the message is so concerned and to which it is so intricately linked? In answer, it may be helpful to bear in mind that, in ancient Israel, the king held legislative, executive, judicial, economic, and military powers.[6] In his examination of the concept, George Ladd found that, in both the Old and New Testaments, the Hebrew word *malkuth* which is used for "kingdom," and its corresponding Greek word *basilea*, speaks of "the rank, authority, and sovereignty exercised by a king."[7] Thus, the kingdom of God is the exercise of God's reign over people. It is a political governance and order at the head of which is God. A couple of generations ago, John Mackay, an American missionary to Latin America, offered a definition of the kingdom that still rings true. According to Mackay, this divine regime entails "the sovereignty of God in all spheres of human life, whether individual, at home, socially, or internationally, and concretely interpreting his sovereignty in the sense of acknowledging Christ as Lord and the application of his teaching to all of life's problems."[8]

While we have zoomed in on the New Testament in our discussion of the message of the kingdom, this is not intended to give the impression that the idea was novel to the New Testament. The Old Testament also has a lot to say about the coming of the divine order along the lines described by Mackay. Throughout the Old Testament we find mention of a king who would descend from the Davidic line, and who would one day appear on the scene of history to rule the world in righteousness (Gen 49:9; 2 Sam 7:12–16; Pss 2; 110; Isa 11:1ff.; 9:6; Mic 5:2). What we find in the New Testament is the irruption, in an unprecedented way, of that divine regime. The gospels present Jesus of Nazareth as the figure who fulfills the Old Testament prophecies about the

---

5. Escobar, *In Search of Christ*, 174.
6. Charles Ryrie, *Basic Theology* (Chicago: Moody Press, 1999), 298.
7. Ladd, *Theology of the New Testament*, 89–90.
8. John Mackay, cited in Escobar, *In Search of Christ*, 174–75.

one who would sit on David's throne.⁹ The angelic announcement to Mary explained that the Lord God would give to her son the throne of his father David, and he would reign over the house of Jacob forever.¹⁰

And Jesus did not object to the messianic claim that was made about him. Even though, during his earthly ministry, the instances of Israel's rejection of Jesus's Davidic kingship were numerous,¹¹ he nonetheless declared that in the world to come the Son of Man would sit on a glorious throne, and that the kingdom of heaven belonged to him.¹² Through meticulous study of the New Testament, it has been recognized that the irruption of the kingdom occurred with the appearance of Jesus Christ on the historical scene. Thus, several scholars, among them C. H. Dodd, have defined the kingdom as the invading of time and space in the person of Jesus, the man of Nazareth.¹³ As Michael Bird states, in the New Testament we find "the announcement that God's kingdom has come in the life, death, and resurrection of Jesus of Nazareth, the Lord and Messiah, in fulfillment of Israel's Scriptures."¹⁴ Bird's succinct statement received a helpful elaboration in Padilla, who writes:

> Throughout the New Testament the doctrine of the two ages is present, but it is interpreted in light of the death and resurrection of Jesus Christ. It is impossible to exaggerate the importance of the fact of Christ for the eschatology of the primitive church. The life and work of Jesus Christ means that God has acted definitively with the aim of fulfilling his redemptive purpose. It is now not possible to restrict his intervention to a cataclysm at the end of "this age." The main actor has appeared, and the eschatological drama of Jewish hope *has begun*! Eschatology has invaded history, and its impact has produced what has been appropriately described as "the new division of time."¹⁵

---

9. Isa 9:7; 2 Sam 7:12–16; Ps 45:6–7.
10. Luke 1:32–33.
11. Matt 8:34; 9:3; 11:20–30; 13:53–58; 15:1–20; 22:15–23; John 1:11; Acts 4:27.
12. Matt 13:41; 19:28.
13. C. H. Dodd, *The Parables of the Kingdom* (New York: Scribner's, 1961), 35, 169.
14. Bird, *Evangelical Theology*, 37.
15. C. René Padilla, "El reino de Dios y la iglesia," in *El reino de Dios y América Latina*, ed. Padilla (El Paso: Casa Bautista de Publicaciones, 1975), 44. Emphasis added. My translation. He makes the same point in *Misión integral: ensayos sobre el reino de Dios y la iglesia* (Buenos Aires: Nueva Creacion, 1986), 181.

We emphasized the words "has begun" in the Padilla quote because they say something important about the kingdom. The kingdom has irrupted with the coming of Jesus, but that irruption has not exhausted its full meaning and scope. The same gospels that speak of its arrival also speak of a "not yet" aspect of the kingdom of God. Hence, according to the Scriptures, the kingdom contains a future as well as a present dimension which brings to fulfillment the messianic promise.[16] This tension must be borne in mind as the church endeavors to devise means to carry out the proclamation of the gospel of the kingdom in its capacity as a herald of the kingdom.

It's Good and Transforming News

But, while the irruption of the kingdom onto the historical scene didn't bring the fullness of God's reign, it was nonetheless good news, and it remains good news. It was and is the gospel. The English word "gospel" is the translation of the Greek noun *euangelion* which has the corresponding verb *euangelizo*. The noun *euangelion*, translated as "gospel," is used seventy-six times in seventy-three verses in the New Testament, while the verb *euangelizo*, most often translated as "bringing glad tidings, or preaching, or proclaiming good news," is used fifty-four times in fifty-two verses.[17] The prefix *eu* means "well" or "good," and *angelion* and *angelizo* are derived from the Greek word *angelos*, which means "messenger," giving the English term "good news." The gospels repeatedly characterize the message of the kingdom as good news, and they show the goodness of that kingdom-related news from several angles.

First, socially, the message of the kingdom uses a narrative that was good news to the less fortunate in society. Jesus opened his public ministry with a declaration that his ministry was intended to alleviate the plight of the marginalized, the poor, and the oppressed (Luke 4:18–19). And, in his interactions with the prominent members of society of his day, he made the case for the inclusion of those who occupied the lower rungs of the social ladder, exhorting them to invite "the poor, the crippled, the lame, [and] the blind" to their social gatherings (Luke 14:13).

Second, from a material standpoint, Jesus's kingdom-prompted ministry was good news to those who were in dire straits. Routinely, his ministry of preaching and teaching the good news of the kingdom was accompanied by the

---

16. Erickson, *Christian Theology* (3rd ed.), 701.
17. Jeremy D. Myers, "The Gospel Is More Than 'Faith Alone in Christ Alone,'" *Journal of the Grace Evangelical Society* (Autumn 2006): 35–36.

performance of works of deliverance from all kinds of conditions that hindered the enjoyment of a decent life (Matt 4:23–25; 8:14–16; 9:35–36; 11:4–6). To the beneficiaries, this ministry was indeed good news.

Third, from a spiritual angle, the appearance of the kingdom was good news to the spiritually bankrupt – those who were marginalized by mainstream society because they were regarded as spiritual misfits. These included the "sinners" and the tax collectors, among others. As part of his kingdom work, Jesus repeatedly reached out to them, offering forgiveness and rehabilitation, to the ire of the religiously respectable, declaring bluntly in one instance that the "Son of Man came to seek and to save the lost" (Luke 19:10).[18]

These instances of religious and spiritual rehabilitation were only a preview of the great and ultimate work of rehabilitation and redemption that he would accomplish on the cross. That work was the pinnacle, the crescendo, of the good news proclamation. It was good news par excellence because it was the act through which God would reverse, once and for all, the disaster of the fall that plunged humanity into its sorry condition. Throughout, the Synoptics intimate this by declaring that the purpose of Jesus's coming was to save his people from their sins, and by Jesus's explanation that such salvation would come by means of his death on the cross (Matt 20:17–19; Mark 8:31–33). In time, that stupendous and ultimate redemptive act came to provide the defining meaning of the gospel. Thus, Paul states in 1 Corinthians 15:3–4: "Christ died for our sins according to the Scriptures, . . . he was buried, . . . [and] he was raised on the third day according to the Scriptures."

This gospel is not only good news, but also transforming news. It is the message that brings about not a superficial makeover, but real and substantive change. We have a glimpse of this in the experience of Zacchaeus following his encounter with Jesus (Luke 19:8). The entrance of salvation into his house brought about a decisive socio-ethical change in his conduct. But Christ's redemptive accomplishment on the cross is intended to do something even greater: it results in a metamorphosis. "If anyone is in Christ, he is a new creation; old things have passed away; behold, all things have become new" (2 Cor 5:17 NKJV). This is so because the gospel is the power of God for the salvation of everyone who believes (Rom 1:16). It is a redemptive message with a broad scope and wide implications. In a joint statement, René Padilla and John Howard Yoder capture the breadth and scope of the gospel that the church is called to proclaim:

---

18. Other references include Luke 11:14ff.; 7:16–50; 15; John 8:1–8.

The gospel is God's good news in Jesus Christ; it is the Good News of the reign he proclaimed and embodies; of God's mission of love to restore the world to wholeness through the cross of Christ and him alone; of his victory over the demonic powers of destruction and death; of his lordship over the entire universe. It is good news of a new creation, a new humanity, a new birth through him by his life-giving Spirit, of the gifts of his messianic reign contained in Jesus and mediated through him by his Spirit; of the charismatic community empowered to embody his reign of shalom here and now, before the whole creation, and make his Good News seen and known. It is good news of liberation, of restoration, of wholeness, and of salvation that is personal, social, global, and cosmic.[19]

It's Incomparable News to Be Proclaimed and Received

If the gospel of the kingdom is such good and transforming news, it is certainly worthy of proclamation. This is indeed the testimony of the New Testament. John shows this in his account of the dialogue Jesus has with Nicodemus about entrance into the kingdom of God. Nicodemus, who had mastered the Jewish sacred writings, was puzzled by Jesus's message that the new birth is the *sine qua non* for entering God's kingdom. Emphatically, this new spiritual genetic reengineering that gives access to the kingdom can be done only through faith in him.[20] God's once-and-for-all gift of his Son to be the perfect sacrifice is the sole provision that grants eternal life to the person who believes.[21] It is worth noting that Jesus equates entering the kingdom to spiritual rebirth or salvation. Paul elaborates on this spiritual genetic remake or regeneration in his letter to the Ephesians, underscoring the problem that the entire human race has with its spiritual genotype since we are all, by nature, "children of wrath."[22] God's perfect law, Paul emphasizes, exposes this sinful nature and silences every mouth at the guilty verdict, as our nature, thoughts, attitudes, and deeds are compared with God's perfect nature and standards.[23] This shows the urgent need for the gospel of the kingdom that proclaims the exclusivity of Jesus's sacrifice as the way to enter the kingdom of God.

---

19. The statement is cited in Douglas, *Let the Earth Hear His Voice*, 1294.
20. John 3:3.
21. John 3:16.
22. Eph 2:3–5 ESV.
23. Rom 3:19–20.

Paul became a bold herald of this gospel, proclaiming the name of Jesus to the Gentiles, their kings, and the people of Israel.[24] Notwithstanding his Christocentric focus, the apostle explains to the Roman believers that this gospel involves all three persons of the Trinity. It is the "gospel of God . . . regarding his Son, who as to his earthly life was a descendant of David, and who through the Spirit of holiness was appointed the Son of God in power by his resurrection from the dead: Jesus Christ our Lord" (Rom 1:1–5). Indeed, Jesus is then the content of the gospel (Rom 1:1–5; 1 Tim 1:11). "Anathema" or "accursed" is anyone who proclaims another gospel. Such a "gospel" is distorted, corrupted, transmuted, or perverted, and in fact is no gospel at all (Gal 1:6–9). At the birth of Jesus, the angelic symphony heralded this *euangelion* of great joy for all people (Luke 2:10). Jesus is the bearer of the kingdom of God, and the gospel of the kingdom is bound up with his person, life, and work (1 Cor 15:1–3). Thus, in 2 Timothy 2:8, Paul admonishes the young pastor Timothy to "remember Jesus Christ, raised from the dead, descended from David. This is my gospel." To Jews who were asking for signs and Greeks who were searching for wisdom, Paul resolved to "preach Christ crucified," a message that was offensive to the first group and foolish to the latter.[25] There is no gospel of the kingdom without Jesus Christ, the inaugurator of the kingdom.

This Christ-centered gospel of the kingdom is not just a theological truth to affirm, but a person to appropriate. Thus, the Synoptic Gospels stress the necessity to enter the kingdom, that is, to become attached to Christ himself, and to do so regardless of the cost. The kingdom is a pearl to which no price can be attached.

The Manner of Heralding the Gospel of the Kingdom of God

In typical pluralist and postmodern fashion, the American singer Madonna Louise Ciccone said, "I do believe that all paths lead to God. It's a shame that we end up having religious wars, because so many of the messages are the same."[26] We join Madonna in bemoaning all too many instances of wars in which the church has played a key role. And for these we need to humbly repent. Christianity, as the faith of the Prince of Peace, need not, indeed should

---

24. Acts 9:15.

25. 1 Cor 1:23.

26. *Madonna Extreme* (blog), "Madonna Interview: Q Magazine (March 1998)," accessed 21 July 2022, http://madonnaextreme.blogspot.com/2018/01/madonna-interview-q-magazine-march-1998.html.

not, be violent. However, we cannot join her call for the dilution of the gospel. Religious wars have indeed caused the destruction of numerous lives. But this does not nullify the truth of the indispensability of Christ for salvation (Acts 4:12; John 14:6). Millard J. Erickson is right in describing the gospel as "the one factor that gives shape to everything the church does, the element that lies at the heart of all its functions."[27] As we argued in chapter 5, the gospel is what God places in the hands of the church to fulfill its mandate as God's representative in the world. But how is the church to carry out this task so that it can result in genuine change? We note three prescriptions.

Proclamation That Aims at Holistic Change

The proclamation of the gospel of the kingdom *must* seek *comprehensive* transformation. It must aim at personal, social, and cosmic change. At a personal level, the gospel is meant to impact the totality of our being. Writing to the Christians in Rome, Paul explains that though they were formerly enemies of God, they had been reconciled through the death of God's Son.[28] And that reconciliation with God made possible the experience of wholeness – shalom – for each of them. "Shalom" is a common salutation among Palestinian and Jewish communities which means "the establishment, and henceforth the presence, of wholeness."[29]

Such wholeness produced by the gospel is not restricted to one part of a person's constitution, but touches the totality of his or her being (3 John 2). And people are not hermits, but entities who relate to others, so the experience of wholeness should also be evident in their multiple relationships.

At a social level, the proclamation of the gospel should result in the creation of communities of reconciliation. Proclamation that is transforming should stress the unity that Christ's sacrificial work on the cross makes possible. On the cross, he *has* torn down the walls of separation. Now it behooves those who are on the various sides to walk across the divisions toward one another in order to form communities of peace and togetherness. In a world plagued by tensions of all sorts – racial, political, ideological, socio-economic, religious – heralding Christ must commend *and* model for a society torn asunder the peace that he brokered on the cross.

---

27. Erickson, *Christian Theology*, 980.
28. Rom 5:9–10.
29. Michael J. Gorman, *Becoming the Gospel: Paul, Participation, and Mission* (Grand Rapids: Eerdmans, 2015), 146.

Most Christians agree with this, yet seldom does this belief translate into reality in the life of the herald of the gospel, the church. Over a generation ago, Martin Luther King Jr. lamented the sad fact that the most segregated hour in the United States was when churches met for worship. Not much has changed since. Yet, heralding the gospel of the kingdom means proclaiming that the Christian community of faith is one single family which includes people from all nations, tribes, and languages.[30] In this regard, René Padilla is correct when he says that to have a socially meaningful impact, churches need to *embody the gospel of reconciliation by being models or representations of reconciled communities.*[31] Indeed, what Christ has accomplished at the cross brought to an end any basis for hopeless alienation for those of any race or nation who believe in the perfect sacrifice of Jesus Christ.[32] Embracing and appropriating this gospel enables the church to be an agent of healing in a fragmented and broken world that wallows in the sea of hate, bitterness, and resentment.

At a more global level, the gospel envisages the transformation of the entire cosmic order. In Romans 8:19–21, Paul makes this amazing declaration:

> The creation waits in eager expectation for the children of God to be revealed. For the creation was subjected to frustration, not by its own choice, but by the will of the one who subjected it, in hope that the creation itself will be liberated from its bondage to decay and brought into the freedom and glory of the children of God.

The entire created order will see the manifestation of that reconciling work of the cross. God's purpose is to reconcile all things to himself through Christ, whether things on earth or things in heaven (Eph 1:9–10).

Proclamation That Fosters Kingdom Living in the Here and Now

The gospel of the kingdom doesn't just provide a ticket or pass to heaven. What it does is transfer those who appropriate Christ from one domain into another. As Paul states, God "has rescued us from the dominion of darkness and brought us into the kingdom of the Son he loves, in whom we have redemption, the forgiveness of sins" (Col 1:13–14). We are then transplanted into the order introduced by Christ. George Eldon Ladd, in his seminal work *The Gospel of*

---

30. Gorman, *Becoming the Gospel*, 146.

31. C. René Padilla, "Mission at the Turn of the Century/Millennium" *Evangel* (Spring 2001), 11.

32. Padilla, "Mission at the Turn of the Century," 11.

the Kingdom, noted that "the redeemed are already in the kingdom of Christ."[33] Paul refers to believers as those who are "in Christ" (2 Cor 5:17).

This transfer of domain or sphere enrolls us in the school of Christ. In that school believers are taught not to live in a way that reflects the life of the old sphere because this is incongruent with the education they receive from Christ (Eph 4:20–21). Their lives should reflect the influence of the instruction they receive at the school of grace (Titus 2:11–13). The mandate that Jesus gave to the original disciples is intended to foster that transformation as believers are taught and learn to obey all his teaching (Matt 28:19–20). For every believer, then, transformation or Christlikeness is an ongoing process that is to be reflected *in every area of our lives*. Proclamation, therefore, must aim at nothing less than the continued shaping and renewal of our minds so that our lives can reflect the values and priorities that operate in the kingdom of God.[34]

To be transforming, the kerygmatic task must include the call to genuine repentance and a firm commitment to follow Christ. Here, the call is for a proclamation that sets people off for a dynamic and transforming walk with Christ. Its aim is a holistic conversion which targets the mind as well as the heart, with a view to replacing the old mentality with one that is shaped by the gospel. As the Latin American theologian Samuel Escobar explains, kingdom living "is a way to live among men, having discovered again the meaning of being human/man in God's design. . . . Anytime we consider the type of society that is desirable, we are really asking about the purpose of the Creator for his creatures."[35] The change that occurs in the believing community, individually or corporately, is beneficial for the society at large. In the words of the African theologian Ermias Mamo, "the integration of the divine encounter with the journey of the believing community toward maturity should work towards the betterment of the society and the transformation of its culture."[36]

Proclamation That's Prophetic with Socio-Cultural Impact

Scripture says that the gospel is the dynamic power of God that produces salvation or wholeness (Rom 1:16). But the experience of this gospel-generated wholeness is not automatic. The fulfillment of that objective requires close

---

33. George Eldon Ladd, *The Gospel of the Kingdom: Structural Studies in the Kingdom of God*, reprint (Grand Rapids: Eerdmans, 2000), 17.

34. Rom 12:1–12.

35. Escobar, *In Search of Christ in Latin America*, 212.

36. Ermias Mamo, *The Maturing Church* (Carlisle: Langham, 2017), 69.

contact between the gospel and the object needing wholeness. Regardless of its power, dynamite cannot blow up a mountain unless it is directly applied to it. In the same way, to unleash the transforming force of the gospel, proclamation needs to wield it in a way that allows it to penetrate, punch, or sting the flesh of the culture. At the risk of using violent language, we can say that the application is more akin to the thrusting of a sword than to the rubbing of an ointment. The latter is a horizontal approach; the former vertical. Horizontal proclamation makes for a merely superficial contact that allows the gospel to float over the surface of the culture. Vertical proclamation gives the gospel a chance to pierce the culture like a sharp object. It brings the culture/society face to face with the challenge of the gospel, and in so doing, gives the culture the opportunity to bend itself in the direction of God's design for it.

In Scripture, we see this kind of proclamation at work on several occasions. After the risen Christ had provided a sharp and trenchant exposition of the gospel to the disciples on the road to Emmaus, their hearts burned within them (Luke 24:24–27, 32). Similarly, following Peter's Spirit-filled and direct proclamation of the gospel to the bewildered crowd at Pentecost, they were "cut to the heart" and their response was, "What shall we do?" (Acts 2:32–37).

Alongside its directness, the kind of proclamation endorsed here needs to be targeted. It needs to aim at the issues that are being faced at a particular moment in a particular milieu. Some use the term "contextualization" to describe this, but I prefer to call it "accentuated proclamation."[37] This mode of gospel proclamation identifies the sinful situation and brings the appropriate edge of the gospel to bear on it.

This manner of wielding the gospel is in keeping with the prophetic tradition. Nathan's proclamation to David was direct and targeted (2 Sam 12:7–15). John the Baptist's preaching of the gospel of the kingdom to his generation was trenchant. His confrontation of Herod for his sin was direct, not oblique (Matt 14:4). Jeremiah, Ezekiel, and Amos conveyed their messages to their society, including the powers that be, directly, not in a beating-around-the-bush manner.

As for Jesus, his proclamation of the gospel of the kingdom couldn't have been more trenchant. His constant use of the parabolic genre, for instance, was a powerful way to bring the message of the kingdom into direct contact with the mores and misguided values of the day.

---

37. For an example, see Jason Valeriano Hallig, "Contextualization of the Life and Ministry of Jesus in the Four Gospels and Its Significance in Proclaiming the Gospel to Asian Cultures in the 21st Century," in *Jesus among the Nations: Christology in Asian Perspective*, eds. Federico Villanueva and Stephen Pardue (Manila: Asia Theological Association, 2017), 123–144.

8

Catalyst of Human Well-Being

The church, we aver, fulfills its role of representing God in the temporal domain at different levels. At one level, it represents God by its sheer presence in the world – a presence that signals the existence of a regime that is different from the prevailing system. At another level, it carries out that task by modeling the divine life before the world. And in a more forceful way, it fulfills its ambassadorial role by communicating to the world the message of the divine order it represents.

Here, we would like to add one final practical element of the church's representational function. We will argue, in a nutshell, that while the steps mentioned above are important, the representational task remains incomplete, and thus the church's engagement in the world less authentic, if it is not accompanied by actions that are designed to champion and promote human well-being. We agree with the Reformed theologian Daniel L. Migliore who says that "the church is a servant community that is called to minister in God's name on behalf of the fullness of life for all of God's creatures. . . . *It serves God by serving the world in its struggle for emancipation, justice, and peace.*"[1] Wherever ecclesial communities are situated, the representational mandate places upon their shoulders the responsibility to carry out a transforming function that is at least threefold: (1) a demonstration of the ways of the triune God; (2) the proclamation of his transforming word; and (3) the performing of works that promote the healing of the context.[2]

---

1. Daniel Migliore, *Faith Seeking Understanding: An Introduction to Christian Theology* (Grand Rapids: Eerdmans, 2004), 25. Emphasis added.

2. Sunday Bobai Agang, Dion A. Forster, and H. Jurgens Hendriks, eds., *African Public Theology* (Carlisle: HippoBooks, 2020).

Well-Being Is God's Desire for Humanity

"Well-being" describes the state of an entity existing in a condition of total satisfaction. In that condition, the entity experiences a pleasant and even euphoric feeling engendered by the satisfaction of all the needs of existence. In psychological terms, we can say that well-being speaks of an existence that is free of tension – a life that is in a state of rest and repose. The absence of tension and inner turmoil makes possible a sense of ease, bliss, contentment, beatitude, enjoyment, serenity, and quietude. Put negatively, the condition of well-being excludes the experience of misery, anguish, and poverty of any sort. But that is not all.

Well-being implies wholeness, which describes the condition of a thing that is complete. An entity that enjoys genuine well-being is also whole. This twin concept describes an entity whose existence reflects integrality and fulfillment. It is an entity whose being lacks nothing and therefore enjoys contentment. But in the biblical perspective, humans are multidimensional entities. Their existence encompasses the physical, the cognitive, the affective, and the spiritual. This means that to be whole and fulfilled, they must experience well-being at all these different levels.

As we open the Scriptures, the bedrock on which the church rests, we note immediately that wholeness and well-being were the conditions that humanity enjoyed when they bore the *unspoiled* image of God. A blessed life lived in the presence of God describes the human condition under the Edenic dispensation before the catastrophic disruption caused by the fall. In the garden, the first human pair enjoyed perfect communion with God and thus lived a life of bliss and fulfillment. There isn't a hint in the Genesis account of discomfort, malaise, and lack of ease in their pristine state.

Sadly, that condition of blessedness was short-lived. The first pair's willful and blatant disobedience in response to the deceitful scheme of the serpent triggered the judgment of God and put the whole experiment on hold (Gen 3:14–19, 22–24). But this disaster did not mean the end of the divine project. For, with God, it is never "one strike and you're out." Judgment indeed came, but in judgment God remembered mercy. Since the discontinuation of that happy existence, a recurring theme of biblical thought is the undoing of the ruin caused by that catastrophic event. And the purpose is to bring about an order that will be conducive to the experience of the paradisiacal life that humans enjoyed in Eden. As we make our way through the biblical story, we observe clearly that it is the state of well-being that God is seeking to restore through his redemptive intervention in the world that reached its high point at the cross of Christ and which will culminate at his return. The purpose of

God in Christ boils down to the repairing of the damaged image, and thereby making possible once again the experience of wholeness and well-being in their fullness (Rom 8:28–29; Eph 4:14, 24; Rev 21:4), to the end that humans, together with the rest of the creation, may ascribe to God the glory that is due to his Name (Rom 11:33ff.). As Christopher Wright puts it: "The *new* creation restores God's *original* purpose for humanity."[3]

Because wholeness is tied to the condition of the *imago Dei* in us,[4] it is never totally lacking in humans. Due to God's common grace, and by virtue of the continued presence of his image in all humans, even in their damaged condition, a degree of wholeness is experienced by all. But God's purpose for us is not to experience a minimum level of wholeness and well-being based on his providential care. His aim for us is the enjoyment of abundant life – an experience that is contingent upon the appropriation of his redemptive provision in Christ. As Scripture makes clear, those who avail themselves of the divine gift embark on a journey of perpetual transformation into the image of God's Son (Rom 8:30; 2 Cor 3:18). They begin to experience a measure of fullness of life and well-being in expectation of its full realization at the end (1 John 3:1–3; Rev 21:1ff.). This means that, while the full realization of that new Edenlike order lies in the future, a foretaste of the blessings it will bring can be experienced in the here and now. And if the understanding of the role of church that we've set out in this book holds true, the ecclesial community is the principal agent through which these deliverables are channeled in the temporal realm. The purpose of the church's engagement in the temporal domain is to nudge the social order in a direction that is conducive to an approximation of the experience of well-being envisaged by God.

Just as the blessedness of the Edenic order required total submission to God's rule, so the future order that Scripture envisages will have as its main feature God's complete hegemony. As Paul states, in that regime, "God [will] be all in all" (1 Cor 15:27). This means that he will be everything to everyone. Not only will his dwelling place be among his people, but also he himself will dwell with them (Rev 21:3). In that God-saturated environment, humans will experience complete wholeness and fulfillment (Rev 21:3–4). Furthermore, under God's just and sovereign governance, they will know perfect well-being (Rev 21:1–4; 22:3–5; Isa 11:6–9).

---

3. Wright, *Old Testament Ethics*, 162.
4. For an explanation of the doctrine of the *imago Dei* and its significance for the pursuit of human well-being see page 123-24 below.

Hindrances to the Experience of Well-Being

It is certainly encouraging to know that the fulfillment of God's good plan for human existence has begun. However, even with this consoling knowledge, much of what we experience now falls far short of God's desire. Jesus's prayer that God's will on earth might reflect his will in heaven is yet to become a reality (Matt 6:10). The abundant life that he came to give is far from being the experience of most of the dwellers of Planet Earth. Wherever we look, we notice that a prominent feature of our world is the prevalence of conditions that are inimical to the experience of human wholeness and well-being.

Why is this the case? The factors that militate against the experience of the good life are multiple, and space does not allow us to enumerate them in detail, but for ease of presentation we may categorize them under three main rubrics. We will briefly mention these broad rubrics before suggesting the ways in which the church, as God's representative in the world, might help to surmount these hindrances, and in so doing, serve as a catalyst for the experience of some level of well-being in anticipation of its full enjoyment in the new heaven and the new earth.

Alienation

The first hindrance to well-being is alienation or estrangement. Alienation is the rupture of relationship experienced by an entity. This problem is multifaceted. We can be estranged from ourselves – personal alienation. We can be estranged from others – social alienation. We can be estranged from God – spiritual alienation. Of these three, the latter is the most serious. Humanity's rejection of God's offer of salvation through the redemptive work of his Son is its predominant expression and *the* cause of the human predicament. According to the Bible, our wretchedness stems from the state of enmity that exists between us and God (Eph 2:11–12). As Paul asserts in the Epistle to the Romans, in their estrangement from God, humans refuse to acknowledge God as God, and this failure leads to a wretched existence. Paul asserts plainly that when people thumb their noses at God, God gives them up, and this divine abandonment results in a futile life (Rom 1:21–30).

This is no exercise in speculative reasoning. This is a matter of lived experience. The world is full of people who live unfulfilled lives *despite* apparently having all that should make them fulfilled and happy. What makes Eden an environment conducive to human well-being is not the environment itself, but the presence of God in it, and the blessing flows from that presence. As Augustine of Hippo realized long ago, we were made to be in relationship with God. Our souls cannot be at rest if they do not rest in God.[5] Augustine's thought is in line with the judgment of the psalmist who says that it is in God's presence that we experience the fullness of joy (Ps 16:11).

It is this somber truth that compels us to hold firmly that the proclamation of the good news of God's reconciling work in Christ must be a prominent feature of any effort by his people to transform the social order. Since we have already made the case earlier, we shall not rehearse it again here. Suffice it to say that this is the strength of the view that stresses evangelistic proclamation as the primary task of the church, and the major deficiency of the unbridled view that makes light of the importance of spiritual and inner change in the effort to transform the world. Paul underlines this with red ink in 2 Corinthians 5:18: "God," he says, "was reconciling the world to himself in Christ . . . and has committed to us the message of reconciliation." The removal of estrangement from God is the prerequisite for the removal of the other forms of estrangement that cause pain and misery in the world.

Devaluation

Next to the rejection of God's great salvation, a formidable impediment to human well-being is the devaluation of personhood. We are speaking here of actions that are an affront to human dignity and an attack on human worth and value. This problem runs like an ugly thread through human history, and to this day it continues to be on display in various parts of the world. It is common knowledge that, for centuries, European powers and the United States used the ideology of racial inferiority to justify the institution of chattel slavery that kept millions in inhumane living conditions. In his book entitled *Africa Betrayed*, George Ayittey describes in vivid terms the negative image Europeans had of Africans. "European colonizers," he writes, "denigrated Africans for centuries as 'sub-humans' and denied them recognition of any meaningful intellectual, cultural, and historical accomplishment or experience. Called 'savages,' millions of Africans were carted off in bondage as slaves to America."[6] In the view of Europeans, he continues, the people of Africa "had no history, no culture, no civilization, and nothing of value to contribute to the creation of the human being."[7] When the transatlantic slave trade was finally abolished, colonialism continued the disparaging policy with the ideology of cultural ethnocentrism.

---

5. Saint Augustine, *The Confessions* (repr., New York: Penguin, 1981), Book I, 21.
6. George B. N. Ayittey, *Africa Betrayed* (New York: St Martins, 1992), 3.
7. Ayittey, *Africa Betrayed*, 4.

That latter ideology regarded non-European and non-American cultures as uncivilized and barbaric. Sadly, even the Christian church, by and large, bought into that misconception and for a long time acquiesced in this human and cultural disparagement. In his excellent book *Theology and Identity*, Ghanaian theologian Kwame Bediako shows that the negative image of Africa (and non-European cultures) that permeated the European mindset was uncritically assumed by European missionaries. This caused them to view the missionary enterprise as embracing a wider civilizing scope: "to elevate the people of Africa to assume their place among civilized and Christian nations."[8]

At last, after centuries of bitter and protracted struggles, those more blatant forms of human devaluation came to an end. But this did not mean the end of the affront to human dignity. The disparagement of humans by other humans persisted in other ways – and does to this day! One current egregious affront to human dignity is statelessness. Despite the Universal Declaration of Human Rights which stipulates that every person is entitled to the rights of citizenship,[9] "there are currently millions of people in the world who are not recognized as citizens of any country."[10] In some cases, this happens by the decision of governments to simply "[strip] individuals or groups of their nationality."[11] In the Dominican Republic, for instance, the status of citizenship was recently withdrawn from hundreds of thousands of Haitian Dominicans, effectively making them people without a country. In Myanmar, the Muslim minority group known as Rohingyas have suffered a similar fate at the hands of the Buddhist majority. Having been made stateless, hundreds of thousands of them have fled the country and wandered like nomads to neighboring countries, in search of a place of refuge.

A similar disregard for human dignity is seen in the marginalization of certain groups of people within their own societies. A case in point is the treatment of the Dalits within the Indian caste system which relegates them to perpetual inferiority by the sheer condition of their birth. We observe similar affronts in Western countries such as the United States where minority groups such as Black people, Asians, and Hispanics are regarded as inferior by the proponents of the pernicious ideology of white supremacy. In recent times in the United States, incidents of hate crimes committed by white supremacists against Black people, Asians, and Jews have increased exponentially throughout

---

8. Kwame Bediako, *Theology and Identity* (Oxford: Regnum, 1992), 227.
9. See Article 5 of the 1948 Universal Declaration of Human Rights.
10. Peter J. Paris, ed., *Religion and Poverty* (Durham: Duke University Press, 2009), 2.
11. Paris, *Religion and Poverty*, 5.

the country, prompting Congress to take additional legislative action to protect these groups.[12] In some countries, political leaders purposely use human denigration as a weapon against political opponents and anyone who dares to disagree with them. They do so with the approval – and, we dare say, the delight – of their supporters – among them Christians! The former American president Donald J. Trump distinguished himself as an artful wielder of this political weapon. During his presidency, Trump used his Twitter account to launch vicious ad hominem attacks and counterattacks on anyone who dared to criticize and oppose him. He was so good at this that he became known as a counterpuncher.

Let us be clear. Assaults on human dignity, in whatever shape or form, constitute a formidable impediment to the experience of well-being. Critical to the enjoyment of well-being is a healthy self-concept. But the devaluation of people's worth injures their view of themselves, engenders low self-esteem, and produces a warped understanding of who they are. When, by the actions of others, people are led to believe that they are beings with diminished personhood, they are susceptible to develop a marred and unhealthy understanding of themselves.[13] Such affronts to people's dignity often inflict deep and crippling wounds, render them numb to their oppression, and cause them to harbor a sense of inferiority[14] that often results in the absurdity of self-contempt.

Deprivation

Human deprivation is the last major enemy of well-being that we'll highlight. Deprivation simply means dispossession or denial. A deprived person is one who is bereft of the necessities required for a humane and decent life. Collium Banda describes it as a "multidimensional reality that precludes the ability to flourish."[15] Further, it is the "denial of opportunities and choices most basic

---

12. In 2021, President Joe Biden signed into law anti-hate legislation which was passed on a bipartisan basis by both the House of Representatives and the Senate. The Act was a response to the alarming rise in the incidence of hate crime committed against Americans of Asian descent who had been blamed for the COVID-19 pandemic that ravaged the country.

13. Bryant L. Myers, *Walking with the Poor* (Maryknoll: Orbis, 1999), 87–88.

14. Myers, *Walking with the Poor*, 76.

15. Collium Banda, "Poverty," in *African Public Theology* eds. Sunday Bobai Agang, Dion A. Forster, H. Jurgens Hendriks (Plateau State, Nigeria: Hippobooks, 2020; Carlisle: Langham Publishing, 2020), 114.

to human development."¹⁶ Deprivation is tantamount to the condition of destitution which manifests itself in an existential reality characterized by abjectness. In short, it is a negative experience of life.

This negative experience takes various forms. In its most severe expression it is manifested in the denial of the right to life itself. This happens when the gift of life is robbed from others, or in some cases from oneself. Daily throughout the world, life is robbed from millions through a variety of social ills. Abortion, gun violence, murder, war, genocide, crime, and politically motivated killings are examples of the robbers of life. Also, for various reasons, people the world over make the fateful decision to deny themselves the precious gift of life through suicide and the increasing practice of euthanasia – the so-called "good death."

Where life is not denied outright, it is put in danger by a plethora of antilife conditions that pervade the world. Chief among them is the damage that is inflicted on the earth by the actions of its inhabitants. In the view of many authoritative voices, this has reached the dimension of a real crisis. It is the consensus of scientists worldwide that, if not abated, the degradation of the environment that results from our unwise and selfish use of it threatens the ability of the earth to sustain life.

Next to the environmental threat is the prevalence of poverty in our world. And by poverty we don't just mean the problem of low income and poor wages. There is no doubt that starvation wages are a huge problem in our world. But as many analysts have pointed out, the problem of poverty is much greater than the lack of adequate financial resources. More critical than the money issue, poverty speaks of the absence, in each context, of the amenities, services, infrastructure, mindsets, and agency necessary to build a quality life. The lack of these necessities, in turn, gives rise to "social crises such as crime, disease, violence, war and prostitution."¹⁷ Years ago, the Swiss theologian Hans Küng and the Parliament of the World's Religions aptly described the situation of human deprivation that we are speaking about here:

> Today we possess sufficient economic, cultural, and spiritual resources to introduce a better global order. But old and new ethnic, national, social, economic and religious tensions threaten the peaceful building of a better world. We have experienced greater technological progress than ever before, yet we see that worldwide

---

16. Banda, 114.
17. Paris, *Religion and Poverty*, x.

poverty, hunger, death of children, unemployment, misery, and the destruction of nature have not diminished, but rather have increased. Many peoples are threatened with economic ruin, social disarray, political marginalization, ecological catastrophe, and national collapse.[18]

Catalytic Ecclesial Actions for the Promotion of Well-Being

The reason for highlighting some of these more egregious impediments to human well-being is to set the stage for the main burden of this chapter. It is not enough to bemoan and lament the predicament that besets the present order. We need to state even in broad strokes the kinds of actions an ecclesial community which is conscious of its role as God's representative can take in its context to blunt, if not nullify, the impact of the obstacles to human well-being we've outlined, and, in so doing, contribute to the transformation of the social environment where God places it. In our view, the following measures readily suggest themselves.

Promotion of Human Worth

Worth and dignity are inherent to every person. These attributes aren't things that we must strive to acquire but intrinsic properties that we possess and that must be acknowledged by all. Yet, as we saw in the preceding section, despite their innate character, seldom are these things automatically recognized and attributed to people by their fellow humans. All too often, they are overlooked and even trampled upon. Indeed, history has shown that, in the realm of interhuman interaction, the default mode has been the denial of human worth rather than its acknowledgment. This travesty in human relations always brings pain and suffering to those who are denied the recognition of these inalienable and innate endowments.

Happily, biblical faith has potent conceptual resources that can be leveraged to uphold the value and dignity of every person, and, in so doing, promote human well-being. Among the most powerful tools that Christian faith puts in the toolbox of the activists of well-being is the doctrine of the image of God, the *imago Dei*. This well-known and most important Christian doctrine

---

18. Hans Küng and the Parliament of the World's Religions, "Towards a Global Ethic: An Initial Declaration" (1993), cited in Agang, Forster, and Hendriks, *African Public Theology*, 183.

affirms that in creating humans God did for them something he did for no other creature, animate or inanimate. He imparted to them his own image and likeness, and declared, with satisfaction, that this unique creature of his was "very good" (Gen 1:27–31).

There is much debate about the meaning of the image of God. But despite the different ways in which it is understood, there are several things about the *imago Dei* on which theologians of all stripes agree. First, the image is recognized as an endowment which God bestows on all. It is a universal gift. Second, it is viewed as a feature that is uniquely human and, therefore, the singular property that distinguishes humankind from the rest of the creation. Third, particularly significant for our purpose here is the fact that the image is understood as a quality that confers value and dignity on every person irrespective of *anything* that may happen to be part of a person's background and living conditions. As the British theologian Alister McGrath puts it: "Being created in the image of God established the common identity and dignity of all human beings."[19]

This high valuation of the human person is not a deduction of speculative reason. No, in creating, God intended humankind to be creatures of incomparable worth and value. This seems to be the point the author of Genesis intended to make when he included in the creation account God's deliberation with himself before proceeding to create humankind. Speaking to himself God said: "Let us make mankind in our image, in our likeness" (Gen 1:26). "God reflects before creating humankind."[20] This suggests that God's express intention was to bring into existence a creature endowed with something that belongs to God himself, thus a creature of inestimable value. And, to ensure that the point is not lost on the reader, Scripture repeats the doctrine of the image of God at critical junctures in the unfolding biblical narrative and puts on the lips of many of its authors statements that affirm human worth and value.[21] In Psalm 8, for instance, in answering the question of the meaning of humanity, the psalmist declares that in the whole of the creation, humans occupy a place that is unique. God made them lower than only the angels. Further, he "crowned them with glory and honor," "made them rulers over the works of [his] hands," and "put everything under their feet" (8:5–6). In Psalm 139, while reflecting on the process of his conception in his mother's

---

19. McGrath, *Christian Theology* (5th ed.), 349.

20. Charles Sherlock, *The Doctrine of Humanity*, Contours of Christian Theology (Downers Grove: IVP, 1996), 34.

21. Sherlock, *Doctrine of Humanity*, 31.

womb, the psalmist describes himself as a magnificent object of art fashioned by God himself: "You created my inmost being; you knit me together in my mother's womb. I praise you because I am fearfully and wonderfully made; your works are wonderful" (139:13–14). In the New Testament, Paul will use similar language when describing believers as God's "workmanship" (Eph 2:8–10 ESV). For his part, Jesus dramatizes the inestimable worth of human beings by declaring that there is nothing in the world that can be given in exchange for a human person (Mark 8:37; Luke 9:25). He further teaches that every person is the object of God's meticulous care and special attention: God knows every one of us by name and watches over the very hairs of our head (Matt 6:30–32; 10:29–30).

Affirmation of Human Worth

To our minds, this high view of the human person should prompt at least two actions on the part of every ecclesial community, regardless of the context, on behalf of human worth and dignity. The first action is human affirmation. Besides being places of spiritual nurture and proclamation, ecclesial communities need to view themselves as centers of existential upliftment and empowerment. They should be places where people of every ethnicity, race, skin pigmentation, level of education, pedigree, social status, and gender are affirmed and encouraged to feel comfortable in who they are in God's eyes. When the church accepts the truth that worth is inherent to the very nature of the human person, it is emboldened to enhance such worth by going against any cultural grain which says otherwise. It sees part of its role, in any social context, as that of counteracting any materialistic mindset that defines value in terms of having, and human worth and value in terms of material possessions and achievements. It does so by proclaiming to men and women, both within the church and outside its ranks, that their value is linked to nothing external to themselves. When it comes to the worth of human beings, it does not matter where they live, what they own, what they achieve, how they look, how well they fit in with their peers, or how well they perform on the job.

Don't get us wrong here. By stressing the need to affirm people as they are, we're not suggesting that the church should discourage them from pursuing wholesome goals and legitimate aspirations. By no means! Any ecclesial community worth its name must spare no effort to motivate people, particularly the young, to fulfill their potential, to strive to scale greater heights and plumb deeper depths. What we would caution against is the temptation to join the culture in its tendency to anchor value and worth in the external dimensions of the human person rather than in what is gratuitously deposited in the person's inner self by God himself.

To make human affirmation a key feature of its modus operandi is perfectly appropriate for any ecclesial community which claims close connection with the triune God. Why? Simply because, as the triune God is revealed in Scripture, he is an affirming community. By being affirming, the church emulates God!

The affirming nature of the triune God is evident. We see it in the love that permeates the life of the members of the Trinity and the support they lend each other. Jesus speaks openly of the bond of love that binds him and the Father (John 15:9; 17:23, 26). This may be what prompted the patristic theologian Augustine of Hippo to view the Trinity as a community of love: the Father is the Lover, the Son the Beloved, and the Spirit the Bond of love that unites them.[22] With respect to mutual support, it is evident in the doctrine theologians call "appropriation." This aspect of the doctrine of the Trinity says that while each member of the Godhead takes lead responsibility for a particular activity on the historical scene, the other members are active in the execution of that work as well. The action of the Father and the Spirit at the scene of Jesus's baptism provides us with a clear example of this. On that occasion, the Spirit anointed the Son who was being baptized as he was about to launch his ministry, while the Father uttered his word of commendation of him from his heavenly abode (Matt 3:14–17). The Father displayed the same affirming attitude at the Mount of Transfiguration vis-à-vis the Son (Mark 9:7–8).

Such a show of support was not superfluous. In his incarnate state, Jesus needed to be affirmed and morally upheld. This is clear from his appeal for support from his disciples and his prayer to his Father in the garden of Gethsemane. We see it as well in his acceptance of help from the angels who came to minister to him after his temptation in the wilderness (Matt 4:11). It was also on display in his cry of dereliction from the cross when he felt the pain of abandonment by his Father (Mark 15:33–35).

Clearly, *affirmation is a human need.* If Jesus Christ the God-man needed to be affirmed, so does every human being. And ecclesial communities which believe in the inherent worth of every person are the primary places where such affirmation should take place. They ought to be places where positive

---

22. Augustine, *On the Trinity* 15.17.31 in *A Select Library of Nicene and Post-Nicene Fathers of the Christian Church*. 1st series. Edited by Philip Schaff. 14 vols. (New York: Christian Literature, 1886–1889. Repr, Peabody: Hendrikson, 1994), 3: 216–217. For a more accessible and fuller exposition of Augustine's explanation of inter-Trinitarian relationship see Gerald O'Collins, *The Tripersonal God: Understanding and Interpreting the Trinity* (New York: Paulist Press, 1999), 146–47.

discourse about the value of humans is held. Emmanuel Katongole makes a similar point but expressed in terms of stories. "Stories," he writes,

> not only shape how we view reality but also how we respond to life and indeed the very sort of person we become.... We are how we imagine ourselves and how others imagine us.... Who we are and [what we can become] depends very much on the stories we tell, the stories we listen to, and the stories we live. Stories not only shape our values, aims, and goals; they define the range of what is desirable and what is possible.[23]

The history of the Black church in the United States provides a good example of the empowerment that is generated when the ecclesial community functions as a place where humans are affirmed and their worth is upheld. As is well known, the Black church in America came into being during the period of chattel slavery that was the order of the day in that country. The African American theologian Dwight Hopkins explains that during the period of slavery, the typical day of the slaves consisted of two parts: sunup-sundown and sundown-sunup. Sunup-sundown was the period of hard labor; it consisted of the daylight hours during which work was done under the watchful eyes of the slave masters. It was the time and space in which the alleged "God-ordained White supremacy over Black inferiority"[24] was on full display. By contrast, sundown-sunup was intended to be a period of respite; it consisted of the night hours when the slaves were supposed to rest in preparation for the resumption of the grueling toil and indignity of the next day. But what the system did not consider was that the enslaved Black people would not use that time just to rest. To them there was something more important than bodily respite. They needed a community that would provide an account of Black humanity to counter the narrative that prevailed in the oppressive sunup-sundown universe. Hence, besides resting, they used many of these night hours to come together and form what would later be known as "the invisible institution" – the Black church! The following excerpt from Hopkins explains what was going on in that alternative universe:

> Under the grace of darkness, [the slaves] sneaked off to some prearranged places deep in the woods, swamps, ravines or in

---

23. Emmanuel Katongole, *The Sacrifice of Africa: A Political Theology for Africa* (Grand Rapids: Eerdmans, 2011), 2.

24. Dwight N. Hopkins, "A Black Theology of Liberation: The Slaves' Self-Creation," in "Black Evangelicalism: A Resource for Social Transformation and Spiritual Renewal," ed. H. Malcolm Newton, unpublished manuscript, 68.

cabins, to *recreate themselves in what is known as the Invisible Institution* – a sacred *space and relationship where the loosely organized and surreptitious religious gatherings of the slave community would take place*. There, the Black chattel renamed themselves as liberated children of God. Before they began their religious rituals, *they called one another "Brother" and "Sister."* They were *siblings of a heavenly Father* whose spirit would descend upon them like a mighty rushing wind. These familial titles also *subversively contradicted the designations they received during the sunup to sundown periods*. No longer were they "nigger," nigra, or black sons of bitches. They were people with their own names; *they identified themselves as divinely created human beings*, and this self-deification confirmed their new cultural initiatives.[25]

Hopkins's description highlights in bright colors the ethos of affirmation and existential upliftment of the ecclesial gatherings that the Black slaves established for themselves. I italicized the statements in his text that express the positive impact that the gatherings had on the psyche of the slaves even in their condition of bondage. These statements show that in stark contrast to the devaluation of Black personhood that reigned supreme in the sunup-sundown world, the culture of the sundown-sunup time was permeated by the ideology of Black somebody-ness. And, as is clear from the excerpt, that affirmation of the worth of Black people was undergirded by a deep-seated conviction of the slaves' relationship with God, their Creator. Hopkins captures this sentiment in his analysis of the slaves' view of themselves in contrast to reigning pro-slavery theological anthropology. Even in bondage, "Black folk felt deeply about their God-given humanity."[26] As the lyric genre known as Negro Spirituals makes clear, it was this sense of inherent worth that would, in turn, provide the stamina to endure the long period of enslavement and the wherewithal to engage in the centuries-long struggle for freedom and liberation.

Defense of Human Worth

Affirmation is an internal action; it takes place within the community and it is directed first and foremost to the members of the ecclesial community itself. We can call it a nurturing act. But while it fulfills an incredibly important

---
25. Hopkins, "Black Theology," 71–72; emphasis added.
26. Dwight Hopkins, "Slave Theology in the 'Invisible Institution'" in *Cut Loose your Stammering Tongue: Black Theology in the Slave Narratives* eds. Dwight Hopkins and George Cummings (Maryknoll: Orbis Books, 1992), 30.

function, it alone does not suffice to promote human worth, and by extension, the championing of human well-being. In a world bent on denying human worth, often the emissaries of God need to add to their affirming actions the *defense* of human worth and dignity. That defense is an act that is directed primarily to the world outside the ecclesial body.

If we need an idea of what such a defense looks like, we need look no further than the praxis that Jesus exercised in the society and culture of his day. Even a rapid reading of the gospels reveals that in the Palestine of Jesus's day there were several social groups that were not held in high esteem by the dominant culture. The reason for the low regard was varied. For some, like the Samaritans, the cause of contempt was their ethnic background (John 4:9). For others, like the tax collectors, the disdain was due to the nature of their profession (Luke 18:9–14; 19:1–7). For still others, the disregard was caused by their moral and spiritual condition (Luke 7:36–39; John 8:1–7). A fourth category of people were ostracized because of the cultic impurity that the diseases with which they were afflicted brought upon them (Luke 17:11–14).

As one reads the gospels, it is difficult to miss the consistency with which Jesus subverted the dominant attitude of his time by standing on the side of those whom society despised. In attitude and actions, Jesus made it abundantly clear that he stood in solidarity with every one of these unfortunate groups. A small sampling of his affirming actions on behalf of the vulnerable demonstrates this: (1) He rejected social mores by openly befriending "outcasts" (Luke 7:36–40); (2) he attracted the ire of the religious class by engaging in table fellowship with "sinners" and tax collectors (Matt 9:11; 11:16–19); (3) he defied the cultic laws by touching a man with leprosy before healing him (Matt 8:1–3); (4) he pleaded the cause of a woman accused of adultery by exposing the hypocrisy of her accusers (John 8:3–11); (5) he openly commended the conduct of a despised Samaritan *and* criticized the moral indifference of the religious class (Luke 10:29–37); (6) he unapologetically placed meeting human needs above the observance of the Sabbath, and, in so doing, again infuriated the religious class (Mark 2:23–28; 14:1–6); (7) he prohibited the use of demeaning language and name-calling, declaring that such behavior would be subject to the most severe divine punishment (Matt 5:22); and (8) in a patriarchal and chauvinistic culture, he elevated the status of women by befriending them and involving them in his ministry (Luke 7:36–38; 8:1–3).

Not everyone toward whom Jesus showed such kindness reacted in a way that allows us to determine the impact of his benevolence on their self-concept. But from the reactions of some of those who were the recipients of his kind actions, we can detect a clear psychological boost and existential upliftment.

As an example, take the story of Jesus's encounter with the Samaritan woman at the well (John 4). Following the private conversation she had with Jesus, she seems to have cast aside what appears to have been a reserved demeanor to become a bold public witness of Jesus. That happened despite her moral condition and the social taboos regarding the value of a woman's testimony (John 4:28–30). We observe an even greater boldness in the attitude of the blind man whom Jesus healed on the Sabbath at the Pool of Siloam (John 9). Having been born blind, the man lived his entire life in dependence upon others for his survival. Such a condition scarcely inspires assertiveness and boldness in interaction with others. Yet, such characteristics are precisely what we observe in the man's heated interchange with the Pharisees after Jesus had healed him. In the face of intimidation and threats by the Jewish religious authorities, the healed man forcefully and adamantly defended the claims of Jesus before the Savior's detractors (John 9:24–33).

The story of Zacchaeus's encounter with Jesus also makes the point but from a different angle – the joy and exuberance he exuded following his encounter with Jesus (Luke 19:1–10). Being a man of small stature and also socially ostracized, all Zacchaeus wanted to achieve by climbing the sycamore tree was to catch a glimpse of Jesus. But when, to his amazement and to the displeasure of the crowd, Jesus paid him a visit *at his house* and acknowledged his identity, Zacchaeus's demeanor and character changed. He was overjoyed and experienced an inner transformation that resulted in concrete and commendable ethical actions.

The point of these stories is that when humans are affirmed, they are invigorated and empowered. Affirmation fans the flames of human agency and unleashes the potential for transforming initiatives that had lain latent within them. At a time when people groups who have suffered centuries of devaluation of their humanity are clamoring for the recognition of their worth by shouting that their lives matter, the people of God should be the first to join such a chorus. Conversely, in a day when the pernicious ideology of white supremacy is rearing its ugly head, the people of God should be the first to condemn such an affront to human worth and dignity, regardless of the quarters from which it originates. For such a stance is antithetical to anything resembling genuine Christianity. This was even acknowledged by none other than Friedrich Nietzsche, the German philosopher who was himself a merciless critic of Christianity. "Christianity," he wrote, "represents the counter-movement to any morality of breeding, of pedigree, of privilege: it is the *anti*-Aryan religion par excellence."²⁷ At stake here is the upholding and defense of a fundamental biblical value. And this should transcend political partisanship and ideological alignment. The Indian philosopher Vishal Mangalwadi has no doubts in his mind about the impact such a stance by the church would have on a society that disregards the value of a certain category of people, including his own. He writes:

> In a caste-ridden country such as India, the church can become a matter of excitement if it is seen to be uniting "untouchable" and the "high caste" into one body. The same applies to other countries where human beings are sharply divided according to race, color, economic status gender, etc. These alienations are the results of sin, features of the kingdom of Satan. Salvation includes becoming one body by overcoming the sin that separates.²⁸

Advocacy for Human Well-Being

In unpacking the contours of human affirmation, we hinted that, in some ways, that action implicates the church in some form of prophetic activity. But there is an activity where the prophetic function is not caught via a side glimpse but comes to full view. We're referring to the role of advocacy that the people of God are called to play in their attempt to steer a given social order in the direction of God's will.

An advocate is a person who argues for a cause on behalf of someone else. The purpose of the argument is to change a given situation by influencing the minds of the relevant power brokers or decision makers. This is the sort of result that defense attorneys seek to wrench from a judge or jury on behalf of their clients.

As the emissary of God in the temporal domain, the church is called to carry out such a function. Just as ambassadors advocate for the policies of their governments in the countries of deployment, so an authentic ecclesial community is God's voice in the corner of the world that it occupies. Part of its role is to plead the cause of God in that place with a view to bringing into being an order that is more conducive to the well-being of humans – particularly the poor. The ecclesial community carries that task based on the conviction that

---

27. Friedrich Nietzsche, *The Twilight of the Idols*, trans Duncan Large (Oxford: Oxford University Press, 1998), 35. Italics his.
28. Vishal Mangalwadi, *Truth and Transformation: A Manifesto for Ailing Nations* (Seattle: YWAM, 2009), 2007.

since God is the one who created the world, he knows best what is good for it, and what the world misses by going its own way.[29] And, as the American theologian Wayne Grudem argues, to seek the good or well-being of others is part of the reason God leaves his people here.[30]

As understood here, advocacy is an exercise in social exegesis. It involves the unearthing, knowing, naming, exposing, and confronting of the hindrances that impede human flourishing in a given milieu. The African theologian Olo Ndukwe likens it to an act of confession which entails the "agreement that a certain state of affairs falls short of what God wants and that as Christians we are committed to setting things right."[31] Through advocacy, the church challenges the social status quo by its refusal to normalize and absolutize the life-stifling features that a society harbors, and by insisting that the society can change for the better.

The function of advocacy is not an outlier that should be regarded as falling beyond the boundaries of the church's regular ministry. Biblical warrants for its support are plentiful. For instance, much of the ministry of the Old Testament prophets consisted in calling Israel to follow God's ways for national life and, by so doing, eliminate the ills that were causing pain and suffering to the poor and vulnerable. The prophets were convinced that the people's abandonment of God's ways was not only causing harm to the poor, but also eroding the moral fabric of the society and jeopardizing its economic well-being. Consider the following examples.

Isaiah advocated passionately for the marginalized by criticizing the religious system of the day. He opened his prophecy by labeling as "worthless" the religious practices of those who engaged in the mistreatment of the poor while claiming to worship God (Isa 1:10–17). He was adamant that their exploitation and oppression of the poor, and their indifference to the plight of the needy, nullified any performance of elaborate religious activity (Isa 58).

Jeremiah was also critical of the religious elite for their corrupt leadership. His critique is interesting. He acknowledged that the people were indeed sinful, but he placed much of the blame for their condition on the shoulders of the leaders who misled them and caused them to live lives of disobedience to God (Jer 6:7; 8:8–13). Similarly, Hosea chastised the leaders for their neglect

---

29. Johannes Reimer, *Missio Politica* (Carlisle: Langham Global Library, 2017), 36.
30. Wayne Grudem, *Politics According to the Bible* (Grand Rapids: Zondervan, 2010), 48.
31. Olo Ndukwe, "Rural Community Development," in Agang, Forster, and Hendriks, *African Public Theology*, 131.

of the need of the people to know the laws and precepts of God. "My people are destroyed for lack of knowledge," he lamented (Hos 4:4–6).

As for Amos, his plea on behalf of the victims of injustice is proverbial. He indicted those who "trample on the heads of the poor . . . and deny justice to the oppressed" (2:6–7), denounced those who engaged in exploitative and unjust economic practices (5:11), and called out judges who engaged in the corruption of justice (5:12). To avert judgment and disaster, he summoned the society to let justice flow freely and mightily (5:24).

In Psalm 82, God issues an indictment against unjust leaders and judges and strongly condemns the abuses they were perpetrating against the weak. The psalmist goes on to make a plea for advocacy on behalf of the vulnerable of the land: "Defend the weak and the fatherless; uphold the cause of the poor and the oppressed. Rescue the weak and the needy; deliver them from the hand of the wicked" (82:3–4).

Besides advocating on behalf of disadvantaged social groups collectively, the prophets also took up the cause of oppressed individuals. Two cases that come immediately to mind are Nathan's masterful and dramatic rebuke of David for the gross injustice the king committed against Uriah (2 Sam 12:1–12), and Elijah's bold confrontation of King Ahab for his blatant injustice against Naboth (1 Kgs 21:17–22). These are powerful stories of prophetic pleading for the cause of the vulnerable. And it is interesting that in both cases, the plea was made even though the victims were dead!

Moving to the New Testament, we hear the note of advocacy loud and clear in the ministry of both John the Baptist and Jesus. John's ministry, as we know, was to prepare the way for Jesus by calling Israel to repentance. But in urging people to repent, John didn't ask them to make a vague profession of faith. He called upon them to abandon specific practices that were causing harm to the well-being of others and were injurious to the common good. These practices included lack of concern for the needy, the charging of exorbitant taxation, and the exacting of payments from the common folk through extortion (Luke 3:7–14). He even chastised the ferocious Herod Antipas, the tetrarch, for the wrong he had committed against his own brother by engaging in an illicit sexual relationship with his wife (Matt 14:3–4).

Jesus's position was no different. We see it clearly in his response to those who were offended by the help that the needy were receiving, and to those who sought to set up roadblocks before people who were seeking relief of one kind or another. He took his stance firmly on the side of those who had received or were seeking relief, and against their critics. Notice how strongly he pushed back against the religious leaders of his day who seemed to suggest that they would rather see people starve or remain sick than let them receive food or healing on the Sabbath (Luke 6:1–7; 14:1–6). He defended the cases of the beneficiaries of these blessings by laying bare the hypocrisy of the critics. Notice, too, the indignation he displayed at his own disciples for seeking to prevent children from having access to him. He summarily overruled their objections and tenderly received and blessed the children in his arms (Mark 10:13–16). Consider how swiftly he dismissed the objections of the crowd and proceeded directly to heal blind Bartimaeus who was desperately seeking his help (Mark 10:46–52).

All this means that when ecclesial communities advocate for the well-being of men and women, they only tread in the trail blazed for them by the prophets and the Lord Jesus Christ himself. Indeed, if their engagement doesn't include such a dimension, they ignore an important part of their representational mandate. The role of a faithful ecclesial community includes being a voice for the voiceless and a defender of the defenseless. Johannes Reimer says it well: "The church of Christ is built on the foundation laid by the apostles and the prophets (Eph 2:20)." Consequently, "[it is urged] to make space for prophecy in [its] midst [in order] to promote edification of its members and their witness in society. . . . *Where prophets act, life is promoted, transformation introduced, and human dignity restored.*"[32]

What we are going to say now should be apparent, but it needs to be stated nonetheless, because of the discomfort and angst many Christians feel about the matter. Here it is: *To say that the church's promotion of human well-being includes prophetic advocacy is tantamount to saying that its role is, in a very important sense, political.* This is where the views that shield the political domain from the prophetic critique of the church fall short.

We are conscious that the mere mention of the word "politics" may provoke the raising of eyebrows. But before putting the book down, please finish reading this section. The term "politics" comes from the Greek words *polis*, which means "city," and *techne*, which means "science." Politics, therefore, literally means the "science of the city." The science in question concerns the administration or management of the affairs of the city. Millennia ago, the Greek philosopher Aristotle said that the purpose of that science is the *pursuit of the highest good for the city* – a "good" defined as *the attainment of the "good" life*.[33]

---

32. Reimer, *Missio Politica*, 58. Emphasis added.

33. W. T. Jones, *History of Western Philosophy: The Classical Mind* (New York: Harcourt, Brace & World, 1969), 288.

Thus understood, politics falls squarely within the purview of God's rule because God is a God of life. As we saw above, Scripture makes it clear that the enjoyment of the good life is God's intent for humanity. John's gospel, which has life as one of its major themes, tells us that the one who is bent on wrecking life is Satan (John 10:8). In stark contrast, John emphasizes that the purpose of the coming of the incarnate Son is to make possible the enjoyment of abundant life (John 10:10). While the fall interfered with that divine purpose, the Bible tells us that even in this dispensation of fallenness, God has not abandoned the project. Indeed, alongside the order of grace, God established the political domain as his servant, and entrusted it with the responsibility to pursue the common good (Rom 13:1ff.). The future messianic reign envisaged by Isaiah and Paul will be a political reign (Isa 11:3–5; 1 Cor 15:24–25). For the church, then, to engage the political domain, in an appropriate manner, is not to engage in something that's antithetical to God's will.

To be sure, the political order has not always lived up to the mandate given to it by God. Indeed, its history is one of countless disappointments. Too often, it betrays its reason for being by failing to pursue the common good. History is replete with examples of it abdicating the responsibility to search for a good life for the dwellers of the city. But such failure is no justification for abandoning it and leaving it to its own devices. We are convinced that it is precisely at such junctures that the engagement of the ecclesial community, the other servant of God, who is also tasked with the promotion of life and well-being, becomes paramount. In our judgment, such engagement is essential if the political domain has any chance of being led back to its God-assigned mandate when it goes astray. If the political domain is left without the church's prophetic witness, the pursuit of the good life runs the risk of being severely jeopardized.

We need to be clear about the kind of political involvement we're advocating. We are not vouching for the ecclesial hijacking of the political domain. This would amount to a trespassing that is clearly contrary to the order that God himself has established. In keeping with Jesus's command, what belongs to Caesar must be given to Caesar (Matt 22:21). Nor are we calling for ecclesial alignment with a particular political party. This too would be problematic since it would mean resorting to a modern version of Constantinianism which would expose the church to all the pitfalls that are attached to that arrangement.

What we are calling for, instead, is a relationship of critical cooperation between the church and the political order. Critical cooperation defines the church's position toward the political realm in terms of measured cooperation and qualified endorsement. The degree of the church's support of any political regime depends upon the merit of that regime's sociopolitical program as measured against basic biblical values such as justice, respect of human dignity and worth, human life, and so on. In this view, the church's cooperation with any political order will always bear the mark of conditionality. No blank check is signed and handed beforehand to a regime irrespective of the name it bears or the name of its standard-bearer. Hence, the stance of critical cooperation discourages political indifference and political naivete. Built within it is a posture of distancing from any prevailing political order. This political distancing serves as a necessary safeguard of the prophetic integrity of the church which is the bedrock of the credibility of its witness.

Granular Engagement

There is no doubt that the actions discussed above are essential to any transforming effort. But there is a level of involvement that they don't quite reach. At times, in the process of fulfilling their representational responsibility, it becomes necessary for ambassadors to be involved in concrete activities in the contexts in which they are deployed. I remember that when our family was living in Jamaica, there was an ambassador of a particular country who invited me and my wife to dinner on several occasions. This diplomat of another country even came to our own humble dwelling place for dinner! The purpose of this ambassador was to persuade me that the policy of their country toward my homeland, Haiti, was correct. The same kind of action is also necessary of the church. In addition to its internal work of affirming and defending human worth, and the external work of advocacy, the ecclesial community must add *its own involvement* in the transforming task itself. This level of engagement includes actions that are granular in nature by virtue of their earthiness and practical character. Through them, the church as a transforming agent seeks to penetrate the soil of a given social milieu and urges it to change.

Subversive Seeding

One such action is the *intentional seeding* of the context in which the ecclesial community is situated with seeds of righteousness to counter the spread of evil. In the parable of the wheat and the weeds or tares (Matt 13:24–30, 36–43), Jesus refers to his disciples collectively as the "good seed" that he himself has sown (13:37–38). This good seed which he also calls "the people of the kingdom" lives in the world it shares with the weeds which are seeds sown by the enemy, the devil, and which are the cause of sin and evil in the world (13:39, 41). Jesus forthrightly says that this uneasy coexistence will continue until the end when he metes out final judgment in which he will rid the world of the weeds

(13:41–42). "The present age is thus one in which human society... is a mixture of those of the evil one and those of the kingdom."[34] The good news is that, in the interim, the field need not be overrun by the weeds. Indeed, it must not. In the parable, Jesus says that the weeds appeared *after* "the wheat sprouted and formed heads" (13:26). This means that the growth and productivity of the good seed can hamper and impede the spread of the germinating weeds! By shedding onto the field seeds that they themselves produce, the good seed can have a greater influence on the field than the weeds. While the good seed is still there, the weeds need not prevail.

This seeding of the context cannot be accomplished by the clergy. It is the work of the church writ large, the scattered ecclesia. It is the work of the laity supplied with the seeds of righteousness, dispatched and dispersed with the order to spread them in every nook and cranny and every field of endeavor of a given context. As the British missiologist Lesslie Newbigin put it, the laity constitutes the "Church's front-line troops in her engagement with the world."[35] This is transformation carried out at the level of the ecclesial grassroots.

Focused Illumination

We term the second action *focused illumination*. To illuminate is to cast light on an object so that it can be seen more clearly. When we illuminate something, we zoom in on it to keep the light from dissipating and thus allow us to get the best view of it possible. With perfect vision, we can perform more flawlessly the work we intend to do on the object. Through illumination, then, we exert a greater influence on the object.

To participate in the transformation of a social context, the church must endeavor to illuminate its life – including its political management. It cannot do that by remaining aloof from the daily life of the city, but instead by keeping abreast of the issues with which it is preoccupied at a given moment. Such engagement gives the church the opportunity to offer gospel-informed perspectives on the issues and persuade the society of the pertinence of these perspectives for the common good. Specifically, this means that ecclesial communities must be keenly attentive to the policies, programs, plans, and legislation put forward by secular government with a view to determining if they are in line with the divine ideals of justice, equity, compassion, and so on. The American public theologian Ronald Thiemann highlighted well the importance of such action when he said that "if persons formed in those

---

34. Hagner, *Matthew 1-13*, 395.
35. Quoted in Nancy Pearcy, *Total Truth* (Wheaton: Crossway, 2004), 67.

communities in which the virtues of faith, hope, and love are nurtured fail to manifest those virtues in public life, then the *polis* will indeed be left to those with a shrunken and desiccated view of the possibilities of the political community."[36]

Both biblical and Christian histories contain instructive and inspiring illustrations of the good that can accrue to society when the people of God seek to influence its life by shedding the light of the gospel on issues of consequence. The influence that biblical figures such as Joseph, Esther, and Daniel exerted on the governments of their societies is proverbial (Gen 41; Esth 7:1–6, 8; Dan 4:16ff.). Enormous calamities were averted because these believers in Yahweh got involved in the political fray. In his book *Under the Influence*, historian Alvin Schmidt catalogs a long list of lasting changes that occurred through the centuries in a number of societies *because Christians mounted sustained challenges against specific evils that were prevalent in their contexts.*[37] To a very large extent, the outlawing of chattel slavery in Great Britain and the United States and the dismantling of the segregationist systems in the United States and South Africa came about because Christians kept insisting that these systems were antithetical to God's will. It took the sustained and relentless efforts of William Wilberforce and Christian abolitionists in Great Britain and the United States to persuade these societies that human bondage and trafficking was contrary to the gospel, and thus morally wrong. Similarly, in the United States, the end of legal sanction for the racist policy "separate but equal" that kept Black people and White people apart from one another necessitated arduous and persistent work on the part of the Black church and some White Christians under the bold and sacrificial leadership of Martin Luther King Jr. When George Wallace kept repeating the mantra "Segregation now, segregation tomorrow, and segregation forever," the Black church responded confidently: "We shall overcome." And for a proponent of nonviolence like Dr King, such confidence to eventually carry the day could not be based on political and military might, but on the power of gospel-grounded and morally unambiguous principles. King's approach was to challenge Americans to bring their attitudes and the policy of the country toward Black people in sync with the basic precepts of the gospel to which they claimed adherence and to the ideals that are expressed

---

36. Ronald Thiemann, *Constructing a Public Theology: The Church in a Pluralistic Culture* (Louisville: Westminster John Knox, 1991), 25.

37. Alvin Schmidt, *Under the Influence: How Christianity Transformed Civilization* (Grand Rapids: Zondervan, 2001). Among them are things we now take for granted, such as the outlawing of pedophilia and infanticide.

in the founding documents of the nation, such as the Constitution and the Declaration of Independence.

The story of the end of the apartheid system in South Africa is particularly relevant to the point we are making here. When we consider the South African experience, one of the pillars that sustained the apartheid system for so long was the erroneous belief that the policy of separate development of the ethnic groups that share the country was biblical and Christian. The proponents of the racist policy went to great lengths to show that there was nothing theologically wrong with it. And for quite some time, most of the church agreed with that understanding. But as Kevin Roy shows in his excellent book *Story of the Church in South Africa*, at one point a sector of the church began to question the correctness of that claim.[38] There was such a groundswell in support of this attitude that in a relatively short time virtually the whole church came to the conclusion that apartheid was a sinful system that was contrary to the gospel, and consequently, any theology that defended it was heretical.[39] This clarity of theological understanding moved the church not only to withdraw its support from the racist policy, but also to call on the government to change it.[40] Following the church's unified stance and collective call, it didn't take long for the government to take the unprecedented decision to dismantle the apartheid system and organize the first free and fair elections in the country's history that resulted in the accession to power of a democratic government.

In relating this story (and, indeed, the others referenced in this section), we are not claiming that the church's push was the only explanation for the changes that occurred in these societies. Certainly in the case of South Africa, there were other important voices who were clamoring for the dismantling of apartheid. Our claim is that in all these instances, the church's decision to beam the light of the gospel on the critical issues that faced these societies was a significant factor in the change that occurred.

Redemptive Defiance

We intentionally mention this aspect last because the step we are proposing here must be taken as a last resort. Indeed, before elaborating on it, we need to state that the default position the church should adopt vis-à-vis the political order is a positive one. Scripture provides several warrants for such a stance.

---

38. Kevin Roy, *Story of the Church in South Africa* (Carlisle: Langham Global Library, 2017), 188.
39. Roy, *Church in South Africa*, 198.
40. Roy, 201.

As a starter, the Bible advises against viewing government qua government as evil, but as an entity that falls under the broader governance of God: "The powers that be are ordained of God" (Rom 13:1 KJV). Further, it admonishes us to be submissive to government: to give government its due (Rom 13:1, 5), to honor political authorities (1 Pet 2:13–17), and to support government financially (Rom 13:7). Moreover, it places upon us the responsibility to pray for political authorities (1 Tim 2:1–2).

Having said that, we must note that the biblical perspective on the temporal authorities includes two principles that might cause a Christian to suspend the default mode at a given moment. The first principle is the Bible's insistence that temporal authority is not ultimate but subordinate to God's authority: secular authorities rule with God's approval and are his servants (Rom 13:2, 4). The second principle is the scriptural assertion that government is not an end in itself but exists for a greater purpose. That purpose is the pursuit of good for the populace of a given *polis* (Rom 13:3–4). Considering this, we must nuance the position stated in the preceding paragraph to say this: *In the context of an overall positive stance, when the temporal authority persists in pursuing actions that clearly usurp divine authority and/or pervert the moral order by upholding evil instead of good, faithfulness demands that the Christian suspends the stance of obedience and withdraws compliance with respect to those acts.* Scripture recognizes that sometimes a political system can be under the total control of evil and act in opposition to God and contrary to the good of the people under its authority (Rev 13). Traditionally, the position we have advocated here is called "civil disobedience." But we think it is more accurate to call it *redemptive defiance* to highlight the fact that in subverting an evil act the purpose of the Christian is not simply to disobey, but to promote an alternative noble act that accords with God's will and is thus beneficial for the common good.

Throughout history, faithfulness to God has compelled many a servant of God to resort to this stance of redemptive suspension. The three young Hebrews' defiance of Nebuchadnezzar's order to commit idolatry by bowing before his statue redounded to the good of Babylon because the act resulted in the repentance of the pagan king (Dan 3:28 – 4:3).[41] By defying Pharoah's order to kill the Hebrew baby boys at birth, the Hebrew midwives saved Moses and thus contributed to the fulfillment of God's plan to rescue his people from Egyptian bondage (Exod 1:15 – 2:2). The magi's refusal to obey Herod's order to report the location of baby Jesus thwarted his evil and murderous plan and

---

41. It is debatable whether Nebuchadnezzar came to truly believe in Yahweh. But what is clear is that, at the least, his attitude toward the God of Israel changed for the better.

saved the Savior from an untimely death (Matt 2:7–12). In the United States, the courageous and firm refusal of a young woman called Rosa Parks to obey the racist and unjust law that required Black people to relinquish their seats on buses to newly arrived White passengers started the American Civil Rights Movement in that land. Martin Luther King Jr., who assumed the mantle of the movement, stepped up the defiance mode, and not only did the effort result in the outlawing of segregation, but in a little over fifty years it led to the election of the first Black man as president of the country – Barack Obama! Similarly, during the Holocaust, Corrie ten Boom, in defiance of the law, hid people in her home to keep them from being captured by the murderous Nazis.

With this we've reached the limit of the actions we believe the church can take to catalyze the transformative process. We are certainly aware that there are well-meaning people who think that the church should push the envelope further by engaging in violent acts. In the 1960s, there were Roman Catholic priests in Latin America who joined revolutionary forces that sought to topple oppressive political regimes throughout the subcontinent.[42] In South Africa, the World Council of Churches supported the use of violence to dismantle the apartheid system.[43] During the Nazi regime in Hitler's Germany, Dietrich Bonhoeffer was convinced that in light of the total breakdown of the order established by God, it was legitimate to resort not only to the temporary suspension of the duty of obedience, but also to the elimination of Hitler through a violent act of disobedience.

We are not saying that God cannot use violent means to bring about change. Clearly, God sanctions the use of coercive force by the state (Rom 13:3–4). In some situations, it may be the only means by which meaningful social change can occur. However, to affirm that such means can be employed by the corporate ecclesial body in its effort to bring about socio-structural changes is seriously problematic. The church is an entity created on the basis of the reconciliation achieved by Christ between formerly alienated elements (Eph 2:13–18). As such, it is a symbol and an agent of peace and reconciliation in the world (2 Cor 5:17–21). "Into this divided world Jesus Christ has come to bring peace, so much so the church came into being and received the task of demonstrating to the world [that] accomplished reconciliation."[44] By its very nature, then, the church is a spiritual-social institution whose contribution to social change can be made only through peaceful means. Recourse to

---

42. See Nuñez and Taylor, *Crisis and Hope*, 278–84.
43. See Roy, *Church in South Africa*, 190–91.
44. Marcus Barth, *Ephesians 1–3*, The Anchor Bible (Garden City: Doubleday, 1974), 322.

violent means will always be incongruent with its vocational integrity. That is why the approach of unbridled engagement oversteps the bounds. Its call for thoroughgoing involvement needs to be tempered by the adoption of a more cautious stance vis-à-vis the church's participation in social change. We believe that the stance of authentic engagement that we advocate does just that. Authentic engagement does not isolate the political domain from the church's purview, but engages it in a way that maintains ecclesial integrity and prophetic credibility.

Part Four

The Stance of Transforming Engagement

9

Hope-Filled Realism

Since we embarked on the search for legitimate ways ecclesial communities can influence their contexts for good, we've traveled a long way. On the road we've trod, we've encountered several important signposts. We saw that, within the overall framework of their representational mandate, ecclesial communities can steer their environment in the direction of God's ideal for community life by their presence, their way of life, their proclamation of God's word, and by taking certain concrete and context-redeeming actions.

As we approach the end of our journey, we remain convinced that the package of ecclesial praxis we've proposed can have a salutary effect on the milieu in which it is applied. In keeping with this conviction, we hope that many an ecclesial community will try it out. Such confidence, however, should not be confused with a boastful triumphalism. We understand that in a fallen world, we can never rule out the possibility, and, indeed, the likelihood, that certain contexts will be bent on resisting the most authentic and credible witness. We need only point to the resistance that was thrown at Jesus's flawless and perfect praxis to make this clear. In fact, Jesus himself warns that "a servant is not greater than his master" (John 15:20). If his efforts were met with a negative response, the church should not be surprised if a similar fate befalls its own. In the face of a raging fire, no dry wood can hope to fare better than the green wood (John 15:18–20)!

Yet, while this warning from our Lord prepares us for what may confront us, it doesn't transform us into apathetic and robotic stoics when we face the ravaging effects of the forces that adamantly oppose the experience of well-being in our world. Like many a saint of old, in such instances we often revolt and lament, sometimes asking angrily "Why?," or impatiently "How long, O Lord, how long?" (cf. Rev 6:10). As I write these words, the confession of a God-fearing mentor of mine who spent decades as a missionary in Haiti comes to mind. He often admitted that repeatedly he argued with God in prayer about the condition of the country he loved so much. And at this very moment as I write, current events in that country cause us to voice these lamenting cries with greater fervor. Farther afield, the news of horrendous atrocities being committed against people in Sudan and Nigeria, and the report of little Afghan girls being sold by their fathers to older men for a pittance, add to our outrage and exasperation.

Happily, as was true of the prophets, the psalmists, and the people of God throughout history, these moments of emotional discharge don't last forever. Eventually, even as our concern persists, the feeling of exasperation subsides. But this doesn't mean that our struggle has ended. For in our eagerness to see the will of God reflected in the temporal domain, we ask: What do we do when faced with a world that resists all efforts to change?

Wrongheaded Directions

In probing a question such as this, it may be helpful to proceed by way of elimination. By this we mean the process of identifying and ruling out options that, though tempting, do not seem congruent with the church's commitment to an engagement that's authentic. We cannot cover them all, but we note the following three.

Fatalistic Resignation

A first course we should avoid is inaction. Inaction is the decision to leave the recalcitrant domain alone because of its refusal to change. We may call it the path of least resistance. In the face of a change-resistant context which saps our energy and weakens our resolve, we can feel constrained to wave the flag of surrender and focus attention on finding ways to cope.

Often, this posture of resignation is due not simply to the toughness of the task but to a deep-seated sense that the situation is unchangeable. And more fundamentally, this sense is itself rooted in the belief that the prevailing situation is the will and action of some transcendent power. With such a conviction, the attitude is then formed that until that power decides otherwise, all efforts to change the situation are futile. We personally know this well. There are people, for instance, who explain the plight of our homeland by an appeal to the belief that Haiti is under some divine curse.[1] For them, the ills that have befallen the country could not be prevented since they were divinely ordained.

We can agree that complete transformation of any social order will be the work of a transcendent power. As Christians we believe that that power is the God revealed in Scripture. Contrary to those who subscribe to the Marxist worldview, we hold that no utopia will result from human efforts. But to say this is a far cry from affirming that our involvement in improving the present order is futile. Such a belief would render meaningless the prayer the Lord taught his disciples, namely, that God's will might be done on earth as it is in heaven. Further, it would nullify the mandate he gives us to be salt of the earth and light of the world. A posture of fatalistic resignation would make the Christian presence irrelevant to the task of making the world a better place.

Nihilistic Retreat

A second path some have taken as a reaction to society's resistance to change is retreat or withdrawal. This option shares the pessimistic outlook of the one mentioned above, but it adds a fundamental element. If the previous stance opts for a presence that is indifferent to the prevailing condition, this approach chooses an *absence* that is nihilistic. Here, the agent is not content simply to turn a blind eye to a recalcitrant reality. Instead, he or she disengages from it *angrily*. The disengagement is fueled by a despair that condemns the status quo and, in some instances, withdraws from it violently. It is akin to the advice of Job's wife to her suffering husband: "Curse God and die!" (Job 2:9). Since the situation holds no hope, the thing to do is to take leave of it – but bitterly.

The protest, of course, is not expressed in the same way in every place. In the Caribbean where we are from, some of those who advocate such a withdrawal give it an ideological form. In the view of some Caribbean writers, the inability of the region to promote human well-being is rooted in its historical experience. In the main, that history is a history of people who were transported violently into a hostile environment, exploited, and then left to swim on their own in the vast Caribbean Sea. Analysts see that experience as consisting of the violation of self and the divestment of being. It is thus devoid of any positive content capable of providing the basis for a new departure. Its only starting point is void, they maintain. But what can come out of a void? The Trinidadian novelist and Nobel Prize-winner V. S. Naipaul

---

1. See my article entitled "Is Haiti under Divine Curse?," *Latin American Journal of Evangelical Theology: Christian Reflection from the Latino South* 6, no. 1 (2011): 86–106.

answered, "Nothing!" He was convinced that since "Nothing" was created in the region, "Nothing" was all that could ever be created there.[2] Given this sense of despair, it is no surprise that some in the Rastafarian movement advocated repatriation to their place of origin – Africa.

At times, the indignation is not so benign. It takes the form of self-inflicted violence; that is, violence that agents of change perpetrate *against themselves*. We see this in the behavior of a cult leader such as Jim Jones. Jones had a vision of an America devoid of such social ills as racism and sexism. When that vision failed to materialize, he withdrew with his followers to the jungle of Guyana in South America, established a commune, and engaged in all sorts of abusive and destructive behaviors. In a confrontation with the American authorities, Jones committed mass murder by forcing some nine hundred persons, among them children, to drink a cyanide-laced drink.

Despair, of course, is no respecter of persons. It can penetrate and overwhelm the strongest of souls. Elijah and Habakkuk would not need to be subpoenaed to testify to its intrusive power (1 Kgs 19:3–5; Hab 1:1ff.). This means that our default response to those who succumb to its weight should be compassion, not a callous and self-righteous condemnation.

But to sympathize doesn't necessarily mean to endorse, and to understand doesn't necessarily mean to agree. To our minds, in none of its forms is the option of nihilistic retreat an appropriate response of a community that represents God and seeks to engage its context authentically. This is so because by giving up on the possibility of renewal of any context, the ecclesial community casts doubt on the renewing power of the God it represents. Furthermore, in withdrawing from a context, it robs it of God's instrument of restoration and renewal. Ezekiel's prophecy of the restoration of Israel recounted in chapters 36 and 37 of his dramatic book shows this. To a people in captivity who had lost the status of nationhood, and whose existence was likened to that of dry bones, God promised full rehabilitation – spiritual and national. This demonstrates that God does possess the power to revitalize and restore the most decrepit of environments. And the promised revitalization was to come about through the ministry of the prophet himself. Of course, in making this argument, we're not claiming the exact replication of Israel's experience in every context. Our argument is for the recognition of God's power and ability to renew any context

---

2. V. S. Naipaul, cited in Gordon Rohlehr, "Man's Spiritual Search in the Caribbean through Literature," in *Troubling of the Waters*, ed. Idris Hamid (San Fernando: Rahaman, 1973), 188. The Haitian playwriter Frankétienne is no less terse. In his play *Dézafi*, he answers the question with the Creole word *anyen*, meaning absolutely *nothing*.

through the instrumentality of his people. If this is so, then despair cannot be an option even in the absence of tangible signs of hope.

Coercive Pursuit

The reference to the Marxist worldview a few paragraphs above may bring to the minds of some readers the idea of the urgency of change that is stressed in that system. In the Marxist construct, the process of displacing an order that inhibits human well-being and of replacing it with a regime that releases humans from the bondage of material insufficiency is a task that cannot wait. In his eleventh thesis on Feuerbach, Marx expresses this urgency when he says that "the philosophers have only *interpreted* the world . . . the point, however, is to change it."[3] For Lenin, taking revolutionary *control* is one of the first things that must be done to begin that process of change.[4]

There are some Christians who, while not embracing full Marxism, find the idea of a coercive push of a recalcitrant context toward change attractive. For them, when facing an environment that resists efforts to change, instead of adopting a laissez-faire stance or resorting to despairing retreat, we should opt for the exertion of coercive pressure to force it to move in the direction they deem correct.

In the early days of liberation theology, several Christians advocated that option.[5] The best-known cases are those of the Colombian Roman Catholic priest Camilo Torres and fellow Nicaraguan priest Ernesto Cardenal. Convinced that a Christian's commitment to structural change for the benefit of the poor could bring the desired result through revolutionary action alone, Torres decided to join the guerrillas in the mountains of Columbia who were trying to topple the government. He was convinced that the way of armed resistance was an appropriate means to demonstrate practical and efficacious love for our neighbor.[6] Cardenal was of a similar conviction. While not participating in actual armed struggle because of his age, he became an active member of the revolutionary movement of Nicaragua which succeeded in toppling the oppressive regime of Anastasio Somoza Debayle. He argued vehemently that

---

3. Tucker, *The Marx-Engels Reader*, 145.

4. Lenin, *State and Revolution*, cited in Heilbroner, *Marxism: For and Against* (New York: W. W. Norton and Co., 1980), 153.

5. In its heyday, there was a movement called Christians for Socialism that numbered several hundreds of Christians.

6. Camilo Torres, *Cristianismo y revolución* (Mexico: Ediciones Era, 1972), 376.

there is no contradiction between Christianity and Marxism, and no difficulty in the church's endorsement of violent revolution for "a just cause."[7]

This option is exercised not only by left-leaning Christians. The history of the church shows that Christians on the right have availed themselves of it as well. An example is the German church's embrace of Hitler's Nazi revolution that resulted in the horrific massacre of the Holocaust. More recently, the attack on the United States Capitol on 6 January 2021 by supporters of former president Donald Trump to force the suspension of the certification by the U.S. Congress of the 2020 presidential elections is another example of forcibly bending the social order in a direction that is different from the one that obtains. Among the rioters were people who revealed their Christian identity by the display of Christian symbols such as the Bible, the Christian flag and the cross, and by the rhetoric they used, the prayers they uttered for the success of the insurrection. Many place these rioting Christians within the group known as Christian nationalism which shares sympathies for the broader Christian nationalism movement which holds to a vision of national life that is binary, exclusionary, and adversarial.[8]

Generally, the question of the use of violence as a means of effecting change is hotly debated. The debate becomes even more intense when the issue turns on the appropriateness of the use of violence by Christians – individually and corporately as the church. Some sanction the discriminate use of violence, while others argue against any recourse to it by the church. For instance, the same passion for social change that impelled the likes of Torres and Cardenal to take the road of coercive force propelled the Brazilian Bishop Dom Hélder Câmara and the American Civil Rights crusader Martin Luther King Jr. to take the option of nonviolent resistance. In doing so they followed the trail of peaceful change blazed by the Indian activist Mahatma Gandhi who led the struggle for India's independence from British colonial rule.

We think that the latter option is the correct one. We believe that it is in sync with the overall thrust of Jesus's praxis revealed in the New Testament. In the Sermon on the Mount, where Jesus lays out, among other things, his

---

7. Cited in Nuñez and Taylor, *Crisis and Hope*, 252.

8. David A. Ritchie, *Why do Nations Rage? The Demonic Origin of Nationalism* (Eugene: Wipf & Stock, 2022), 3–4, 21. In the aftermath of the riot, a slew of newspaper reports highlighted the connection between the event and Christianity. See, for instance, Michelle Boorstein, "A Horn-wearing Shaman. A Cowboy Evangelist. For Some, the Capital attack was a kind of Christian revolt," *The Washington Post* (July 6, 2021); Kathryn Joyce, "How Christian Nationalism drove the insurrection: A religious history of January 6," *Salon* (January 6, 2022); Jack Jenkens, "How Christian nationalism paved the way for January 6," *National Catholic Reporter* (June 13, 2022).

directives for his disciples' response to a hostile environment, he commends the way of peace (Matt 5:9), love for enemies (5:43ff.), and nonretaliation toward an aggressor (5:38ff.). In the parable of the wheat and the tares or weeds (13:24–30, 36–43) that we referenced earlier, we see Jesus's peaceful approach on display once again. To the servants who asked him for permission to root out the weeds that were growing in the same field as the wheat, Jesus commanded restraint. He advised against such violent uprooting and recommended patient waiting instead. The uprooting of the weeds and their separation from the wheat is the work of the gardener, and this will take place at the end (13:30). Until then, evil is to be tolerated, and no violent effort is to be made by the disciples of Jesus to bring it to an abrupt end.

Hope-Filled Realism: A Better Option

If our judgment is correct that none of the options reviewed above is a legitimate course of action an ecclesial community can take in response to a stubborn reality, what are we left with? Does this mean that, in such instances, we are trapped in a proverbial cul-de-sac, a dead-end? Is there a path that can be followed beside immobilism, nihilistic retreat, and violent revolution? In our pursuit of a social order that lends itself to the promotion of human well-being, must we settle for either a calcified and absolutized status quo or an elusive utopia?

We don't think our options need to be so limited, nor our objective cast in starkly opposing and contrasting terms. Our response to an obstinate milieu need not take the form of a pessimistic cynicism nor an unrealistic naivete. It should always include hope for the possibility of change without any overblown claims to transform a context into an instant paradisiacal order. We call this mediating approach "hope-filled realism." Hope-filled realism is the path that seeks to straddle two lanes. It has one foot firmly planted in the reality, with the other in possibility. On the one hand, it steers clear of a position that is oblivious to the configurations of the context, and on the other, it keeps the agent from being so overwhelmed by the negative features of the milieu that it rules out all prospect of its alteration.

The notion of realism is not a novel idea. We encounter it in its secular version in the works of many well-known political philosophers, among them Thomas Hobbes's *Leviathan* and Machiavelli's *The Prince*. But it is primarily to the patristic theologian Augustine of Hippo and the American ethicist Reinhold Niebuhr that we owe the Christian expression of the concept. Our elaboration will follow the path of these latter thinkers but will add an emphasis that we find missing in their formulations.

According to Reinhold Niebuhr, realism is the disposition to take all factors that are relevant to a particular situation into account in our consideration of it.[9] For his part, in his classic work *City of God*, which provides analysis of life in the earthly city compared with life in the city of God, Augustine argues that in considering the sociopolitical situation that obtains in the earthly city, one must consider the conflictual nature of that domain. Social reality in the *civitas terrena*, he argues, is not characterized by harmony and peace, but by tensions, competitions, frictions, and factions at every level of community life.[10] In searching for the cause of this unsettling reality, Augustine parts company with classical thought in laying the blame for the conflictual nature of the earthly city not in inability of reason to take control of humanity's subrational impulses, but in the *nature of the self itself*. The cause of the ills that beset community life in the earthly city is that it consists of people who are polluted by evil, consumed with self-love, and bent on pursuing their own interests.[11] The city is permeated and dominated by an egocentricity that propels people to make themselves their own ends or the centers of the communities they inhabit.

This blunt realism doesn't lead Augustine to total despair, however. He finds two factors that can moderate the recalcitrance against change that prevails in the earthly city. The first is the capacity of humans for self-transcendence. While the corruption of human freedom is universal, it need not become normative, he argues. Humans can moderate their egocentrism and seek God rather than themselves. This is possible (and this is his second factor) because the earthly city doesn't constitute the totality of reality. Existing alongside it, and comingled with it, is the city of God, which is dominated by the love of God, and where God, not the self, is the end. There is thus some tension between the two cities, and that tension involves the leavening of the earthly city by the city of God.

More than fifteen hundred years separated Augustine and Niebuhr. Yet, their analysis of the human condition and their assessment of the threat it poses to community life, and of how the danger that results can be mitigated, in the main converge. Niebuhr addresses the issue of realism in his *Moral*

---

9. Reinhold Niebuhr, *Christian Realism and Political Problems* (repr., Fairfield: Augustus M. Kelly, 1997), 119.

10. Saint Augustine, *City of God*, trans. Henry Bettenson (repr., New York: Penguin Books, 1980), 19.7.

11. Augustine, *City of God*, 15.5.

Man and Immoral Society and *Christian Realism and Political Problems*.[12] In the latter work, he provides a thorough analysis of Augustine's perspective on the sociopolitical reality. While he finds weaknesses in Augustine's construal that need correction,[13] for him the Augustinian account is basically correct. Indeed, he considers it superior to the proposals of those who came before and after the bishop of Hippo.[14] He joins Augustine in locating the roots of sociopolitical problems in the control that egocentricity exerts on humans. In doing so, he parts company with modernity's overly optimistic appraisal of the human person, particularly its twin ideas of the "perfectibility of man" and human progress. He sees this optimistic assessment as contributing to the flawed and unrealistic examination of the social scene.[15]

But, as with Augustine, Niebuhr's clear-eyed examination of the social reality doesn't lead him to the conclusion that society is desperately doomed. The self that is at the center of the social predicament is not a one-sided entity, capable only of causing damage. No: in the human self resides the capacity to reach "the heights of human creativity and the depths of destructiveness."[16] In this balanced view of personhood, he thinks, there is some way to escape both the pitfalls of an unanchored naivete and a pessimistic cynicism. Channeling Augustine and agreeing with him, Niebuhr says:

> A realism becomes morally cynical or nihilistic when it assumes that the universal characteristic in human behavior must also be regarded as normative. The biblical account of human behavior ... can escape both illusion and cynicism because it recognizes that the corruption of human freedom may make a behavior pattern universal without making it normative. Good and evil are not determined by some fixed structures of human existence.[17]

For those concerned with the possibility of change in the social domain, the crack left open in the Augustinian-Niebuhrian construct is welcome. It leaves open the possibility of prodding the self-centered egos that inhabit the earthly city to embark on a path that might be more conducive to the well-being of the collectivity. As Ronald H. Stone remarks in his analysis of Niebuhr's brand of

---

12. Reinhold Niebuhr, *Moral Man and Immoral Society* (New York: Charles Scribner's Sons, 1960); *Christian Realism*.
13. Niebuhr, *Christian Realism*, 137.
14. Niebuhr, 2, 120, 130, 145.
15. Niebuhr, 3.
16. Niebuhr, 2.
17. Niebuhr, 130.

realism, for Niebuhr, although tragic, "[history] contains possibilities of gains as well as loss. . . . Its configurations were continually producing surprises to both pessimists and optimists."[18]

While acknowledging the possibilities inherent in the Augustinian-Niebuhrian construal, we cannot, however, close our eyes to the fact that in this version of realism the balance tips decisively on the side of the tragic features and the dark side of reality. While it contains hints of the possibility of change in the status quo, the prospect of the *eventuality* of such change is acknowledged only tepidly. We see this clearly in Augustine's sober description of social existence in its various forms. In his analysis, which Niebuhr endorses, Augustine likens social life to the river of Babylon. Babylon for him is a symbol of the earthly city which is bound to disappoint its inhabitants because it cannot ultimately deliver what is expected of it. That is why the Christian who belongs to the city of God is admonished by both thinkers not to put too much stock in the earthly city. And if we ask what the Christian can do to improve the prospect of meaningful change in the earthly city, we meet with a lukewarm response on two fronts. First, the Christian can engage the world, but his or her engagement must be light and cautious. Augustine advises us to "sit *by* the waters, not *beneath* the waters, of Babylon." We are to take our place "*by* the waters, not *in* the waters, not *under* the waters," he emphasizes.[19] Second, in engaging the world, we are asked to use the resources and tools available in the earthly city, even though these means are known to be corrupt.

What accounts for this praxiological lukewarmness and nonchalance, we might legitimately ask? To our minds, the explanation lies in the absence of an adequate ideology to drive the Christian's effort to countervail the negative features of the earthly city. An ideology is a set of ideas and beliefs that are unique to a system. It is a particular view of the world and of life that drives actions and behaviors in the world. Without ideology, engagement in the world is bound to be directionless and anemic.

We submit that in the biblical perspective, the concept that provides a strong enough ideological backing for a robust engagement in the world is the kingdom of God. The kingdom is, fundamentally, the sovereign rule of God. It speaks of a rule which frees people from the forces that oppress and inhibit their lives in the fallen world, and places them in a "commonwealth that is governed by the only power that is capable of meeting human needs."[20] Paul

---

18. Ronald Stone, *Realism and Hope* (Washington: University Press of America, 1976), 123.
19. Augustine, as cited in Niebuhr, *Christian Realism*, 145. Emphasis added.
20. Stone, *Realism and Hope*, 17.

speaks of our being rescued from the dominion of darkness and brought into the kingdom of the Son (Col 1:13). The kingdom, then, is a divinely engineered socio-spiritual order tailor-made for the experience of true human well-being. It is the "Christian expression of social hope."[21]

The linking of the kingdom and hope in the preceding paragraph shouldn't give the impression that the kingdom is ethereal, distant, out of this world. Not at all. While not reducible to the historical and temporal, the kingdom's this-worldly presence is no less real. As the late American New Testament scholar George Eldon Ladd puts it, "the kingdom of God is the redemptive reign of God dynamically active to establish his rule among men."[22] While it will appear in its full and final form only at the end of the present age, "it has already come into human history in the person of and mission of Jesus to overcome evil, to deliver men from its power and to bring them into the blessings of God's reign."[23] It is a dialectical construct which embraces "both fulfilment within history and consummation at the end of history."[24]

It is our contention that to be efficacious, Christian realism needs to take seriously both the reality and the hope of the kingdom. When it does, it accomplishes two things. First, because the presence of the kingdom is real, not some symbolic notion as Niebuhr seems to hold, realism becomes less lopsided and more balanced. Reality includes a positive counterweight to its dark side. Second, thus understood, realism constitutes a more robust challenge to the negative features of reality. The kingdom is "a protest against the reality of oppression and a promise of a new order."[25] Where it is taken seriously, oppressive reality comes under pressure.

As we have stated repeatedly in the pages of this book, the church is God's representative in the temporal domain. It is called to engage the world in the name of God. In its engagement with the world on behalf of God, it has no greater tool than the ideological platform provided by God himself: his kingdom. This is the tool that the church is to wield in its effort to encourage, prod, and chastise any context to come into alignment with God's will and design for community life. Jürgen Moltmann, whom we have referred to several times in these pages, puts it graphically: "Those who hope in Christ can no longer put up with reality as it is, but begin to suffer under it, to contradict

---

21. Stone, 17.
22. Ladd, *Theology of the New Testament*, 91.
23. Ladd, 91.
24. Ladd, 91.
25. Stone, *Realism and Hope*, 17.

it. Peace with God means conflict with the world. For the goad of the future stabs inexorably into the flesh of every unfulfilled present."[26] But this task must be carried out with a healthy dose of realism. The effort of the church to influence any social order must always be tempered by the knowledge that the realization in history of the perfect human society will ultimately be the work only of God himself.[27] Our efforts, while important, have their limits; their results will always fall short of the outcome that will be realized only in the perfect order that God will establish.

All this means that the engagement we are calling for is for an age that is sandwiched between two worlds – this world and the next. It is an engagement for "the interim," or as the late Latin American evangelical theologian René Padilla called it, an engagement "between the times."[28] In this "in-between" order, existence is characterized by an uncomfortable suspension. It is hanging between the "already" and the "not yet," between the real and the ideal, between the "is" and the "ought," between reality and possibility. In this order, the church's efforts to steer society in the direction of conformity to God's will, will inevitably meet with mixed responses, and the results reached will be ambivalent. As it challenges the present social order to align itself with the ideals and values of the kingdom, it will not hit a home run all the time. Indeed, it is more likely that its efforts will receive varied responses. Sometimes, they will meet with delayed acceptance, at other times with partial agreement, and in some instances with total rejection. But these outcomes, unsatisfactory as they are, should not lead us to succumb to despair and resignation, or to resort to impulsive actions. Instead, we advocate a posture that is realistic yet hopeful, producing an engagement that is resolute, persevering, and unflinching.

The resoluteness of this stance is not baseless. The praxis we are commending here rests on two solid load-bearing pillars. The first is this: because of the presence of the kingdom, there is the real *possibility* that the negative forces that are at work in any context can, at any moment, crack under the pressure of a kingdom-inspired engagement. The fall of the Berlin Wall, the collapse of apartheid, the outlawing of segregation in the United States through the efforts of the Civil Rights Movement, the dismantling of the slave trade through the arduous and persistent efforts of Wilberforce and

---

26. Moltmann, *Theology of Hope*, 18.

27. Wolfhart Pannenberg, *Theology and the Kingdom of God* (Philadelphia: Westminster, 1969), 76.

28. C. René Padilla, *Mission between the Times: Essays on the Kingdom of God* (Grand Rapids: Eerdmans, 1985; 2nd ed., Carlisle: Langham Monographs, 2010).

his fellow abolitionists across the Atlantic, all clearly indicate that this is not wishful thinking. The second pillar is the *assurance* of the coming kingdom and the accompanying elimination of all the forces of evil from any social order. Such assurance provides the motivation to persevere even in the absence of any concrete signs of change. The writer of Hebrews gives this as the reason why the heroes of faith, who did not see the fulfillment of the promises made to them at the time of their death, *continued* to live by faith. They continued to act based on these promises because they "saw them and welcomed them from a distance" (Heb 11:13).

10

Expectancy

If the thought with which we ended the previous chapter is true, we must add yet another element to our argument for the church's engagement in social change. To say that the features of the present order that inhibit life can yield at any moment under the pressure of the inaugurated kingdom, and to assert that the evil that undergirds and props up these negative elements will assuredly be defeated when the kingdom comes in its fullness, suggests that the church cannot be content with merely enduring the current frustrating order in a fatalistic way. Its posture can and indeed must be more confident and uplifting. This is so because the possibility of change in the present order, and the assurance of the impending doom of the evil that stands behind it, says that real *hope* for change exists in any context. No reality needs to be absolutized and doomed to remain the way it is.

The Necessity of Hope

Hope is not superfluous to existence; it is an essential commodity for the sustenance of life. Hope sustains the human spirit; it lifts the human psyche, and keeps it from sinking in even the direst of situations. We see this whenever a disaster strikes, whether it is the collapse of a building, an earthquake, a tornado, or a plane crash. In such instances, the frontline responders go straight into search and rescue mode and stay there as long as possible, sometimes beyond the time that seems reasonable. The reason for this is that, so long as the rescue operation is in force, there is hope of finding people alive. This hope keeps people's spirits from succumbing to despair – especially those who have loved ones caught up in these tragic events. Hope also helps preserve the will to live for those who are trapped and in need of rescue. For instance, the knowledge that people on the outside, whether government or family, are working for their release gives many hostage victims the inner fortitude and strength to live one more day. Similarly, "Christian hope offers a coherent and *energizing basis for work in today's world.*"[1]

Martin Luther King Jr.'s stance provides a powerful illustration of the sustaining and energizing power of hope for engagement in the here and now. In his famous Mountaintop speech, King gave a lengthy recital of the sundry vicissitudes that he and the throng of oppressed Black Americans suffered at the hands of the White establishment in their struggle for justice and social equity. While at the time the obstacles were intense and brutal, King did not expect them to subside. "We've got some difficult days ahead,"[2] he predicted. Indeed, as he drew the speech to a close, he revealed that he had a premonition that his own life would be cut short violently. Yet, he declared that the prospect of that tragic event did not deter him from pursuing the march toward freedom. His reason for this resoluteness was his vision from afar of the sure triumph of the freedom campaign. "I've been to the mountaintop," he declared. "I've seen the Promised Land. I may not get there with you. But . . . we, as a people, will get [there]," he declared confidently.[3] The hope for the sure fruition of the liberation process that King expressed then was an echo of the note he sounded five years earlier in his memorable "I Have a Dream" speech.[4]

But, if the presence of hope sustains life, its absence is detrimental to existence. Where hope is lacking, the negative features of reality fuel despair, which in turn is given free rein to invade the human spirit and even snatch life away. The field of psychiatry defines hopelessness as a set of negative expectations about the near and/or distant future.[5] History has shown that where hopelessness prevails, the appetite for life diminishes and life itself is endangered. Millennia ago, the ancient Greek writer and philosopher Sophocles wrote: "Not to be born at all is best, far best that can befall. Next best, when born, with least delay, to trace the backward way."[6] In more recent times, the French existentialist philosopher Jean-Paul Sartre said in his play *No Exit* that

---

1. N. T. Wright, *Surprised by Hope* (New York: HarperCollins, 2008), 5. Emphasis added.
2. Martin Luther King Jr, "I've Been to the Mountain Top," April 3, 1968, https://kinginstitute.stanford.edu/encyclopedia/ive-been-mountaintop. Accessed October 25, 2022.
3. King, "I've Been to the Mountain Top."
4. The Avalon Project, "I Have a Dream by Martin Luther King, Jr; August 28, 1963," Yale Law School, accessed 25 July 2022, https://avalon.law.yale.edu/20th_century/mlk01.asp.
5. A. T. Beck, A. Weissman, D. Lester, and L. Trexler, "The Measurement of Pessimism: The Hopelessness Scale," *Journal of Consulting and Clinical Psychology* 42, no. 6 (1974): 861–65.
6. *Sophocles I: Oedipus the King, Oedipus at Colonus, Antigone*. 2nd ed. David Grene and Richard Lattimore, eds. (Chicago: University of Chicago, 1991), 1224.

"life begins on the other side of despair."[7] For his part, Saul Bellow, the 1976 Nobel Prize-winner in Literature, gave the following somber description of an existence that finds itself in the throes of hopelessness:

> But what is the philosophy of this generation? Not God is dead, that point was passed long ago. Perhaps it should be stated Death is God. This generation thinks – and this is its thought of thoughts – that nothing faithful, vulnerable, fragile can be durable or have any true power. Death waits for these things as a cement floor waits for a dropping light bulb. . . . You think history is the history of loving hearts? You fool! Look at these millions of dads. Can you pity them, feel for them? You can do nothing! There were too many. We burned them to ashes, we buried them with bulldozers. History is the history of cruelty, not love as soft men think.[8]

Things have not gotten better since Bellow painted that gloomy picture. In 2021, the World Health Organization reported that suicide accounts for the deaths of more than 700,000 people every year and is the fourth leading cause of death among 15–19-year-olds.[9] Hopelessness is currently having an impact on families, schools, churches, and communities. As I write, that gloomy climate is being exacerbated by the devastating effects of the COVID-19 pandemic on social strata that were already being pulled apart by other sociopolitical problems such as racism, poverty, and the environmental crisis. The current conditions have led some people to wonder if we have reached the final hour of human history, as many hearts have sunk into despair.

Hope is badly needed to counteract this sorry state of affairs. Happily, by including hope in its vision of reality, Christian faith puts in the hands of the church a weapon that can be wielded in its engagement with any recalcitrant context.

The Surprising Irruption of Hope

Those who don't think that the church can play any meaningful role in alleviating the social problems that confront the world may shrug off the appeal

---

7. Jean-Paul Sartre, cited in M. Shanthi and Lizella Faria Gonsalves, "Hope amidst Despair: Revisiting John Steinbeck's Novel *The Grapes of Wrath* in the Times of COVID-19 Pandemic," *Rupkatha Journal on Interdisciplinary Studies in Humanities* 12, no. 5 (2020): 1–9.

8. Saul Bellow, *Herzog* (New York: Penguin, 1976), 315.

9. World Health Organization, "Suicide," 17 June 2021, https://www.who.int/news-room/fact-sheets/detail/suicide.

to hope as a cop-out, as illusory, even delusional. But this only reveals their failure to appreciate the ability of hope to irrupt into the historical present and impact it in meaningful ways. In his book *Surprised by Hope*, the British biblical theologian N. T. Wright argues vehemently that the ultimate hope that God has wrought in Jesus's resurrection, in which he inaugurated the new order, ought to inspire transforming and hope-instigated actions in the present order on the part of God's people.[10] Sometimes, these actions of hope may be low-key, run-of-the mill, and barely noticeable. But at other times they may be astounding, jaw-dropping, causing major shifts in the operation of the present order. When, for instance, at the height of the Civil Rights Movement in the United States, President Lyndon B. Johnson uttered the words "We shall overcome" (the first line and refrain of the protest song of the movement), that was an instance of hope's surprising breakthrough into the here and now. From that point on, life changed for the better for the oppressed Black people in that land. The same can be said of the tearing down of the Berlin Wall in 1990, which ended the almost thirty-year division of the city of Berlin and the continent of Europe. The event put an end to the Cold War period during which the threat of a nuclear Armageddon hung like the sword of Damocles over the human race. In 1983, during a visit to Haiti, Pope John Paul II made a statement that had similar historical import. While in Port-au-Prince, the pontiff said that things needed to change. That declaration contributed in no small measure to the collapse of the almost thirty-year Duvalier dictatorship that was supposed to be "for life"!

Hope as Expectation of the Good

At this point, the question that may be lingering in our minds is "What is hope?" Viewed from a strictly human perspective, hope has been defined as an emotion that helps people cope with despair.[11] This emotional energy to fight despondency is self-generated. Thus, for psychologist C. R. Snyder, hope is "the perceived capability to derive pathways to desired goals and motivate oneself via agency thinking to use those pathways."[12] Indeed, in an influential article

---

10. Wright, *Surprised by Hope*, 221–22.

11. Richard S. Lazarus, "Hope: An Emotion and a Vital Coping Resource against Despair," *Social Research* 66, no. 2 (1999): 654.

12. C. R. Snyder, "Hope Theory: Rainbows in the Mind," *Psychological Inquiry* 13, no. 4 (2002): 249.

entitled "Hope Theory: Rainbows in the Mind," Snyder argues that integral to the concept of hope is the mental capacity to achieve specific goals.[13]

While triumph over despair and confidence in the human ability to pursue worthy goals are important elements of a hopeful life, there is an element that is missing in the above construal. In the biblical perspective, the concept includes the element of expectation – either good or bad.[14] In the New Testament, the root Greek word that is translated hope, trust, or faith is *elpis*, which denotes the sense of anticipation with pleasure, a confident expectation. Hence the German New Testament scholar Rudolf Bultmann explained that "hope as expectation of good is closely linked with trust, and expectation is also yearning, in which the element of patient waiting or fleeing for refuge is emphasized."[15]

In the biblical view, therefore, hope goes behind the human person and is directed toward a transcendent Other. And as biblical characters relate their experience, this Other is God. Thus, biblically speaking, hope is directed toward God as people seek to find deliverance from their present earthly woes. The psalmist expresses these sentiments in the following words:

> Deliver me, my God, from the hand of the wicked,
>   from the grasp of those who are evil and cruel.
> For you have been my hope, Sovereign LORD,
>   my confidence since my youth.
> From birth I have relied on you;
>   you brought me forth from my mother's womb.
> I will ever praise you.[16]

Similarly, other psalms (e.g. 9, 27, 34, 37, 58, 62, to name just a few) emphasize these expectations of the manifestation of the goodness, justice, and faithfulness of God on earth. Bereft of this divine referent, the church does not have the wherewithal to create pathways of authentic engagement that represent the kingdom of its Creator and is thus hopeless.

---

13. Snyder, "Hope Theory," 249.

14. Emeka C. Ekeke and Ubong E. Eyo, "The Necessity of Hope: A Philosophical and Theological Appraisal," *European Scientific Journal* 12, no. 5 (2016): 376.

15. Rudolph Bultmann, cited in *Theological Dictionary of the New Testament*, eds. Gerhard Kittel and Gerhard Friedrich, trans. Geoffrey W. Bromiley (Grand Rapids: Eerdmans, 1964–1976), 2:522–23.

16. Ps 71:4–6.

The God of Hope

Happily, God is indeed that referent! He is the ground that makes it possible for the church to be hope-filled, even in the darkest of times.

From Genesis to Revelation, God is presented as the God of hope. His presence and power, his faithfulness and plan, his goodness and mercy, brought hope to people again and again. Hope is present in the creative act. As Paul Wells puts it, "[hope] is hardwired into the human constitution by God's promise of life, by the eschatological perspective of the creation week, and by the fact that the human psyche, created in the image of God, is programmed with a memory of eternity."[17] And when the Edenic scene presented a grim picture of humankind's condition as they strayed away through disobedience, hope was seen in God clothing them with garments of skin and promising a seed from Eve that would crush the head of the serpent, signifying that this tragedy was not the end (Gen 3:10–15). The divine voice that uttered the immediate and future consequences of sin made provision in his plan for the redemption of humanity and for the restoration of creation through the sacrifice of the lamb slain before the foundation of the world (1 Pet 1:19–20). In Genesis 6, the God of hope rescues Noah and his family as a wicked world perishes in a deluge that is an execution of divine retribution. Was it not hope that appeared when God called Abraham from pagan ancestry to become a pioneer of faith, the father of those who would come to believe? The birth of Isaac from the barren womb of Sarah to begin a nation that would be a source of blessing for gentile nations, a promise that would find its realization in the Messiah's crucifixion, resurrection, and ultimate establishment of his kingdom (Gen 12:2), surely testifies to the reliability and omnipotence of the God who made the promise. In Romans 4, Paul describes and applauds the posture of hope of Abraham in a hopeless situation:

> Against all hope, Abraham in hope believed and so became the father of many nations, just as it had been said to him, "So shall your offspring be." Without weakening in his faith, he faced the fact that his body was as good as dead – since he was about a hundred years old – and that Sarah's womb was also dead. Yet he did not waver through unbelief regarding the promise of God, but was strengthened in his faith and gave glory to God, being fully persuaded that God had power to do what he had promised. (Rom 4:18–21)

---

17. Paul Wells, "Editorial: Hope against Hope," *Unio cum Christo* 7, no. 1 (April 2021): 6.

This clearly indicates that even in desperate situations where human capabilities cease, hope can be found in the God who by nature is good, just, and faithful, and whose power greatly surpasses human limitations.

Why is hope such a recurrent theme in the biblical narrative? Because the story is about the God who creates, provides, and protects to accomplish his plan. Abraham's descendant Joseph was protected from his brothers' wicked and deadly schemes and raised to leadership in a foreign land to safeguard the nation that carried the promised seed. Israel multiplied in abundance under the Egyptian yoke and was delivered from this hopeless situation through Moses, a Hebrew child who by divine providence was brought up in Pharaoh's court and educated in all the wisdom of Egypt. It was the God of hope who paved a way through the Red Sea for his people in spite of their stubbornness, fed them with the bread of angels, and satisfied their thirst in the wilderness of Zin with water from a rock.[18] Songs of hope echoed from their lips as they witnessed the God of Abraham, Isaac, and Jacob, in his loyal kindness or *hesed*, conquer their enemies with the strength of his bow.[19] These incidents show that the God of hope is not intimidated by hopeless situations; he is not paralyzed by human depravity, nor is he ever bankrupt of mercies. Even when the nation of Israel wandered after foreign gods, the prophetic voice in Israel would often concomitantly utter judgment and hope. For instance, the prophet Amos, after addressing Israel's false piety, hopes for a change that will be brought about by God where all might partake in his justice. Similarly, addressing a nation that knows the taste of God's judgment for disobedience, idolatry, and pride, Isaiah emphasizes the theme of hope in God who will fulfill the promise that nations shall one day come to Israel's light, and kings to the brightness of his dawn (Isa 60:3). As Jürgen Moltmann asserts, "In the prophets, despite all the newness of their message, the God who confronts Israel with his claims is no other than the *Deus spei*, the God of hope."[20]

And hope does not withdraw from the scene in the New Testament. Indeed, there it blooms and flourishes with the coming of the Messiah, the promised seed, who made a public spectacle of the diabolical and demonic foes, "triumphing over them by the cross" (Col 2:15). And the realization of the promise that the Gentiles will be included as recipients of God's blessings, as per the Abrahamic covenant, becomes evident in the establishment of the multi-ethnic church. In his epistle to the Romans, Paul, a Greek-speaking Jew from Asia Minor who

---

18. Ps 78:24–25.
19. Ps 42.
20. Moltmann, *Theology of Hope*, 126.

before his conversion was a strict adherent of Judaism, appeals to the believers to accept one another as Christ has accepted them. And the ministry that Christ has rendered the Jews was done "on behalf of God's truth, so that the promises made to the patriarchs might be confirmed" (Rom 15:8). The references that Paul cites in the subsequent verses of that chapter from the Law, the Psalms, and the Prophets pinpoint the present inclusion of Jews and Gentiles in Christ through the church and the future reign of Christ over the nations. Paul concludes, "May the God of hope fill you with all joy and peace as you trust in him, so that you may overflow with hope by the power of the Holy Spirit" (15:13). In view of the untarnished reputation of the God of Abraham who always keeps his promises, those who have placed their hope in him will not be disappointed.

The Emitter of Hope

As we argued in chapter 4, the church is rooted in God; it is a community of the triune God. If God to whom it is intrinsically connected is a God of hope, then his people must also be. A people who belong to the *Deus spei* must themselves be a *populi spei*. They must be a people who can confidently expect God to manifest his power to transform lives and situations. He is a God who, by his Holy Spirit, empowers his people to maintain determination and optimism "in the face of hardship," and to have "the audacity to [hope] and believe despite all the evidence to the contrary."[21]

In his fine book *Realism and Hope*, Ronald Stone, whom we have referenced several times already, asks a question which is relevant for our argument here: "Where can hope come from if not from the church?"[22] The people of God ought to be people of hope not only by virtue of their connection to God, but because they carry within themselves the seed of what will be manifested in them when they are transformed into what God intends them to be (2 Cor 5:5; 1 John 3:2; Rom 8:18). For it is only in hope that they are saved (Rom 8:24). Therefore, amid trials, disappointments, heartache, and tribulations caused by a world that resists change, their calling is to labor resiliently for change based on the knowledge of the possibility that the God of hope will break through to change things, and more importantly, on the expectation of his final irruption to make all things new (Rev 21:1–5). In the meanwhile, they persevere in being an ambassador and exemplar of that coming new order, a herald of its message, and the catalyst for the well-being that God wants all people to enjoy.

---

21. Barack Obama, *The Audacity of Hope* (New York: Crown Publishers, 2008), 356.
22. Stone, *Realism and Hope*, 16.

11

Prayer

In the previous chapter we argued that authentic engagement must include the church's brandishing the lantern of hope in a world fraught with hopelessness, even when its effort doesn't seem to yield positive results. Like Abraham of old, it must hope against hope (Rom 4:18). But how is hope maintained? In this final chapter we will argue that to uphold hope and avert despair, the people of God must constantly look to the God of hope. In humility, they need to tap into the Reality that transcends what meets the eyes. They need to rely on the Sovereign of the universe who is the "Ruler of the kings of the earth."[1] This upward look is intended to accomplish three important objectives.

Empowerment to Stay the Course

Those involved in authentic engagement are human. When facing dire situations, they can feel powerless and hopeless. They therefore need divine empowerment that comes through the spiritual discipline of prayer for the courage, strength, endurance, wisdom, and boldness to maintain the course. We see this recourse to prayer in several biblical instances. When Nehemiah felt called to lead the project to rebuild the wall of Jerusalem, he accompanied that effort with prayer. When the king asked him to request what he needed to accomplish the work, Nehemiah prayed before responding (Neh 2:4). Later, when in the thick of the construction project opposition came in the form of intimidation and mockery (4:1–3), he again resorted to prayer (4:4–6). The influence Daniel exerted on Babylonian society during his long career as a government official in that pagan land is well known. That influence, too, was due to a large extent to his dependence upon God through a disciplined

---

1. Rev 1:5.

prayer life. By reliance upon God, he gained the ability to relay and interpret Nebuchadnezzar's dreams and, in so doing, prevented the proud king from massacring the wise men of his kingdom (Dan 2). On at least two further occasions, Daniel's unswerving dependence upon God miraculously saved his life and the lives of his fellow Jews and served as a powerful witness to the society and its kings of the power of the God of Israel (Dan 3; 6). Similarly, when Esther agreed, at the request of Mordecai, to intervene with the powerful king Ahasuerus to prevent the massacre of the Jews that Haman had plotted, knowing the gravity of the task, she asked the people to fast for her, even as she also humbled herself before God in fasting (Esth 4:15–17). Turning to the New Testament, when the apostles received threats from the Sanhedrin for preaching the good news and attesting to what they had witnessed of Jesus Christ, their only recourse was prayer (Acts 4). They did not give up and become discouraged; instead, they prayed. The mandate to make disciples of all nations had come from their Lord. Hence, in doing so, they were fulfilling his will. Yet, divine enablement was needed for them to persevere and access divine power through prayer. They did not assume that God would automatically grant them courage and strength for the journey. They asked for it!

In the effort to persuade society to align itself with God's will, we can easily allow self-sufficiency and adequacy to be the drivers of our efforts. We may believe that organizational structures, marketing ingenuity, political clout, and numerical strength are sufficient to guarantee the desired outcome. This is a temptation to avoid at all costs. For, while engagement does entail the performance of activity in society on the part of the church, it cannot be accomplished effectively if it is not divinely energized. The authentically engaged church is one that humbly seeks divine power above all in the execution of the task.

Leadership to Fulfill God's Purpose

In prayer, the church doesn't only seek divine help for staying power for itself, it also looks to God for his work in the hearts and minds of those he has entrusted with the responsibility to seek the good of the city – the political authorities. The Christian church was birthed in political and religious milieux that were hostile to its survival and growth. Yet, Paul instructed his young mentee Timothy to pray for the political rulers. "I urge, then, first of all, that petitions, prayers, intercession and thanksgiving be made for all people – for kings and all those in authority, *that we may live peaceful and quiet lives in all godliness and holiness."*[2] When Paul wrote these words, the Roman emperor Nero was unleashing fierce persecution on Christians. Yet, even in that context, Paul underscores the importance of prayer for the fulfillment of God's purpose.

In Romans 13:1–7, Paul makes it clear that the God-given role of the government is to carry out justice and act in righteousness. Consequently, those who do what is right should live free from fear. Such governance promotes the good and discourages injustice. Our involvement with the political realm should include fervent intercession for it to fulfill that God-given purpose. By praying for those in political authority, the church acknowledges the sovereignty and power of God over that realm – to establish, to humble, to remove, and to change. Political leaders have repented and changed their governance; some have been ousted while others have been firmly established. As the church kneels for political authorities, it requests God's intervention to help leaders act according to God's just and compassionate rule. Even when they aren't faithful in pursuit of that mandate, God can be counted on to accomplish his purpose. Some of the apostles suffered the most severe persecution, yet the early church grew to such an extent that Tertullian could write in his *Apologeticus* that "the blood of the martyrs is the seed [of the church.]"[3]

Discernment to Act Wisely

Prayer is God's instruction to his church and serves to uphold hope, but this does not mean inactivity. In his sermon "The Misuse of Prayer," Martin Luther King Jr. said that we should "never make prayer a substitute for work and intelligence."[4] The kneeling posture does not entail inactivity or passivity. Throughout this book, we have emphasized the importance of a high-level, multipronged engagement by the church in its effort to influence society for good. Paul, in his letter to Titus, accentuates the necessity of the believer's zeal for good works and the collective kingdom impact that we must have in the world (2:11–14). Nonetheless, just as prayer is not a substitute for work and intelligence, so work and intelligence are not substitutes for prayer. Prayer is indispensable to the upholding of hope and the effecting of change. Dwight L. Moody once said that "every great movement of God can be traced to a

---

2. 1 Tim 2:1–2.

3. Tertullian, *Apologeticus*. Translated by S. Thelwall. From *Ante-Nicene Fathers*, vol. 3. Edited by Alexander Roberts, James Donaldson, and A. Cleveland Coxe (Buffalo, NY: Christian Literature Publishing Co., 1885), 50.13.

4. Martin Luther King Jr., cited in *Revives My Soul Again: The Spirituality of Martin Luther King Jr.*, eds. Lewis V. Baldwin and Victor Anderson (Minneapolis: Fortress, 2018), 144.

kneeling figure."[5] In prayer, the church turns to the God of hope to obtain a sustained awareness of the One who is in control and to draw from that connection the strength to do what God intends for this moment and this time. As Reinhold Niebuhr famously prayed: "God, grant me the serenity to accept the things I cannot change, courage to change the things I can, and wisdom to know the difference."

---

5. Dwight L. Moody, cited in Andre Dagger, *Prayer: Your Own Letter to God; A Practical Prayer Guide Inspired by the Major Motion Picture* Letters to God (Grand Rapids: Zondervan, 2010), 17.

Bibliography

Agang, Sunday Bobai, Dion A. Forster, and H. Jurgens Hendriks, eds. *African Public Theology*. Carlisle: HippoBooks, 2020.
Agence France Presse. "Risking Jail and Church Ire, Russian Priests Condemn Ukraine Conflict." France24. 1 May 2022. https://www.france24.com/en/live-news/20220501-risking-jail-and-church-ire-russian-priests-condemn-ukraine-conflict.
The Avalon Project. "I Have a Dream by Martin Luther King, Jr; August 28, 1963." Yale Law School. Accessed 25 July 2022. https://avalon.law.yale.edu/20th_century/mlk01.asp.
Ayittey, George B. N. *Africa Betrayed*. New York: St Martins, 1992.
Baldwin, Lewis V., and Victor Anderson, eds. *Revives My Soul Again: The Spirituality of Martin Luther King Jr*. Minneapolis: Fortress, 2018.
Banda, Collium. "Poverty" in *African Public Theology* eds. SundayBobai Agang, Dion A. Forster, and H. Jurgens Hendriks. Plateau State, Nigeria: Hippobooks, 2020; Carlisle: Langham Publishing, 2020.
Barth, Karl. *Church Dogmatics* I/1. *The Doctrine of the Word of God*. Edited by G W. Bromiley and T. F. Torrance. Edinburgh: T&T Clark, 1975.
———. *Dogmatics in Outline*. New York: Harper Touch Books, 1959.
Barth, Marcus. *Ephesians 1–3*. The Anchor Bible. Garden City: Doubleday, 1974.
Beck, A. T., A. Weissman, D. Lester, and L. Trexler. "The Measurement of Pessimism: The Hopelessness Scale." *Journal of Consulting and Clinical Psychology* 42, no. 6 (1974): 861–65.
Bediako, Kwame. *Theology and Identity*. Oxford: Regnum, 1992.
Bellow, Saul. *Herzog*. New York: Penguin, 1976.
Bettenson, Henry. *Documents of the Christian Church*. 2nd ed. Oxford: Oxford University Press, 1963.
Bird, Michael. *Evangelical Theology*. Grand Rapids: Zondervan, 2013.
Boff, Leonardo. "La Iglesia es una Casta Meretriz." *Cristianismo y Sociedad* 84 (1985): 115–124.
———. *Jesus Christ Liberator*. Maryknoll: Orbis, 1979.
———. *Salvation and Liberation*. Maryknoll: Orbis, 1984.
———. *Trinity and Society*. Maryknoll: Orbis, 1988.
Bonhoeffer, Dietrich. *Letters and Papers from Prison*. Rev. ed. New York: Macmillan, 1963.
Bosch, David. *Transforming Mission: Paradigm Shifts in Theology of Mission*. Maryknoll: Orbis, 1991.
Boyd, Greg. *The Myth of a Christian Nation*. Grand Rapids: Zondervan, 2005.

Braaten, Carl E., and Robert W. Jenson, eds. *Christian Dogmatics*. Vol. 1. Philadelphia: Fortress, 1984.
Bratton, Susan Power. "The Undoing of the Environment." In *Earth at Risk*, edited by Donald B. Conroy and Rodney Lawrence Petersen, 213–36. Amherst: Humanity, 2000.
Bray, Gerald. "One God in Trinity and Trinity in Unity." In *Trinity among the Nations*, edited by Gene Green, Stephen Pardue, and K. Yeo, 1–17. Grand Rapids: Eerdmans, 2015.
Brower, Kent E., and Andy Johnson. *Holiness and Ecclesiology in the New Testament*. Grand Rapids: Eerdmans, 2007.
Bruce, F. F. *The Epistles to the Colossians, to Philemon, and to the Ephesians*. Grand Rapids: Eerdmans, 1984.
Carson, D. A. *Showing the Spirit: The Farewell Discourse and Final Prayer of Jesus*. Grand Rapids: Baker, 1980.
Carvajal, Rafael Tomas, Filemon Escobar, et al. *America Latina: Movilización popular y fe Cristiana*. Montevideo: ISAL, 1971.
Chafer, Lewis Sperry. *Systematic Theology*. Edited by John F. Walvoord. Wheaton: Victor, 1988.
Clowney, Edmund. *The Church*. Downers Grove: IVP, 1996.
Colson, Charles. *How Now Shall We Live?* Wheaton: Tyndale House, 1999.
Cox, Harvey. *The Secular City*. New York: Macmillan, 1965.
Dagger, Andre. *Prayer: Your Own Letter to God; A Practical Prayer Guide Inspired by the Major Motion Picture* Letters to God. Grand Rapids: Zondervan, 2010.
Dawkins, Richard. *The God Delusion*. New York: Houghton Mifflin, 2008.
Dodd, C. H. *The Parables of the Kingdom*. New York: Scribner's, 1961.
Douglas, J. D., ed. *Let the Earth Hear His Voice: International Congress on World Evangelization, Lausanne, Switzerland; Official Reference Volume: Papers and Responses*. Minneapolis: Worldwide Publications, 1975.
Dragas, Father George. "Orthodox Ecclesiology in Outline." *The Greek Orthodox Theological Review* 26, no. 3 (1981):1 –2.
Dulles, Avery. *Models of the Church*. Garden City: Doubleday, 1978.
Ekeke, Emeka C., and Ubong E. Eyo. "The Necessity of Hope: A Philosophical and Theological Appraisal." *European Scientific Journal* 12, no. 5 (2016): 371–85.
Erickson, Millard. *Christian Theology*. 2nd ed. Grand Rapids: Baker Academic, 1998; 3rd ed. Grand Rapids: Baker Academic, 2013.
Escobar, Samuel. *In Search of Christ in Latin America: From Colonial Image to Liberating Savior*. Carlisle: Langham Global Library, 2019.
Fee, Gordon. *God's Empowering Presence*. Peabody: Hendrickson, 1994.
Feinberg, John. *No One Like Him*. Wheaton: Crossway, 2001.
Feinberg, John, and Paul Feinberg. *Ethics in a Brave New World*. 2nd ed. Wheaton: Crossway, 2010.

Fleming, Dean. "On Earth As It Is in Heaven." In *Holiness and Ecclesiology in the New Testament*, edited by Kent Brower and Andy Johnson, 343–62. Grand Rapids: Eerdmans, 2007.

Gener, Timoteo. "Divine Revelation and the Practice of Asian Theology." In *Asian Christian Theology: Evangelical Perspectives*, edited by Timoteo Gener and Stephen Pardue, 13–37. Carlisle: Langham Global Library, 2019.

Giles, Kevin. *What on Earth Is the Church?* Downers Grove: IVP, 1995.

Gill, Robin. *A Textbook of Christian Ethics*. London: Bloomsbury, 2014.

Gladwin, John. *God's People in God's World: Biblical Motives for Social Involvement*. Leicester: Inter-Varsity Press, 1979.

Glasser, Arthur. *Announcing the Kingdom: The Story of God's Mission in the Bible*. Grand Rapids: Baker, 2003.

González, Justo. *Mañana: Christian Theology from a Hispanic Perspective*. Nashville: Abingdon, 1990.

Gorman, Michael J. *Becoming the Gospel: Paul, Participation, and Mission*. Grand Rapids: Eerdmans, 2015.

Graham, Billy. "Why the Berlin Congress?" In *One Race, One Gospel, One Task*, edited by Carl F. Henry and Stanley Mooneyham, 22–34. Minneapolis: Worldwide Publications, 1967.

———. "Why Lausanne?" In *Let the Earth Hear His Voice*, edited by J. D. Douglas, 22–36. Minneapolis: Worldwide Publications, 1975.

Green, Gene L., Stephen T. Pardue, and K. K. Yeo, eds. *The Church from Every Tribe and Tongue: Ecclesiology in the Majority World*. Carlisle: Langham Global Library, 2018.

Green, Joel B. "Living as Exiles: The Church in the Diaspora in 1 Peter." In *Holiness and Ecclesiology in the New Testament*, edited by Kent Brower and Andy Johnson, 311–25. Grand Rapids: Eerdmans, 2007.

Grenz, Stanley. *Theology for the Community of God*. Grand Rapids: Eerdmans, 2000.

Grudem, Wayne. *Politics According to the Bible*. Grand Rapids: Zondervan, 2010.

Gunton, Colin, and Daniel W. Hardy. *On Being the Church: Essays on the Christian Community*. Edinburgh: T&T Clark, 1989.

Hagner, Donald. *Matthew 1–13*. Word Biblical Commentary 33. Dallas: Word, 1993.

———. *Matthew 14–28*. Word Biblical Commentary. Dallas: Word, 1995.

Hallig, Jason Valeriano. "Contextualization of the Life and Ministry of Jesus in the Four Gospels and Its Significance in Proclaiming the Gospel to Asian Cultures in the 21st Century." In *Jesus among the Nations: Christology in Asian Perspective*, edited by Federico Villanueva and Stephen Pardue, 123–144. Manila: Asia Theological Association, 2017.

Harink, Douglas. *Paul among the Postliberals*. Grand Rapids: Brazos, 2003.

Harper, Brad, and Paul Louis Metzger. *Exploring Ecclesiology: An Evangelical and Ecumenical Introduction*. Grand Rapids: Baker, 2009.

Harris, Sam. *Letter to a Christian Nation*. New York: Knoft, 2007.

Hastings, W. Ross. *Theological Ethics: The Moral Life of the Gospel in Contemporary Context*. Grand Rapids: Zondervan, 2021.

Hay, Andy. *God's Shining Light: A Trinitarian Theology of Divine Light*. Eugene: Pickwick, 2017.

Heilbroner, Robert L. *Marxism: For and Against*. New York: W. W. Norton and Co., 1980.

Henry, Carl F., and Stanley Mooneyham, eds. *One Race, One Gospel, One Task*. Minneapolis: Worldwide Publications, 1967.

Hick, John. *God Has Many Names*. Philadelphia: Westminster, 1980.

Hitchens, Christopher. *God Is Not Great: How Religion Imprisons Everything*. New York: Twelve, 2007.

Holmes, Stephen R. "Divine Attributes." In *Mapping Modern Theology: A Thematic and Historical Introduction*, edited by Kelly M. Kapic and Bruce L. McCormack, 47–65. Grand Rapids: Baker, 2012.

Hopkins, Dwight N. "A Black Theology of Liberation: The Slaves' Self-Creation." In *Black Evangelicalism: A Resource for Social Transformation and Spiritual Renewal*, edited by H. Malcolm Newton, 62–84. Unpublished manuscript.

———. "Slave Theology in the 'Invisible Institution'" in *Cut Loose your Stammering Tongue: Black Theology in the Slave Narratives* [1–45] eds. Dwight Hopkins and George Cummings. Maryknoll: Orbis Books, 1992.

Hunter, Archibald M. *Introducing the New Testament*. Philadelphia: Westminster Press, 1957.

Jones, W. T. *History of Western Philosophy: The Classical Mind*. New York: Harcourt, Brace & World, 1969.

Kaiser, Walter C. *The Promise-Plan of God: A Biblical Theology of the Old and New Testaments*. Grand Rapids: Zondervan, 2008.

Kane, J. Herbert. *A Global View of Christian Missions*. Grand Rapids: Baker, 1977.

Kärkkäinen, Veli-Matti. "Ecclesiology and the Church in Christian Tradition and Western Theology." In *The Church from Every Tribe and Tongue: Ecclesiology in the Majority World*, edited by Gene L. Green, Stephen T. Pardue, and K. K. Yeo, 15–34. Carlisle: Langham Global Library, 2018.

Katongole, Emmanuel. *The Sacrifice of Africa: A Political Theology for Africa*. Grand Rapids: Eerdmans, 2011.

Kelly, J. N. D. *Early Christian Doctrines*. New York: Harper & Row, 1978.

Kierkegaard, Søren. *The Point of View of My Work as an Author*. San Francisco: Harper & Row, 1962.

Kittel, Gerhard, and Gerhard Friedrich. *Theological Dictionary of the New Testament*. Translated by Geoffrey W. Bromiley. 10 vols. Grand Rapids: Eerdmans, 1964–1976.

Küng, Hans. *The Church*. New York: Sheed and Ward, 1968.

Kuyper, Abraham. "Sphere Sovereignty." In *Abraham Kuyper: A Centennial Reader*, edited by James D. Bratt, "Sphere Sovereignty" in *Abraham Kuyper: A Centennial Reader*. 461–90. Grand Rapids: Eerdmans, 1998.

LaCugna, Catherine. *God for Us: The Trinity and the Christian Life*. New York: HarperCollins, 1991.

Ladd, George Eldon. *The Gospel of the Kingdom: Structural Studies in the Kingdom of God*. Reprint. Grand Rapids: Eerdmans, 2000.

———. *A Theology of the New Testament*. Grand Rapids: Eerdmans, 1974.

Lazarus, Richard S. "Hope: An Emotion and a Vital Coping Resource against Despair." *Social Research* 66, no. 2 (1999): 653–78.

Madonna Extreme (blog). "Madonna Interview: Q Magazine (March 1998)." Accessed 21 July 2022. http://madonnaextreme.blogspot.com/2018/01/madonna-interview-q-magazine-march-1998.html.

Mamo, Ermias. *The Maturing Church*. Carlisle: Langham, 2017.

Mangalwadi, Vishal. *Truth and Transformation: A Manifesto for Ailing Nations*. Seattle: YWAM, 2009.

Marx, Karl. "Theses on Feuerbach." In *The Marx-Engels Reader*, edited by Robert C. Tucker, 143–45. 2nd ed. New York: Norton & Co., 1978.

McFague, Sallie. *Models of God: Theology for an Ecological, Nuclear Age*. Philadelphia: Fortress, 1987.

McGrath, Alister E. "Challenges from Atheism." In *Beyond Opinion: Living the Faith We Defend*, edited by Ravi Zacharias, 21–39. Nashville: Thomas Nelson, 2007.

———. *Christian Theology: An Introduction*. 5th ed. Oxford: Wiley-Blackwell, 2011; 6th ed. Oxford: Blackwell, 2016.

Merdjanova, Ina. "Russia's War in Ukraine and the Limits of Religious Diplomacy." *Occasional Papers on Religion in Eastern Europe* 42, no. 4 (2022): Article 3.

Migliore, Daniel. *Faith Seeking Understanding: An Introduction to Christian Theology*. Grand Rapids: Eerdmans, 2004.

Minear, Paul. *Images of the Church in the New Testament*. Philadelphia: Westminster Press, 1960.

Moltmann, Jürgen. *Theology of Hope*. Translated by James Leitch. New York: Harper & Row, 1967.

———. *Trinity and the Kingdom: The Doctrine of God*. Minneapolis: Fortress, 1981.

Morris, Leon. *The Gospel According to John*. Grand Rapids: Eerdmans, 1971.

Mott, Stephen Charles. *Biblical Ethics and Social Change*. New York: Oxford University Press, 1982.

Myers, Bryant L. *Walking with the Poor*. Maryknoll: Orbis, 1999.

Myers, Jeremy D. "The Gospel Is More Than 'Faith Alone in Christ Alone.'" *Journal of the Grace Evangelical Society* (Autumn 2006): 33–56.

Ndjerareou, Abel. *De quelle tribu es-tu?* Abijan: Editions PBA, 2007.

Ndukwe, Olo. "Rural Community Development." In *African Public Theology*, edited by Sunday Bobai Agang, Dion A. Forster, and H. Jurgens Hendriks, 127–41. Carlisle: HippoBooks, 2020.

Niebuhr, Reinhold. *Christian Realism and Political Problems*. Reprint. Fairfield: Augustus M. Kelly, 1977.

———. *Moral Man and Immoral Society.* New York: Charles Scribner's Sons, 1960.
Nietzsche, Friedrich. *The Twilight of the Idols.* Translated by Duncan Large. Oxford: Oxford University Press, 1998.
Niringiye, David Zac. *The Church: God's Pilgrim People.* Carlisle: Langham Global Library, 2014.
Noëlliste, Dieumeme. "Enlisting Theology in the Project of Human Reconciliation." In *Confronting the Legacy of Racism*, edited by Dieumeme Noëlliste, 1–28. Denver Seminary: Vernon Grounds Institute of Public Ethics, 2016.
———. "Is Haiti under Divine Curse?" *Latin American Journal of Evangelical Theology: Christian Reflection from the Latino South* 6, no. 1 (2011): 86–106.
———. "Poverty and the Gospel: The Case of Haiti." *Evangelical Review of Theology* 34, no. 4 (2010): 313–18.
Nuñez, Emilio, and William Taylor. *Crisis and Hope in Latin America.* Pasadena: William Carey Library, 1996.
Obama, Barack. *The Audacity of Hope.* New York: Crown Publishers, 2008.
Padilla, C. René. *Misión integral: ensayos sobre el reino de Dios y la iglesia.* Buenos Aires: Nueva Creacion, 1986.
———. "Mission at the Turn of the Century/Millennium." *Evangel* (Spring 2001): 6–12.
———. *Mission between the Times: Essays on the Kingdom of God.* Grand Rapids: Eerdmans, 1985; 2nd ed. Carlisle: Langham Monographs, 2010.
———. "El reino de Dios y la iglesia," in *El reino de Dios y América Latina*, 44–65. El Paso: Casa Bautista de Publicaciones, 1975.
———. "La teología de la liberación: una evaluación crítica." *Misión* 2, no. 2 (March–June 1982): 16–21.
Padilla, C. René, and Tetsunao Yamamori, eds. *La Iglesia local como agente de transformación: una eclesiologia para la misión integral.* Buenos Aires: Kairos, 2003.
Panikkar, Raimundo. *The Trinity and the Religious Experience of Man.* New York: Orbis, 1973.
Pannenberg, Wolfhart. *Theology and the Kingdom of God.* Philadelphia: Westminster, 1969.
Paris, Peter J., ed. *Religion and Poverty.* Durham: Duke University Press, 2009.
Pearcy, Nancy. *Total Truth.* Wheaton: Crossway, 2004.
Rae, Scott. *Doing the Right Thing.* Grand Rapids: Zondervan, 2008.
Ramachandra, Vinoth. *The Recovery of Mission: Beyond the Pluralist Paradigm.* Grand Rapids: Eerdmans, 1996.
Reimer, Johannes. *Missio Politica.* Carlisle: Langham Global Library, 2017.
Rohlehr, Gordon. "Man's Spiritual Search in the Caribbean through Literature." In *Troubling of the Waters*, edited by Idris Hamid, 187–205. San Fernando: Rahaman, 1973.
Romain, Charles-Poisset. *Le Protestantisme dans la société haïtienne.* Port au Prince: Editions Henry des Champs, 1985.
Roy, Kevin. *Story of the Church in South Africa.* Carlisle: Langham Global Library, 2017.

Ryrie, Charles. *Basic Theology*. Chicago: Moody Press, 1999.
Saint Augustine. *City of God*. trans. Henry Bettenson. Reprint. New York: Penguin Books, 1980.
———. *The Confessions*. Reprint. New York: Penguin, 1981.
———. "Sermon 71.32" in *Works of Saint Augustine: A Translation for the 21st Century*. Hyde Park, NY: New York City Press, 1997, 3/3: 265–66.
———. *The Trinity*. Trans. Edmond Hill. Edited by John E. Rotelle. New York: New York City Press, 1991.
Sanders, Fred. *The Deep Things of God: How the Trinity Changes Everything*. Wheaton: Crossway, 2010.
Satyavrata, Ivan. "Jesus and Other Religions." In *Asian Christian Theology: Evangelical Perspectives*, edited by Timoteo Gener and Stephen Pardue, 221–43. Carlisle: Langham Global Library, 2019.
Schmidt, Alvin. *Under the Influence: How Christianity Transformed Civilization*. Grand Rapids: Zondervan, 2001.
Segundo, Juan Luis, S.J. *The Community Called Church*. Maryknoll: Orbis, 1976.
———. *The Liberation of Theology*. Translated by John Drury. Maryknoll: Orbis, 1974.
Shanthi, M., and Lizella Faria Gonsalves. "Hope amidst Despair: Revisiting John Steinbeck's Novel *The Grapes of Wrath* in the Times of COVID-19 Pandemic." *Rupkatha Journal on Interdisciplinary Studies in Humanities* 12, no. 5 (2020): 1–9.
Sherlock, Charles. *The Doctrine of Humanity*. Contours of Christian Theology. Downers Grove: IVP, 1996.
Sider, Ronald. *One-Sided Christianity? Uniting the Church to Heal a Lost and Broken World*. Grand Rapids: Zondervan, 1993.
Sider, Ronald, and Ben Lowe. *The Future of Our Faith*. Grand Rapids: Brazos, 2016.
Skillen, James W., and James R. Skillen. "Evangelical Double-Mindedness in Support of Donald Trump" in *The Spiritual Danger of Donald Trump: 30 Evangelical Christians on Justice, Truth, and Moral Integrity*, edited by Ronald J. Sider and Bandy Lee, 164–68. Eugene: Cascade, 2020.
Snyder, C. R. "Hope Theory: Rainbows in the Mind." *Psychological Inquiry* 13, no. 4 (2002): 249–75.
Sophocles I. *Oedipus the King, Oedipus at Colonus, Antigone*. 2nd ed. David Grene and Richard Lattimore, eds. Chicago: University of Chicago, 1991.
Stone, Ronald H. *Realism and Hope*. Washington: University Press of America, 1976.
Stott, John R. W. *Christian Counter-Culture: The Message of the Sermon on the Mount*. Downers Grove: IVP, 1978.
———. *The Message of Timothy and Titus*. Leicester: Inter-Varsity Press, 1997.
Thiemann, Ronald. *Constructing a Public Theology: The Church in a Pluralistic Culture*. Louisville: Westminster/John Knox, 1991.
Thiselton, Anthony. *The First Epistle to the Corinthians: A Commentary on the Greek Text*. The New International Greek New Testament. Grand Rapids: Eerdmans, 2000.
———. *The Hermeneutics of Doctrine*. Grand Rapids: Eerdmans, 2007.

Torres, Camilo. *Cristianismo y revolución*. Mexico: Ediciones Era, 1972.

Van Gelder, Craig. *The Essence of the Church. A Community Created by the Spirit*. Grand Rapids: Baker Publishing Group, 2000.

Volf, Miroslav. *After Our Likeness: The Church as the Image of the Trinity*. Grand Rapids: Eerdmans, 1998.

Wagner, C. Peter. *Latin American Theology: Radical or Evangelical? The Struggle for the Faith in a Young Church*. Grand Rapids: Eerdmans, 1970.

Wallace, Daniel B. *Greek Grammar Beyond the Basics: An Exegetical Syntax of the New Testament*. Grand Rapids: Zondervan, 1997.

Ware, Frederick L. *African American Theology: An Introduction*. Louisville: Westminster John Knox, 2016.

Wells, Paul. "Editorial: Hope against Hope." *Unio cum Christo* 7, no. 1 (April 2021): 5–7.

Westcott, B. F. *The Gospel According to St. John*. Reprint. Grand Rapids: Eerdmans, 1973.

White, James R. *The Forgotten Trinity*. Minneapolis: Bethany House, 1998.

White, Lynn. "The Historical Roots of Our Ecological Crisis." Reprinted in *Ecology and Life: Accepting Our Environmental Responsibility*, edited by Wesley Granberg-Michaelson, 125–37. Waco: Word, 1988.

Willard, Dallas. *Renovation of the Heart: Putting on the Character of Christ*. Colorado Springs: NavPress, 2002.

World Health Organization. "Suicide." 17 June 2021. https://www.who.int/news-room/fact-sheets/detail/suicide.

Wright, Christopher. *Thinking Clearly about the Uniqueness of Jesus*. Crowborough: Monarch, 1997.

———. *Old Testament Ethics for the People of God*. Downers Grove: IVP Academic, 2004.

Wright, N. T. *Surprised by Hope*. New York: HarperCollins, 2008.

Yoder, John Howard. *Body Politics: Five Practices of the Christian Community before the Watching World*. Nashville: Discipleship Resources, 1999.

———. *For the Nations: Essays Evangelical and Public*. Grand Rapids: Eerdmans, 1997.

———. *The Politics of Jesus, Vicit Agnus Noster*. 2nd ed. Grand Rapids: Eerdmans, 1994.

Zizioulas, John. *Being as Communion: Studies in Personhood and the Church*. Crestwood: St. Vladimir's Seminary Press, 1985.

Subject Index

A
authentic engagement 35–39, 142

C
Christ
  likeness 113
  reconciliation 112, 119
  sacrifice 111
  school of 113
church
  hope 164, 166
  identity 155
  violence 150
  work 155–56, 159, 161
Church
  unity 52, 59
community 89, 92, 95–96, 98–99, 104, 109, 112, 115, 117, 125, 127, 131, 134–36, 155
Constantinianism 135
COVID-19 93, 161
cross 8–9, 26, 59–60, 87–88, 92–93, 108–9, 112, 116, 126

E
eschatological
  community 60, 66
  creation 164
  hope 5, 7, 9
  transformation 3–4
evangelism 27–28

G
God
  grace 117
  judgment 116
  purpose 117–18, 124
  triune 126

H
Holy Spirit 19, 51, 57, 62–63, 65–66, 72, 86–87, 95, 99, 166

I
imago dei 93, 116–17, 123–24, 164

J
justice 40, 61, 115, 133, 136–37, 163, 165, 169

K
kingdom of God 37, 75, 104–5, 107, 109–10, 113, 154–55

L
lament 145
Lausanne Covenant 26, 28

M
Martin Luther King 112, 138, 141, 150, 160, 169
Marxism 81, 149–50

P
politics, political 88, 135, 137–40, 142, 152, 168–69
Putin, Vladimir 32

R
race 56, 59–60, 92–93, 112, 125, 131
reconciliation 92–93, 103, 111, 119, 141

S
salt and light 10, 42–46, 147
salvation 18, 21, 26, 52, 59, 87, 103, 108–9, 111, 113, 118–19, 131
shalom 3, 109, 111

slavery 119, 127, 138

T
Trinity 53, 64, 83–86, 91, 126
Trump, Donald 32, 121, 150
two kingdoms 23–24

W
witness 22, 24–25, 28, 37, 42–44,
    46–47, 82, 98–99, 130, 134–36,
    145, 168

Author Index

A
Augustine 60, 64, 118, 126
Ayittey, George 119

B
Banda, Collium 121
Barth, Karl 19, 84
Bediako, Kwame 120
Bellow, Saul 161
Bird, Michael 68, 70, 106
Boff, Leonardo 30–31, 84
Boileau 36
Bonhoeffer, Dietrich 30
Bosch, David 82
Boyd, Greg 17
Bultmann, Rudolf 163

C
Chafer, Lewis Sperry 62
Clement of Alexandria 60
Clowney, Edmund 63
Colson, Charles 27
Cox, Harvey 30
Cyprian 52

D
Dodd, C. H. 106
Dragas, George Dion 54
Dulles, Avery 18, 104

E
Erickson, Millard J. 68, 111
Escobar, Samuel 33, 113

F
Fleming, Dean 95

G
Giles, Kevin 8, 18
Gill, Robin 99

Gladwin, John 20
Glasser, Arthur 4
González, Justo 10
Graham, Billy 15–16, 26, 33
Green, Gene L. 69
Green, Joel B. 96
Grenz, Stanley 66
Grudem, Wayne 132

H
Hagner, Donald A. 44
Harink, Douglas 88
Harper and Metzger 60
Hay, Andrew 85
Henry, Carl F. 27
Hopkins, Dwight 127–28

K
Kärkkäinen, Veli-Matti 67, 72
Katongole, Emmanuel 127
Küng, Hans 19, 122
Kuyper, Abraham 24

L
Ladd, George Eldon 9, 105, 112, 155
Luther, Martin 23

M
MacFague, Sallie 83
Mackay, John 105
Mamo, Ermias 113
Mangalwadi, Vishal 131
Marx, Karl 29
McGrath, Alister 2, 56, 124
Migliore, Daniel L. 115
Minear, Paul 56, 69, 74
Moltmann, Jürgen 6, 155, 165
Moody, Dwight L 169
Mott, Stephan Charles 38

N
Naipaul, V S 147
Ndjerareou, Abel 93
Ndukwe, Olo 132
Newbiggin, Lesslie 137
Niebuhr, Reinhold 152–53, 170
Nietzsche, Friedrich 130
Niringiye, David Zac 47, 56
Nuñez, Emilio 22, 24, 28

P
Padilla, René 18, 24, 39, 108, 112, 156

R
Reimer, Johannes 134
Romain, Charles-Poisset 23
Roy, Kevin 139

S
Sartre, Jean-Paul 160
Satyavrata, Ivan 104
Schmidt, Alvin 138
Segundo, Juan Luis 15, 30
Snyder, C. R. 162
Stone, Ronald H. 153, 166
Stott, John 11, 47

T
Taylor, William 22, 24, 28
Tertullian 53
Thiemann, Ronald 137
Thiselton, Anthony 64, 72

V
Van Gelder, Craig 67, 76, 81
Volf, Miroslav 84

W
Ware, Frederick 83
Wells, Paul 164
Westcott, B F 91
Willard, Dallas 98
Wright, Christopher 40, 96, 117
Wright, N. T. 162

Y
Yoder, John Howard 88–89, 108

Scripture Index

OLD TESTAMENT

Genesis
1–2 20
1:26 124
1:27–31 124
3:10–15 164
3:14–19 116
3:15 .... 9, 88
3:22–24 116
6 164
12:1–3 55
12:2 164
12:2–3 39
12:3 9
18:18–19 9
18:19 40
41 138
49:9 105

Exodus
1:15 – 2:2 140
15:13 55
15:16 55
19:4–5 41
19:5 54
19:5–6 .... 40, 72

Leviticus
19 40
19:1 96
19:2 .... 40, 86, 95, 97
19:9–10 40
19:13 40
19:14 40
19:15 40
19:16 40
19:23 40
19:32 40

19:33–34 40
19:35–36 40

Numbers
22:30 11

Deuteronomy
7:6–11 55
9:1–6 55
14:2 55
32:9–10 55

2 Samuel
7:12–16 105
12:1–12 133
12:7–15 114

1 Kings
19:3–5 148
21:17–22 133

2 Kings
17 47
17:15 47

2 Chronicles
7:13–14 94

Nehemiah
1:4–11 2
2:4 167
4:1–3 167
4:4–6 167

Esther
4:15–17 168
7:1–8 138

Job
2:9 147

Psalms
2 105
8:5–6 124
16:11 119
24:1 .... 6, 20
51:11 95
71:4–6 163
82:3–4 133
110 105
139:7–12 71
139:13–14 125

Proverbs
23:7 51

Isaiah
1:10–17 132
2:4 .... 3, 5
9:6 105
11:1 105
11:1–9 4
11:3–5 135
11:6–9 .... 3, 117
11:8 3
12:6 95
28:16–17 61
35:6 3
35:8 4
40:1–2 101
40:9 102
40:25 95
41:2 11
41:10 71
42:6 39

43:3 95	**Ezekiel**	**Joel**
49:6 39	36:25–28 63	2:28–32 8
52:7 102		2:29 87
54:5 95	**Daniel**	
55:1 101	2 168	**Amos**
58 132	3 168	2:6–7 133
60:3 165	3:28 – 4:3 140	5:11 133
62:4 55	4:16 138	5:12 133
63:10 95	6 168	5:24 133
65:17–18 4	9:4–19 2	
		Micah
Jeremiah	**Hosea**	5:2 105
6:7 132	2:23 55	
8:8–13 132	4:4–6 133	**Habakkuk**
12:7–10 55		1:1 148
29:1–7 25		

NEW TESTAMENT

Matthew	6:30–32 125	18:20 .... 57, 71
2:7–12 141	8:1–3 129	20:17–19 108
3:1–2 105	8:14–16 108	22:21 135
3:1–3 102	9:11 129	24:14 105
3:14–17 126	9:35–36 108	25:31–46 25
4:11 126	10:7 102	28:18 73
4:23 102	10:29–30 125	28:19 .... 10, 73
4:23–25 .... 24, 108	11:1 10	28:19–20 113
5:1–12 42	11:4–6 108	28:20 .... 57, 59, 65, 71
5–7 41	11:16–19 129	
5:9 151	12:28–29 87	**Mark**
5:13 44–45	13:24–30 .... 136, 151	1:14–16 105
5:13–14 10	13:26 137	1:15–16 102
5:13–16 42	13:30 151	1:24 95
5:14–15 44	13:36–43 .... 136, 151	2:23–28 129
5:15 44	13:37–38 136	3:14 102
5:16 .... 10, 21, 28, 45, 75	13:39 136	8:31–33 108
5:17 – 7:27 42	13:41 136	8:37 125
5:22 129	13:41–42 137	9:7–8 126
5:38 151	14:1–6 129	10:13–16 134
5:43 151	14:3–4 133	10:45 86
5:44–45 86	14:4 114	10:46–52 134
5:48 96	16:16–19 58	12:10 61
6:8 46	16:17–20 87	15:33–35 126
6:10 .... 10, 75, 118	16:18 58	
6:12 86	18:19–20 20	

Luke

1:35	95
2:10	110
3:3	102
3:7–14	133
4:18	10, 102
4:18–19	107
4:34	95
6:1–7	134
7:36–38	129
7:36–39	129
7:36–40	129
8:1–3	129
9:25	125
10:29–37	129
14:1–6	134
14:13	107
17:11–14	129
18:9–14	129
19:1–7	129
19:1–10	130
19:8	108
19:10	108
24:24–27	114
24:32	114
24:44–47	102
24:45–47	59

John

1:4	44
1:11–12	62
1:18	73
3	62
3:3	62
4	130
4:9	129
4:28–30	130
6:1–15	24
6:69	95
7:37	62
8:1–7	129
8:1–11	28
8:3–11	129
8:11	28
9	130
9:24–33	130
10:1–21	61
10:8	135
10:10	135
13–17	59
14:6	111
14:9	74
14:16–17	63
14:20	62
15:1–3	20
15:1–5	61
15:9	126
15:18–20	145
15:20	145
17:4	74
17:9–10	65
17:9–17	59
17:11	21, 90
17:14–15	21
17:18	9
17:20	10
17:20–23	90
17:21	65
17:23	126
17:26	126
20:21	10, 73
21:15	59

Acts

1:8	59, 62
2	62
2:1–13	87
2:16–17	8
2:27	95
2:32–37	114
4	168
4:12	111
5:14	62
8:1	62
9:3–9	59
9:5	57
13:1	62
18:1–11	55
20:28	57

Romans

1:1–5	110
1:16	108, 113
1:21–30	118
4:18	167
4:18–21	164
5:12	62
8	62
8:6–11	64
8:9	63
8:9–11	86
8:15–17	64
8:18	6, 166
8:19–21	112
8:24	166
8:26	64
8:28–29	117
8:30	117
9:24–26	56
10:9	59
11:25	86
11:25–26	60
11:33	117
12:1–2	85, 96
12:3–10	64
12:16	90
13:1	135, 140
13:1–7	169
13:2	140
13:3–4	140–41
13:5	140
13:7	140
14:10–12	25
15:8	166
15:13	166
16:1–5	20
16:3	20
16:16	58

1 Corinthians

1:2	20, 55, 57
2:10	64
3:1	90
3:5–11	55
3:11	61

3:12–15 25	**Ephesians**	**1 Thessalonians**
3:16 63	1:1 57	1:1–2 20
3:16–17 72	1:4 87	4:18 6
3:17 72	1:9–10 112	5:13 90
6:19 .... 51, 63, 72	2:1–4 62	
10:11 8	2:8–10 125	**1 Timothy**
12 64	2:11–12 118	1:11 110
12:3 63	2:12 54	2:1–2 140
12:13 .... 59, 63, 87	2:13 7	3:15 54
12:27 20	2:13–18 141	
15:1–3 110	2:15 60	**2 Timothy**
15:3–4 108	2:19 .... 54, 59	1:10 9
15:23 9	2:20 .... 61, 134	2:8 110
15:24–25 135	2:20–22 20	3:13–17 85
15:27 117	3:1–6 87	3:16–17 85
15:55–57 87	3:6 60	
15:58 6	3:8 .... 54, 102	**Titus**
	4:3–7 90	2:11–13 113
2 Corinthians	4:11–16 33	2:11–14 .... 41, 169
1:1 57	4:14 117	2:12 7
3:18 .... 86, 117	4:15 61	2:14 6
5:5 166	4:15–16 86	3:3–5 62
5:14–15 28	4:20–21 113	
5:17 .... 62, 108, 113	4:24 .... 95, 117	**Hebrews**
5:17–20 103	5:18 86	9:12 57
5:17–21 141	5:25–27 61	11:13 .... 74–75, 157
5:18 119		12:22–23 20
6:16 54	**Philippians**	13:5 71
13:14 65	1:1 57	13:20 61
	2:5–8 86	
Galatians	2:13–18 41	**1 Peter**
1:6–9 110	2:14–15 .... 10, 43	1:1 .... 41, 74
1:15–16 102	2:14–16 98	1:1–2 .... 41, 54
2:20 86	3:20 75	1:4 62
3:28 59		1:16 .... 41, 95–96
4:4–6 62	**Colossians**	1:18–19 57
4:6 64	1:2 57	1:19–20 164
5 86	1:13 .... 62, 155	2:9 .... 54, 56, 72
5:22 86	1:13–14 112	2:9–10 41
5:25 64	1:18 .... 20, 61	2:11 74
6:16 54	2:1–15 9	2:12 10
	2:15 .... 87, 165	2:13–17 140
	3:1–4 86	
	3:3–4 61	
	3:11 7	
	3:17 33	

2 Peter
3:9 5
3:13 .... 5, 7
3:14 6
3:18 33

1 John
1:5 44
2:7–12 86
2:15–17 20
3:1–3 .... 86, 117
3:2 166
3:3 6

3 John
2 111

Revelation
1:6 .... 54, 72
1:12–13 58
4:8 95
5:1 9
5:10 72
6:10 145
7:9–13 60
7:16–17 5
13 140
19:7 61
20:1–3 9
21:1 117
21:1–4 .... 37, 117
21:1–5 166
21:3 .... 54, 117
21:3–4 117
21:4 117
21:5 .... 5, 11
22:3–5 117

Langham Literature and its imprints are a ministry of Langham Partnership.

Langham Partnership is a global fellowship working in pursuit of the vision God entrusted to its founder John Stott –

> *to facilitate the growth of the church in maturity and Christ-likeness through raising the standards of biblical preaching and teaching.*

Our vision is to see churches in the Majority World equipped for mission and growing to maturity in Christ through the ministry of pastors and leaders who believe, teach and live by the word of God.

Our mission is to strengthen the ministry of the word of God through:
- nurturing national movements for biblical preaching
- fostering the creation and distribution of evangelical literature
- enhancing evangelical theological education

especially in countries where churches are under-resourced.

Our ministry

Langham Preaching partners with national leaders to nurture indigenous biblical preaching movements for pastors and lay preachers all around the world. With the support of a team of trainers from many countries, a multi-level programme of seminars provides practical training, and is followed by a programme for training local facilitators. Local preachers' groups and national and regional networks ensure continuity and ongoing development, seeking to build vigorous movements committed to Bible exposition.

Langham Literature provides Majority World preachers, scholars and seminary libraries with evangelical books and electronic resources through publishing and distribution, grants and discounts. The programme also fosters the creation of indigenous evangelical books in many languages, through writer's grants, strengthening local evangelical publishing houses, and investment in major regional literature projects, such as one volume Bible commentaries like *The Africa Bible Commentary* and *The South Asia Bible Commentary*.

Langham Scholars provides financial support for evangelical doctoral students from the Majority World so that, when they return home, they may train pastors and other Christian leaders with sound, biblical and theological teaching. This programme equips those who equip others. Langham Scholars also works in partnership with Majority World seminaries in strengthening evangelical theological education. A growing number of Langham Scholars study in high quality doctoral programmes in the Majority World itself. As well as teaching the next generation of pastors, graduated Langham Scholars exercise significant influence through their writing and leadership.

To learn more about Langham Partnership and the work we do visit **langham.org**

www.ingramcontent.com/pod-product-compliance
Lightning Source LLC
Chambersburg PA
CBHW050758160426
43192CB00010B/1557